Situationism and
The New Morality

Contemporary Problems in Philosophy

George F. McLean, O.M.I., *editor*

SITUATIONISM AND
THE NEW MORALITY

Robert L. Cunningham
University of San Francisco

APPLETON-CENTURY-CROFTS
EDUCATIONAL DIVISION
New York   MEREDITH CORPORATION

Copyright © 1970 by

MEREDITH CORPORATION

772-2

Library of Congress Card Number: 73-105878

390-24800-2

To my wife Margery

Foreword

Contemporary Problems in Philosophy, a new series initiated with this volume, is a response to needs generated by a period of rapid change in which systems of thought and even methods of approach seem ever more short-lived. We search less after permanent principles than after those shifting circumstances which define the growth and articulation of basic issues or problems. These circumstances include our heritage from the past, but they are also considered now as decisive dynamisms for the future.

Thus there is a need to search out the influential forces (particularly from the recent past), to identify the way in which they have been coordinated in the actual situation in order to constitute the chief philosophical problems of the present day, and to indicate the direction indicated by the interplay of these forces for new and creative steps in the ongoing process of self understanding and of comprehending one's world in the broadest sense. This is the aim of the present series, in which each volume will be devoted to a different key problem in the field of present-day philosophy.

In each volume an extensive introductory essay by the author will set out the main lines of the development of the issue and identify the creative possibilities inherent in possible interaction of the various approaches presently being followed. Then, extensive passages from key works will illustrate this development and allow the student to share firsthand in the growth and the contemporary dynamisms of the particular philosophical issue.

This volume by Dr. Robert L. Cunningham of The University of San Francisco focuses upon an issue which not only is central in the area of contemporary ethical thought but which typifies the change that is taking place in the field of philosophy as a whole. In the past, ethical thought veered either toward a somewhat deterministic calculus of the circumstances on the one hand, or a rigorous analysis of the nature of individual human acts on the other. With the shift to person-centered values in recent decades, a new constellation of factors arose, and with it a new approach to man's moral assessment of himself and his actions. Where a universal law, based on the nature of an act, might previously have been evoked, there has been a shift to evaluating on the basis of the person's response in love. The result has forced each of us, in making moral decisions, to face a number of issues. What, for instance, is the source, and hence the nature and import, of love in our life; if love is—at least poetically speaking—blind, in what way do circumstances specify and direct its imperatives; and if the nature of the individual act does not determine a universal norm, what is the basis for the norms or guidelines that figure in evaluating particular sets of circumstances in order to provide context and constancy for one's response of love?

To shed light upon these issues the introductory essay by Dr. Cunningham has traced the intricate work done by the Utilitarians on the significance of concrete circumstances in making moral judgments. To this he has added a study of the new significance attached to love in ethics. From the combination of these two he has both drawn out those implications which have already appeared for contemporary man's self understanding and pointed out the issues which yet remain, illustrating each step by extensive and pertinent passages from those writings which stand as landmarks in this development.

In thus launching the *Contemporary Problems in Philosophy Series* with SITUATIONISM AND THE NEW MORALITY by Robert L. Cunningham, it is hoped that a lively and creative element is hereby added to man's most trying but central task—to understand himself in his present and total context so that he might thereby direct his destiny.

G.F.McL.

Contents

Foreword   vii

I. INTRODUCTION
  Overview   1
  Existentialism   6
  Relativism   15
  Intrinsically Wrong Acts   24
  Christian Ethics   27
  Utilitarianism vs. Formalism   34
  Dewey's Pragmatism   44
  Natural Law   46
  The Readings   50

II. READINGS
  A. The Fletcher-McCabe Debate
     Love is the Only Measure, *Joseph Fletcher*   55
     The Validity of Absolutes, *Herbert McCabe*   66
     Agreement and Disagreement, *Joseph Fletcher*   79
     The Total Context, *Herbert McCabe*   84

  B. Themes and Issues in Situationism
     Situation Ethics and Objective Morality, *Louis Dupré*   88
     A proof of Objectivity of Morals, *Renford Bambrough*   103
     'Whatever the Consequences', *Jonathan Bennett*   125
     Christian Ethics and Utilitarianism, *A. C. Ewing*   150
     Rules and Utilitarianism, *B. J. Diggs*   168
     Towards an Ethics of Relationships, *Eugene Fontinell*   197

ix

II. READINGS—continued

General Standards and Particular Situations in
Relation to the Natural Law, *Charles DeKoninck*   214

Natural Law, *Charles Fried*   221

C. Old or New Morality: Kolnai vs. Fletcher

A defense of Intrinsicalism Against
Situation Ethics, *Aurel Kolnai*   230

A Situationist's Feedback, *Joseph Fletcher*   272

Situationism and
The New Morality

I. Introduction

OVERVIEW

Man today faces a whole array of social problems having important moral dimensions, at the very time that traditional moral standards and values have begun to seem irrelevant. Bonds between civil and moral law are stretched by movements which justify civil (and, sometimes uncivil) disobedience. Opposite views on sexual morality—on contraception, abortion, divorce, and homosexuality—are defended, and, when taken to be appropriate matter for civil legislation, often make for social division. A consensus is hardly to be found on any of a variety of issues such as the location of responsibility for the direction of human beings by mass media, or for helping the two-thirds of the earth's population who are poor, or on the possibility of "just war." If one adds to all this the problems of personal alienation that are signalized, in an extreme form, by the "Hippie" rejection of white-collar morality, and the problems having to do with automation and leisure in an affluent welfare society, one will hardly be surprised to find a growing moral disorientation. All this makes one suspect that traditional moral theory to which one looks for justified solutions to such problems is, to put it mildly, in a state of flux.

In the not too distant past, a man could live his whole life without encountering anything like such serious questionings of the given social and moral order. The range of goals and responsibilities was fairly fixed and clear. To be sure, one could decide to disobey given norms—but there was little difficulty in knowing just what they were. By contrast, today's milieu is radically open, and man sees within his grasp the power to change himself and his environment. More than ever before, the values in terms of which these changes, accom-

1

plished and prospective, are made, seem to be *themselves* matters of human choice and decision.

A common first reaction is often enough a kind of scepticism about the very possibility of knowing and adhering to moral norms. It is surely a sign of the modern temper that a version of the existentialist doctrine that salvation of self is achievable only by the "transvaluation of values," by the repudiation of "morality" itself—by going Beyond Good and Evil—and by an emphasis on freedom, especially from the "ungenuine" demands of normative rationality, is found fitting and familiar.

This, however, is but one part of the picture, for one must distinguish between the undeniable weakening of the practice of traditional morality and the attempt to see that there is a difference between right and wrong. W. D. Ross has pointed out, for example, that both the advocates and the opponents of a relaxed sexual code are concerned with moral right and wrong.

Both alike think there is *some* right way of arranging the relations between the sexes. And even if some go so far as to say that all rules for individual behaviour in this matter ought to be abolished, they say they *ought* to be abolished, i.e. that legislators *ought* to abolish certain laws and that public opinion *ought* not to visit certain acts with its displeasure . . . . In fact the difference that divides us is not a difference on the question whether there is a right or wrong, but a difference on the questions, 'What are the characteristics of acts that make them right or wrong?' and 'How far do certain types of acts in fact possess these characteristics?'[1]

Among the attempts to deal with moral issues generated by an increasingly humanized and humanizing environment, none is more strikingly obvious than that set of positions known popularly as "The New Morality" or "Situation Ethics." (Other designations include "contextual ethics," "existential ethics," "antinomianism," "nominalism," and "ethics of inspiration." Here, the preferred term will be the brief "situationism.") Its main thrust is the rejection of what is referred to as traditional, legalistic, anti-humanist morality.[2] But since there

---

[1] *Foundations of Ethics* (London: Oxford University Press, 1939), p. 29.
[2] A good many advocates of the "new morality" believe in freedom and "sitting loose to the rules" in personal life, but believe in rigor and being bound by unbreakable rules in civic and social life. Thus quite relaxed sexual mores are, for example, seen to be quite compatible with absolute condemnation of any and every war as unjust. One might say rather vaguely that the "old morality" demands categorical imperatives in personal life and expediency in civic life while the "new morality" calls for the opposite, categorical imperatives in civil life and expediency in personal life.

are many moral "traditions," many "legalisms" to which reactions take place and many "humanisms" which are defended, there is really no one *school* of situationists whose common tenets can be easily isolated and discussed. It is even true, as James Gustafson has remarked,[3] that under the umbrella of situationism are placed thinkers whose views on some issues are as significantly different from one another as they are from those of certain opponents. Nonetheless it is generally conceded that there is a striking "family resemblance"[4] among situationists which warrants a common name.

Agreement on a name, however, will not carry us very far. The present discussion of situationism is truly a mare's nest, a confusing tangle of reactions to various philosophical and theological traditions, presuppositions, and idioms. It is the aim of these pages to identify a few of the more obvious thematic strands of situationism, especially utilitarianism, existentialism, pragmatism, and relativism. This should enable the reader to see in a general way the pros and cons of philosophical positions which influence situationists or against which they react; it will also set the stage for a critical appreciation of the readings which follow.

Situationism is worth serious effort, for it appeals to a great many for a variety of reasons. It is congenial to the atheistic existentialist who denies that man is morally nature-bound, to the secular humanist who gives primacy to personal values, to the "practical" men who emphasize the actual facts of the case, to the "scientific-minded" who

---

[3] "Context versus Principles: A Misplaced Debate in Christian Ethics," *Harvard Theological Review*, LVIII (1965), pp. 171–202, at p. 173; reprinted in *New Theology No. 3*, edited by M. E. Marty and D. G. Peerman (New York: The MacMillan Company, 1966).

[4] The term "family resemblance" is Wittgenstein's; see his *Philosophical Investigations* I, 66. In "Universals and Family Resemblances," *Proceedings of the Aristotelian Society LXI* (1960–1961), pp. 207–222, Renford Bambrough uses "the Churchill face" as an example of a "family resemblance:" "It may be that there are ten features in terms of which we can describe 'the family face' (high forehead, bushy eyebrows, blue eyes, Roman nose, high cheek-bones, cleft-chin, dark hair, dimpled cheeks, pointed ears and ruddy complexion). It is obvious that the unmistakable presence of the family face in every single one of the ten members of the family is compatible with the absence in each member of the family of one of the ten consistent features of the family face. It is also obvious that it does not matter if it happens that the feature which is absent from the face of each individual member is present in every one of the others. The members of the family will then have no *feature* in common, and yet they will all unmistakably have the Churchill face in common." (p. 210).

demand full use of the personal and impersonal sciences in ascertaining the facts of the situation, to some Protestants who see the Christian moral decision as a response to a call by God in the actual situation, and to some Catholics who, especially in continental Europe, are disenchanted with traditional natural law theory and who wish to emphasize the role of Christian love. To an equally broad spectrum of critics, situationism appears to be a chaotic antinomian wasteland in which the role of reason and principle is minimized almost to the vanishing point, in which moral acts consist of virtually nothing but circumstances, "a wage packet with nothing but deductions,"[5] and in which there is excessive reliance on intuitive, quasi-mystical responses to the facts of the situation.

A brief outline of this Introduction may prove helpful.

Existentialism. Perhaps the most important, and certainly the most obvious philosophic ancestor of situationism is existentialism, in view especially of its concern not so much with the rightness or wrongness of what is chosen as with the nature of authentic moral choice. Here we see themes characteristic of situationism carried perhaps to their extreme, the radical criticism of traditional morality and the positive emphasis on human subjectivity, freedom and authenticity. An attempt will be made here to delineate the crucial existentialist notions which illuminate situationist themes.

Relativism. We shall next examine a major critical charge against situationism, that it is excessively "relativistic." Since contemporary analytic ethics has made considerable progress in clarifying the issues involved in the relativism vs. absolutism controversy, and in providing a satisfactory non-relativistic basis for ethics, this section of the Introduction will sketch the distinctions which have been developed and will indicate the line often taken by "absolutistic" analysts. This will also provide the background for Renford Bambrough's defense of an absolutist position.

Intrinsically wrong acts. Often closely associated with the charge of relativism is the claim that situationists deny the existence of intrinsically wrong acts or the moral relevance of the "intrinsic nature"

---

[5] George Woods, "Situational Ethics," in *Christian Ethics and Contemporary Philosophy*, ed. Ian T. Ramsey (New York: The Macmillan Company, 1966), p. 33. This collection of essays is cited below as *Christian Ethics . . .*

of acts in favor of an exaggerated emphasis on the moral relevance of circumstance, motive, and consequence. Here we shall investigate the issues involved in this criticism, and provide background for the objections to situationist "extrinsicalism" leveled by Aurel Kolnai and Herbert McCabe, and for Jonathan Bennett's analysis of the moral relevance of the act/consequence distinction.

Christian ethics. Another charge against situationism is that, being a species of "Christian ethics," [6] it confuses the realms of faith and reason. Is the existence or non-existence of God relevant ethically? Is ethics autonomous, or does ethics depend crucially upon metaphysics or revelation? Some discussion of these questions will help one see better some implications of the religious dimension of situationism, and will provide background to the Fletcher–McCabe debate and to parts of the articles by Louis Dupré and A. C. Ewing.

Utilitarianism vs. Formulism. It is noteworthy that situationism has developed in isolation from linguistic analysis, the way of doing philosophy now dominant among professional philosophers in North America and the British Commonwealth. The philosophy journals representing this tradition contain little more than casual passing references to situationism. However, the situationist vs. traditionist controversy has a highly sophisticated analogue in contemporary Anglo-American analytic philosophy in the on-going controversy between utilitarians and formalists. An examination of the main lines of this latter controversy, and later the articles of A. C. Ewing and B. J. Diggs, will make for a deepened understanding of what is involved in opting for a situationist stance in ethics.

Dewey's pragmatism. Of special importance on the American scene is the influence exerted by Deweyian pragmatism on exponents of situationism. The direction and scope of this influence will be discussed here and in the article by Eugene Fontinell, who defends a pragmatic position.

Natural law. Only recently have a number of Roman Catholic

---

[6] In the past, few Roman Catholics would have distinguished the referent of "moral theology" from that of "Christian ethics"; though the former was the preferred term. Today an increasing number use the term "moral theology" to refer to Christian metaethical doctrine and "Christian ethics" to refer to normative Christian moral doctrine.

philosophers and theologians taken a positive interest in situationism.[7] To them it has appeared mainly as providing possible lines of attack on what goes by the name of "traditional natural law theory," which they considered incapable of providing a sound analysis of such moral issues as contraception, divorce, and abortion. This section sketches an analysis of natural law theory as it might be developed by a situationist; and the articles by Charles DeKoninck, Charles Fried, and Louis Dupré present versions of natural law theory having contrasting emphases.

EXISTENTIALISM

One of the strongest influences on most situationists is that of the existentialists, with whom they share a great many similarities of emphasis, if not of precise positions. A view of this matrix of situationism will provide helpful background for the articles below, especially those of Fletcher, Kolnai, and Dupré.

It is difficult to say anything that is true of all or even of the major existentialists.[8] Like the situationists, they form no "school". Heidegger,

---

[7] Interest in situationism was especially noticeable on the continent following the condemnatory addresses of Pius XII in 1952 and the Instruction of the Holy Office in 1956. For a bibliography of early continental writings on situationism, see Karl Rahner, "On the Question of a Formal Existential Ethic, *Theological Investigations*, Volume II: Man in the Church, trans. Karl-H. Kruger, (Baltimore: Helicon Press, 1963), footnote 7, pp. 217–18; and for a selection of pertinent Roman documents with lengthy interpretation and bibliography, see John C. Ford, S. J. and Gerald Kelly, S.J., *Contemporary Moral Theology I* (Westminster, Md.: Newman Press, 1958), pp. 104–40. More recently in Catholic as well as in Protestant circles, interest has been aroused by Bishop John A. T. Robinson's *Honest to God* (Philadelphia: Westminster Press, 1963), by Harvey Cox's situationist approach to sexual morality in *Secular City* (New York; The Macmillan Company, 1965), and by the Fletcher–McCabe *Commonweal* debate: Joseph Fletcher, "Love is the Only Measure," LXXXIII (Jan. 14, 1966), pp. 427–32, and Herbert McCabe, "The Validity of Absolutes," LXXXIII (Jan. 14, 1966), pp. 432–37. For the history of situationism, see Louis Monden, S.J., *Sin, Liberty and Law* (New York: Sheed and Ward, 1965), pp. 73–87, and John G. Milhaven, S.J., and David J. Casey, S.J., "Introduction to the Theological Background of the New Morality," *Theological Studies*, XXVIII (1967), pp. 213–34; and for an outline of the positions of major situationists, see James M. Gustafson, "Christian Ethics," *Religion* (Englewood Cliffs, N.J.: Prentice-Hall, Inc., 1965), pp. 285–354.

[8] Probably every list of existentialists would include these five; Kierkegaard, Heidegger, Marcel, Sartre, and Jaspers. Longer lists would probably include at last some of the following: Nietzsche, Camus, Teilhard de Chardin, Dostoevsky, Kafka—and might run even to Norman Mailer and Juliet Greco.

Sartre, and Jaspers have disavowed even the name 'existentialist,' and at most one can see a "family resemblance" among them. Their writings are generally unsystematic, often appearing in the form of novels or plays. The precise questions in which one is interested are sometimes not even raised, at least not in easily recognizable ways.

To do justice even to a single one of the existentialists in a few pages is no little challenge. But since, as Chesterton once said, a job worth doing is worth doing badly, an attempt will be made here to highlight the moral theory of one of the standard-bearers of existentialism, J-P. Sartre. The emphasis will be upon those of Sartre's views which seem most relevant to situationism.[9]

After presenting Sartre's analysis of the "student's dilemma" (1), we shall look to what it can tell us of existentialist concern with radical decisions (2), and with moral inauthenticity of phoniness (3). We shall then consider the quality of existentialist opposition to moral values (4), and some grounds for questioning the compatibility of moral responsibility with the existentialist version of absolutely free moral choice (5). Finally, we shall conclude by examining the charge that Sartre's own analysis of the dilemma is inconsistent with his rejection of moral rules (6).

1. We begin with a summary of Sartre's much-discussed "student's dilemma." In his *Existentialism and Humanism*,[10] he tells of a student of his who during World War II approached him for help in making a difficult choice. The circumstances were these. The young man's elder brother had been killed by the Germans during their offensive in 1940, and he burned to avenge his brother's death. He was living with his mother—his father collaborated with the Germans and was no longer a member of the household—and she was deeply affected by the semi-treason of her husband and the death of her eldest son. Her one consolation was her young son. At the time he approached Sartre for advice, this young man saw himself faced with the choice between going to England to join the Free French Forces and remaining behind

---

[9] For further discussion, see Mary Warnock, *The Philosophy of Sartre* (London: Hutchinson & Co., 1965); Anthony Manser, *Sartre: A Philosophic Study* (London: Athlone Press, 1966); A. Manser and A. Kolnai, "Symposium on Existentialism," *Aristotelian Society Supplementary Volume XXXVII* (1963), p. 11–51. Alisdair MacIntyre, "Existentialism," *A Critical History of Western Philosophy*, ed. D. J. O'Connor (London: Collier-Macmillan Ltd., 1964), pp. 509–29.

[10] Trans. Philip Mairet (London: Methuen, 1948), pp. 35–38.

to comfort his mother. He felt he owed his country something and that under the circumstances he ought to be willing to make great sacrifices.

But on the other hand he was fully aware that his mother lived only for him and that his departure would cause her anguish and despair. If he stayed with his mother, moreover, he was sure to be of help; but if he went abroad, he might fail to accomplish anything useful—even if he successfully escaped he might end up in an office filing papers. Should he choose to direct his life to helping one individual, his mother? Or should he choose to direct his life to a "higher" end, to a national collectivity, despite the fact that he might be ineffective? Who or what could help him choose between these two alternatives? Could Christian doctrine help, Christian doctrine which says, Love your neighbor, do the hardest thing, and so on? But who is the relevant neighbor, his suffering mother or his suffering country? And which is the hardest thing to do, to stay or to leave? Could the Kantian ethic, perhaps, help in this choice? That ethic says, Never regard another as a means, but always as an end. But is not the logic of the situation such that if he regards his country as an end he is making a means of his mother, and if he takes his mother as an end, he is making a means of his fellow countrymen who are fighting in his behalf?

Sartre believes that in a case like this, where values are too uncertain and abstract to determine the right choice, "nothing remains but to trust in our instincts." But if one is to trust one's instincts or feelings, how does one estimate the strength of a feeling? Is the student's feeling of love for his mother stronger than his love for his country? Sartre answers that the only way to tell the strength of a feeling is by the action which defines and ratifies it. One can, for example, know one loves a friend enough to sacrifice a large sum of money for him only if one actually does sacrifice that sum of money. One can know one loves one's mother enough to remain with her only if one does actually remain with her.

Sartre concludes: "In coming to me, he knew what advice I should give him, and I had but one reply to make: you are free, therefore choose—that is to say, invent. No rule of general morality can show you what you ought to do: no signs are vouchsafed in this world."

Sartre gives us a moral dilemma that he feels to be unanswerable. Neither Christian doctrine, nor the Kantian ethic, nor expert advice can break down the dilemma, one can only feel and then choose—

in a state of agonizing uncertainty, abandonment, and forlornness.

2. One of the first things to note about existentialist moral teaching is that very little is said about the day-to-day problems of morality such as ordinary obligations, duties, and roles. Honesty, faithfulness to promises, and the daily demands of parenthood, etc., all allegedly make up the content of "bourgeois morality." The existentialist, like the situationist, is aware of living, not in a world where social norms are stable, social conflict minimal, and ordinary morality supported by custom and habit, but in a world of war and conscription, of civil strife and the totalitarian state. In such a world people must learn to justify — the radical decision for which the situation calls. To what norm can one appeal when faced with the student's dilemma, where consequences can hardly be evaluated? Can ordinary moral reasons be relevant when part of what one must choose is what is going to count as a reason for choice in the future?[11] One might wonder, nonetheless, whether an ethics whose paradigm of moral decision is so radical a choice of a way of life (for Sartre himself *the* moral question appears to be: Shall I join the Communist Party?) has chosen the most illuminating paradigm.

Compromise with the demands of authentic non-legalistic morality is impossible.

Such is the real paradox of morality: If I occupy myself with treating as ends in themselves certain human beings, my wife, my son, my friends, the needy beggar I meet in the street, if I really try to carry out all my duties toward them, I shall spend my whole life in doing so, I shall be compelled to *pass over* in silence the injustice of the epoch, the class-struggle, colonialism, anti-semitism, etc., and, in the last resort to profit from oppression in order to do good.[12]

Sartre goes on to say that if, on the other hand, he throws himself into struggle against injustice and oppression, he will be compelled to neglect *completely* his family and his friends. But just why it is that

---

[11] ". . . either decision in effect marks the adoption on the part of the agent of a changed moral outlook. It does not seem to have been much observed by ethical philosophers that, speaking psychologically, the adoption of a new morality by an agent is frequently associated with the confrontation of a moral dilemma. Indeed, it is hard to see what else would be likely to bring about a change of moral outlook other than the having to make a difficult moral decision." John Lemmon, "Moral Dilemmas," *Christian Ethics* . . . p. 276. Cf. Robert O. Johann, S.J., "Rules and Decisions," *America*, *CXVII*, (July 15, 1967), p. 61.

[12] Quoted by Manser, *Aristotelian Society* . . . , p. 23.

compromise is so totally impossible, why one cannot act morally in dividing his attention between family and society, is by no means entirely obvious.

Existentialist ethics contrasts sharply with analytic ethics where, it is sometimes said, the paradigm of moral decision is the decision to return or not to return a borrowed library book or to keep a promise made on a desert island to a dying man. As Anthony Manser has said:

I have never seen a discussion in a philosophical journal of a moral problem of the type that many of our students now face: should I sleep with this girl whom I have no intention of marrying? What Sartre has to say is relevant to issues like this, to a world where there is the possibility of total annihilation. This constitutes his strength and his importance.[13]

One might add that it is a similar concern with relevant and pressing moral issues that is the strength and importance of the situationists.

3. Sartre fails to give any concrete moral advice. He directs: Be authentic! but provides no criteria of authenticity. This or that objectively describable act might be generally characterized as a good act. Nevertheless since it may be done wrongly and then be counted as a bad act, the existentialist feels he must emphasize a motive-like characteristic similar to intensity of choice. Mary Warnock has suggested that the typical Sartrean moral question is: What, here and now, would be the least *phoney* thing for me to do? Phoniness or inauthenticity constitutes virtually the only criterion for evaluating decisions. When, as for Sartre's student, neither choice would be clearly phoney, pure decision is king.

One might discern in Christian ethics a similar concern with authentic purity of intention, of non-phoney intensity of choice. Witness the condemnation of the lukewarm and self-righteous as contrasted with a milder judgment of sinners, especially in the parables of the Pharisee and the Publican, and of the woman taken in adultery.[14] Concern with acting in accordance with a given code is phariseeism; what God looks for is loving response to this situation. Forget the moral code that comes out of the past, even if it proved satisfactory in past situations. Acting in this way is, of course, risky; but for a Christian it is, presumably, not an excessive source of "dread."

4. "Where there are rules, there is no morality: where there is

---

[13] *Sartre: A Philosophic Study* (London: Athlone Press, 1966), p. 139.
[14] Cf. Kolnai, p. 35.

morality, no rules" is proposed by Anthony Manser as the characteristically existentialist slogan. Sartre agrees with Kierkegaard that the
answers to the problems of life are not given, as are the answers to
mathematics problems, in the back of the book.[15] Anyone who believes
in given standards is trying to "lay off" responsibility for what he does
on the shoulders of others, and so lives in "bad faith." Ordinary
morality is one of the main sources of bad faith; it tends to conceal
the extent to which man is free and must choose what he is and is to
become. There is no choice if choice is a kind of deduction from given
and necessary premises, and if conscience is simply the introjection of
the rules and attitudes of society. True morality is more radical, beyond
any given good and evil:

In all previous studies of morality, one thing was lacking, strange as that may
sound: the problem of morality itself; what was lacking was the suspicion that
there was anything at all problematic here. What the philosophers called a
'rational foundation for morality' and tried to supply was, properly considered, only a scholarly variation of a common *faith* in the prevalent
morality; a new means of *expression* of this faith . . . in the last analysis, a
kind of denial that this morality might ever be considered problematic . . .[16]

---

[15] For still another ground for opposition to decisions based on given rules, see
George Polya, *Patterns of Plausible Inference*, Volume II of *Mathematics and
Plausible Reasoning*, (Princeton, N.J.: Princeton University Press, 1954). "I remember
a conversation on invention and plausible reasoning. It happened long ago. I talked
with a friend who was much older than myself and could look back on a distinguished
record of discoveries, inventions, and successful professional work. As he talked of
plausible reasoning and invention, he doubtless knew what he was talking about.
He maintained with unusual warmth and force of conviction that invention and
plausible reasoning have no rules. Hunches and guesses, he said, depend on
experience and intuition, but not on rules: there are no rules, there can be no rules,
there should be no rules, and if there were some rules, they were useless anyway.
I maintained the contrary—a conversation is uninteresting if there is no difference
of opinion—yet I felt the strength of his position. My friend was a surgeon. A wrong
decision of a surgeon may cost a life and sometimes, when a patient suddenly starts
bleeding or suffocating, the right decision must come in a second. I understand that
people who have to make such responsible quick decisions have no use for rules. The
time is too short to apply a rule properly, and any set pattern could misguide you;
what you need is intense concentration upon the situation before you. And so people
come to distrust rules and to rely upon their intuition or experience or intuition-and-
experience.
  In the case of my friend, there was still something else, perhaps. He was a little
on the domineering side. He hated to relinquish power. He felt, perhaps, that
acknowledging a rule is like delegating a part of his authority to a machine, and so
he was against it." (pp. 109–110).
[16] Friedrich W. Nietzsche, *Beyond Good and Evil*, Section 186.

To the extent that good and evil are not given, and do not exist till the moment of choice, one cannot act in a distinctively human fashion in choosing good over evil. "It is decision," says Jaspers, "that makes existence real." Values are not to be found or discovered; like artistic values they are to be invented. Nietzsche put it: "This is now my way, what is yours? As for *the* way—it does not exist."

Moral philosophy, the existentialist would insist, is not like philosophy of science in its analysis of universally accepted examples of successful scientific discovery and progress. If moral philosophy had a similar function, it would demand demonstrably successful examples of high morality—but who is to furnish such examples? The only possible criteria would be that given by one's own society; but as this would entail accepting society's evaluation, it would be impossible to get beyond the given good and the given evil. Morality is rather like the artistic process: *given* criteria of aesthetic or moral evaluation serve only for comparing an individual's performance with past successes. Such criteria do not help to answer the question: is this artifact or way of life a present success? Nietzsche's words about morality apply just as well to the artist: "good and evil are creations of man, nothing eternal, stable, but change with changes in man's image of himself." No true artist follows a given pattern, even one given by himself; this would make of him a mechanic. The critic may formulate rules; the artist ignores them in order to achieve authentic beauty. Freedom is inseparable from creativity. Neither aesthetic nor moral values exist before the artist or the moral man sets to work; values appear in the work itself.[17]

5. Sartre accepts the Kantian categorical imperative, "Act only on that maxim which you can at the same time will also to be universal law." Earlier in the above quoted essay Sartre writes:

... in creating the man that we want to be, there is not a single one of our acts which does not at the same time create an image of man as we think he ought to be ...

... if I want to marry, to have children; even if this marriage depends solely

---

[17] Helen Oppenheimer points out a crucial weakness in the "artist as model" view of morality: "It is the stringency rather than the universality of rules which is really in question ... In the last resort the trouble is not that each painter's task is individual to himself, but that it is not properly analogous to the moral task of doing one's duty." ("Moral Choice and Divine Authority," *Christian Ethics* ... p. 227.).

on my own circumstances or passions or wish, I am involving all humanity in monogamy and not merely myself. Therefore, I am responsible for myself and for everyone else. I am creating a certain image of man as my own choosing. In choosing myself, I choose man.

In criticism of Kant, Sartre writes:

... though the content of ethics is variable, a certain form of it is universal. Kant says that freedom desires both itself and the freedom of others. Granted. But he believes that the formal and universal are enough to constitute an ethic. We, on the other hand, think that principles which are too abstract run aground in trying to decide action. Once again take the case of the student. In the name of what, in the name of what great moral maxim do you think he could have decided to abandon his mother or to stay with her? There is no way of judging. The content is always concrete and thereby unforseeable; there is always the element of invention. The one thing that counts is knowing whether the inventing that has been done, has been done in the name of freedom.

Kant believed that the categorical imperative was the adequate test of the moral rules or "maxims" to be followed. If you propose to follow a rule that says: "Do x," but would be unwilling to have that rule made a universal law or a rule for everybody, then you ought not do x. For example, since you would not want everybody to follow the rule "Tell a lie when it suits your convenience," do not tell a lie. For Kant, though not for Sartre, one might say that human reason provides definite limitations on universalizable maxims: given human reason, there are certain maxims one could not possibly wish to see everybody follow. For Sartre there is but one limitation on choice: an authentic moral choice must respect the freedom of everyone alike. It is difficult to see how this is consistent with his assertion that whatever I do I do freely, choosing my dispositions, my attitudes, and even my wishes. Why must I respect the freedom of all alike; in terms of what given categories is this limitation proposed? Doubtlessly, emphasis on the scope of human freedom tends to strengthen one's sense of human dignity. However, if nothing is given by God, or "nature", or moral codes, and if we choose absolutely everything, not only are we made aware of responsibility for more attitudes, emotions, etc. than we usually like to think, but the very meaning of *choice* is distorted beyond recognition.

Alvin Plantinga considers the very possibility of morality to be undercut by Sartre's doctrine that "man's absolute freedom entails man's absolute responsibility":

Every choice, [Sartre] tells us, is unconditioned and completely contingent, there is nothing to which it can appeal, and it is therefore "absurd" . . . Every choice defines both values and rationality. But if that is so, then it is impossible to make a wrong choice . . . my choice can never be mistaken. *Whatever* I choose is right by definition. Sartre is surreptitiously holding on to the meaning of responsibility appropriate to a world in which there are objective values which I may decide to realize or to reject. But if there is no value exterior to choice, then this notion of responsibility is no longer appropriate or even meaningful.

. . . the notions of responsibility and anguish lose their point. Sartre tells us of a military commander who has decided to send men on a mission that may cost them their lives. The man is anguished. But why should he be? If we think of the preservation of human life as a value prior to any choice on our part, we can understand his anguish—he is forced to choose a positive disvalue. But if his very choice constitutes value, then no matter what he chooses, he will be right. Why then be anguished? [18]

A similar critique might be made of the situationist who would claim seriously—if any do—that love or agapé is the only rule of moral action. The difficulty is something like that which might be brought against the claim that intuition is the only source of truth. Unless one knows how to recognize the presence of intuition, or knows a sign of intuition (i.e. some independently knowable characteristic which correlates with intuition, and so indirectly with truth), the claim about intuition would not really help distinguish truth from falsity. And likewise if one is told that nothing is moral but loving makes it so, then one needs to know how to recognize either the presence of love or some independently knowable characteristic which correlates with the loving act, and so with the moral act. In the absence of either of these, it might be argued that the usefulness of knowing that love is the only rule of moral action is diminished, for identification of the loving action is beyond one's practical reach.

6. To return to Sartre's student, it would appear that, as Bambrough says, Sartre has a pretty good idea of what considerations are relevant to the solution of the dilemma:

It is as plain to him as it is to us that loyalty to parents and resistance to tyranny are both good: the dilemma arises because these two good things conflict. It is as plain to him as it is to us that the young man would be doing *wrong* if he went to South America to escape both his conflicting obligations.

[18] "An Existentialist's Ethics," *Review of Metaphysics*, XII (1958), pp. 248–49.

This and a hundred other possible answers are so clearly ruled out that they are not so much as mentioned.[19]

A defender of moral rules might further contend with Sartre: "The model of morality you (rightly) reject is that the mention of a moral rule together with the mention of the facts of the case are enough to give a decision. True, in a case like this, such a model is not enough (if it ever is), here there is a conflict of principles and the application of a single principle is unsatisfactory. But does this mean that the decision has to be made with no regard for principles? Is not this decision difficult for the student, not because no principles are relevant—for then decision would be easy—but because principles of equal or nearly equal weight must be evaluated in the light of the circumstances? Decisions are easy when there is no conflict of principles, and hard only when conflicting principles are relevant and of very nearly equal weight. You have, I am afraid, hardly given us an example which would convince us that rules and principles are irrelevant in crucial moral decisions."

RELATIVISM

Situationists are sometimes accused of, and sometimes glory in "relativism" in morals. Since the term 'relativism in morals' is used in so many ways today, and since it is unlikely that it has the same meaning (intension) when used as a pro-word and a con-word, it will prove useful to look at some main types of relativism in order to clarify what is involved in legitimately referring to someone's metaethical stance in morals as "relativist."

Philosophers today generally distinguish two types of relativism:

---

[19] J. R. Bambrough, "Unanswerable Questions," *Aristotelian Society Supplementary Volume XL* (1966). Bambrough concludes that Sartre's discussion of his own example is partial and inadequate, and we see "hence how inaccurate and inadequate is the epistemology of morals that he bases on that example and that discussion." Further, Sartre "implicitly claims to know the right answer to the young man's dilemma. He claims to have shown that the considerations in favor of the two possible answers—Mother or France—are exactly equal in weight. And that is to claim to have shown that the right answer to the dilemma is that it is *a matter of moral indifference* which of the two choices the young man makes. If this is so (and it is important to notice that Sartre does not supply *us* with sufficient data to know whether or not it is so) then indeed the young man may freely and even arbitrarily choose between the two alternatives." It is also rather odd that Sartre does not tell us what the (expressed?) preference of the student's mother is.

cultural and ethical. Cultural relativism may be defined as the view that the ethical judgments supported by different individuals or groups are sometimes different and conflicting in a very fundamental way. Ethical relativism may be defined as the view that cultural relativism is true and that conflicting ethical judgments may be equally correct.

Thus every ethical relativist is a cultural relativist, but not necessarily vice-versa. One can be a cultural relativist, but not an ethical relativist, if one maintains that fundamental judgments conflict, but that there is a way of showing which of the conflicting judgments is more correct.[20]

What is important to see here is that many who are accused of being, or claim to be, "relativists" do not deserve the name, for they say nothing inconsistent with cultural absolutism, the view that there are no fundamental disagreements in morals. Suppose in one society it is judged morally right to strangle one's father when he reaches old age; and in another society, it is judged morally wrong ever to strangle one's father. Or: in one society at a given time, slavery or contraception or abortion or infanticide or capital punishment is judged morally wrong; and in another society, or in the same society at a later time, an opposite judgment is made. The issue seems clear enough and could be put as follows: parricide—right or wrong? If one answers "In one society right, and in the other society wrong," then surely this is moral relativism.

However, the issue is not so simple. The question that might appropriately be raised is whether these two apparently disagreeing judgments are really about the same moral act?[21] Are these two groups

---

[20] Thus there are three possible options: one can be a cultural absolutist, denying that there are fundamental differences in morals; one can be a cultural relativist, but an ethical absolutist; or one can be an ethical relativist.

[21] S. Toulmin writes about Christian and Muslim "marriage": "The ramifications, both in Christian and in Muslim societies, of the institution of marriage, its relation to the institutions of property, of parenthood and so on, are so complex that there is no question of simply replacing the one institution by the other. Such different parts does the institution of 'marriage' play in the ways of life of a Christian society and of a Muslim one that we might even feel it hardly right to describe Christian and Muslim marriage as being instances of the 'same' institution at all." *Reason In Ethics*, pp. 152–53. P. Winch writes of the practice of child sacrifice in pre-Abrahamic Hebrew society: "This is a practice which, in terms of our own way of living and the moral ideas that go along with it, is just unintelligible . . . the main problem about this is one of *understanding* what is involved . . . not just taking up an attitude, for without understanding we should not know what we were taking up an attitude to." "Nature and Convention," *Proceedings of the Aristotelian Society*, *LX* (1959–60), p. 235.

talking about the same thing? Suppose one group believes in an eternal life after death, lived by the individual in the very same body he had at the moment of death, whether healthy or sick, sound or crippled. Is it clear that we, who now disapprove of strangling superannuated parents, would continue to disapprove if we thought that by strangling our fathers we would be acting piously, be ensuring for them an eternal life with relatively healthy bodies rather than with worn-out bodies racked by illness? [22] If we believed this, would we not think it right to act as they act? Apart from the cases in which quite different circumstances call for the application of quite different moral principles, it would appear that differing religious or philosophical beliefs about life after death are certainly relevant to deciding whether strangling one's father is a moral act. One might either say that the two opinions about strangling one's father are not opinions about the same moral act, i.e. about the same action *qua* constituting a morally judgeable action; alternatively one might say that the two groups do not hold different basic moral principles, i.e. that all differences can be accounted for in terms of different beliefs about putative properties of the act, and that such an example offers evidence of a relativity of *beliefs*, but not of relativity of *morals*. Certainly, any dispute about a non-trivial moral question involves beliefs and assumptions, sometimes rudimentary and only half-formulated, about psychological, cosmological, sociological, philosophical, and theological questions.[23] In sum, there is certainly

[22] Cf. Franz Boas, *The Mind of Primitive Man* (New York: The Macmillan Company, 1922), pp. 57–58: "The person who slays an enemy in revenge for wrongs done, a youth who kills his father before he gets decrepit in order to enable him to continue a vigorous life in the world to come, a father who kills his child as a sacrifice for the welfare of his people, act from such entirely different motives, that psychologically a comparison of their activities does not seem permissible. It would seem much more proper to compare the murder of an enemy in revenge with destruction of his property for the same purpose, or to compare the sacrifice of a child on behalf of the tribe with any other altruistic action performed on account of strong altruistic motives, than to base our comparison on the common concept of murder."

[23] Thus Aurel Kolnai has written: "Erroneous conscience may lean on intellectual delusion or misconception as a kind of collateral support, or indeed be occasioned by it. In such cases, theoretical error not only causes the agent's conscience to be misapplied in fact but colours its intrinsic content and distorts its emphasis. Thus, the moral error that it is not wrong to maltreat animals is often fused with, perhaps conditioned by, the factual error that animals are scarcely more than unconscious automata and incapable of feeling pain in any sense comparable to human suffering. The erroneous conscience of Pacifists is mostly linked up with false opinions about the nature and causes of war; that of nationalists and racialists, with certain historical delusions; that of Marxists, with their sham-scientific theory of social institutions.

good reason to believe that moral divergencies are seldom arbitrary and are mainly the understandable product of large differences in, and conflicting interpretations of, beliefs and experiences.

Granting all this, as will virtually everyone today, the question now to be considered is whether there are any *fundamental moral* differences between peoples, societies, groups or individuals? Apparent moral differences of the most drastic sort abound, and one can be easily fascinated by tales of the strange doings of the Ba-Ila and the Kwakuitl. But is it possible to divide without remainder all these differences into those which rest on variations in attendant circumstances (e.g. the circumstance of an abundant or scarce water supply is certainly relevant to the rules concerning the unrestricted use of water), and those which rest on different views of questions of "fact?" Is A. J. Ayer right when he says that any argument on a question of value reduces itself to an argument about a question of logic or about an empirical matter of fact? Are moral arguments liable to "break down" only on "matters of fact?" What is the nature of the evidence that would help decide these issues one way or the other? What is the import of the evidence of moral differences and similarities gathered by social scientists—psychologists, sociologists, and anthropologists? Since Herodotus we have been aware of different cultural and ethical practices, but the work of several generations of cultural anthropologists has extended almost unimaginably our knowledge of the extent of ethical diversity. It is hard to imagine a social practice or rule, no matter how odd it appears to us, which has not been tried somewhere.

One thing seems clear. There is no incontrovertible evidence of basic moral differences between peoples, societies, groups or individuals.[24] If not all, at any rate most differences are only apparent and are reducible to differences in attendant circumstances or to differences in

In general, our vision of things as they are is largely dependent on our emotive and valuational attitudes; and conversely, our valuations, including our moral views, are largely contingent upon our perception and construction of reality and our appraisal of the factual importance of various things and forces in its order." "Erroneous Conscience," *Proceedings of the Aristotelian Society*, *LVIII* (1957–1958), p. 180. Cf. Also Morris Ginsberg, *Essays in Sociology and Social Philosophy*, Vol. 1: On the Diversity of Morals (London: Heinemann, 1956).

[24] "We must concede that no anthropologist has offered what we should regard as really an adequate account of a single case, clearly showing there is ultimate disagreement in ethical principle." R. Brandt, *Ethical Theory* (New Jersey: Prentice Hall, Inc., 1959), p. 102.

views about questions of beliefs, whether theological, philosophical, scientific, sociological, or economic.[25] If this is so, many a *soi-disant*

---

[25] If, for example, a man claims to be a relativist about divorce, holding that it was wrong, but is now all right, he might well be challenged: Does "divorce" have the same meaning for you and for your adversaries? Do both of you agree about the prospective consequences of change, about the changing understanding of marriage and of the role of women, and the like? If you believed what your opponent believes about these non-moral matters, would you continue to draw the moral conclusions you draw?

Here is an example of the kind of "factual" analysis which, if accepted, might well lead to a re-evaluation of the morality of divorce:

It is essential that we begin . . . by exorcizing the myth that divorce constitutes a threat to our present concept of the family. Moralistic rhetoric would have us believe that, at some vague era in the past, a familial idyl prevailed, and the sanctity and inviolability of the family as we now know it were the unchallenged pillars of society. Our rising divorce rates are then presented as the degeneration from this golden age. However, knowledge of social history indicates that our present notion of the family, upon which these appeals to home and motherhood are based, is a recent one which became possible only with the privatizing of marriage and the new idea of the child that began to arise during the 18th century. In an earlier period marriage was a multifunctional socio-economic institution and had little to do with these personal values. The whole concept of child-rearing as an intensive project of the family, engaging the wife as a full-time occupation, would have seemed incredible before our present period. Children in earlier societies were left very much to fend for themselves and grew up higgledy-piggledy among the extended family, servants, children of servants and older siblings. Lower-class parents were too busy with the many economic tasks upon which their existence depended to waste much time with the psychology of their children. The whole concept of childhood as a special process is a modern novelty. So the two most distinctive characteristics of modern marriage, intense emotional relationship between the spouses and conscious dedication to child-rearing, are specifically modern traits which had only a minor role in the institution of marriage before the 19th century.

Our present divorce trends, far from threatening this concept of marriage, are the condition which makes this use of marriage possible. Now that practically all the productive functions which once characterized marriage—food and goods production, political alliances—have fled from this institution to other spheres, marriage loses its public character and survives today primarily as an interpersonal relationship. Divorce is the escape hatch which makes possible this use of marriage for a purpose for which it is, in some ways, rather poorly adapted. Only by keeping open the back door of divorce, are we able to maintain unchallenged a view of marriage that is almost impossibly overloaded with expectations of interpersonal fulfilment. Rosemary Ruether, "Divorce: No Longer Unthinkable," *Commonweal, LXXXIV* (April 14, 1967), pp. 117–18.

The author is saying that since marriage means something different today from what it meant in the past, we must be consistent and see that divorce must mean something different. One might of course question the adequacy of this account of social history; but one could hardly refer to its author as a relativist simply on the basis of an allegedly false or inadequate reading of social history. If the author is right, then "moral relativist" may deserve the name no more than he who cries shame at moral relativism.

Today a number of philosophers argue for ethical relativism. Non-cognitivists, who hold that ethical sentences are emotive-directive in function, and so neither true nor false, are sometimes taken to be ethical relativists on the ground that such a position offers no rational basis for ethical preference.[26] More relevant to our concerns here is the form of ethical relativism which might be stated as follows: even if there are no fundamental differences at the level of moral prinicples or rules, might not two persons holding identical sets of non-moral beliefs nonetheless basically disagree on the hierarchy of values or on the best "way of life?" Such a position is defended by R. M. Hare:

. . . Thus a complete justification of a decision would consist in a complete account of its effects, together with a complete account of the principles which it observed, and the effects of observing those principles—for, of course, it is the effects (what obeying them in fact consists in) which give content to the principles too. Thus, if pressed to justify a decision completely, we have to give a complete specification of the way of life of which it is a part. This complete specification it is impossible in practice to give; the nearest attempts are those given by the great religions, especially those which can point to historical persons who carried out the way of life in practice. Suppose, however, that we can give it. If the inquirer still goes on asking "But why should I live like that?" then there is no further answer to give him, because we have already, *ex hypothesi*, said everything that could be included in this further answer. We can only ask him to make up his own mind which way he ought to live; for in the end everything rests upon such a decision of principle.[27]

"divorce is wrong" when said in the 18th century and "divorce is right" when said in the 20th century are both true and non-contradictory. There is no basic moral change, since "divorce" is understood in two different ways.

[26] But cf. Charles L. Stevenson, "Relativism and non-Relativism in the Theory of Value," *Proceedings and Addresses of the American Philosophical Association, 1961–62 XXXV* (Yellow Springs, Ohio: Antioch Press, 1962), pp. 25–44.

[27] *The Language of Morals* (London: Oxford University Press, 1952), p. 69. Cf. Brian Medlin, "Ultimate Principles and Ethical Egoism," *The Australasian Journal of Philosophy*, XXXV (1957). "It is now pretty generally accepted by professional philosophers that ultimate principles must be arbitrary . . . To arrive at a conclusion in ethics one must have at least one ethical premise. This premise, if it be in turn a conclusion, must be the conclusion of an argument containing at least one ethical premise. And so we can go back, indefinitely but not forever. Sooner or later we must come to at least one ethical premise which is not deduced but baldly asserted. Here we must be a-rational: neither rational nor irrational, for there is no room for reason even to go wrong."

In the face of this form of relativism—common to some empiricist and existentialist philosophers—it is the task of the absolutist to determine the criteria that a man must meet if he is to make a rational choice of a way of life or comprehensive moral code.

Space is not available here to develop the excellent analysis offered by Paul Taylor [28] to meet this demand, but a few words may be in order. One could not be said to choose anything rationally unless his choice was free, informed, and unbiased. A man would not be said to have made a rational choice among alternatives unless first, he had chosen freely, that is, unless his choice was undetermined by internal or external constraint; second, unless his choice was made with full knowledge of the various alternatives; and third, unless his choice was free of bias and he was free of so-called "vicious" dispositions or habits.

To be sure, one can seldom, if ever, make decisions which are perfectly free, informed, and unbiased. But one can reasonably be committed to changing one's decision when it is shown that the decision is based on less than optimal information, even given the constraints of time and effort, or that bias or lack of freedom has not been adequately discounted.

If one asks: why try to meet the conditions of rational choice in choosing between ways of life? the answer may be given: because a choice which meets these conditions will offer the best chance of achieving what you want to achieve by choosing. If it be asked: why do you say that these are the criteria of rational choice? The answer is that no choice which failed to meet and every choice which did meet these criteria would be called "rational."

One might object that the notion of "rationality" itself is comprehensible only in terms of a given culture, and therefore that the very criteria of rational choice are culture-bound and ultimately personal. The short answer is that one cannot make a personal decision about the criteria of rationality in morals or in any other value-system. One can no more make a personal decision about what is to count as evidence in moral argument than one can make a personal decision about what is to count as a rule of etiquette. It belongs to the grammar

---

[28] *Normative Discourse* (Englewood Cliffs, N. J.: Prentice-Hall Inc., 1961). Cf. John Hospers, *Human Conduct* (New York: Harcourt, Brace & World, 1961); W. K. Frankena, *Ethics* (Englewood Cliffs, N.J.: Prentice-Hall, Inc., 1963); and my "How to Defend Ethical Absolutism," *Proceedings of the American Catholic Philosophical Association*, XXXVII (1963), pp. 78–81.

of the word 'rational' that it is intelligible to speak of not acting in a rational way; but this is not to say that it is intelligible to speak of altering the criteria of rationality. The private enterprise theory of moral or rational criteria is simply untenable. The desire to avoid the charge of making a verbal decision in favor of one's own moral code or way of life, though a reasonable desire, is not in much danger of going unfulfilled because of the language one happens to speak. No doubt moral vocabulary is determined to a degree by one's accepted way of life; but not so the criteria for accepting a way of life, the criteria of rationality. Doubtless at times "when we call certain actions or attitudes 'rational,' 'reasonable,' 'valid,' or 'sound' we are using these terms in a purely *moralistic* sense,"[29] but this is not always the case. One can discount settled non-rational attitudes which are the source of expressions of moralistic approval or disapproval; but one cannot "make words mean anything one likes"—Humpty-Dumptyism is an absurdity.[30]

It is evident that if there are criteria of rational choice between ways of life, then in principle, moral disputes are always ultimately resolvable in terms of competing ways of life and, it may well be, often only at that level. This is to say that most, if not all, moral disputes implicitly involve comparisons between ways of life as wholes. Thus, when a dispute about birth control or the desirability of suicide under some circumstances is being carried on, even between two opponents who share many of the same moral principles, the dispute is basically resolvable to the question: is a way of life which includes birth control or suicide rationally preferable to a way of life without birth control or suicide? In this light, the disputants *tend* to concentrate attention on circumstances and consequences of acts, immediate and mediate, direct and indirect, obvious and subtle, personal and institutional. For this

[29] Kai Nielson, "Conventionalism in Morals and the Appeals to Human Nature," *Philosophy and Phenomenological Research*, XXIII (1962), p. 217. On the "private enterprise theory of moral criteria," see "Moral Arguments" by Mrs. Philippa Foot, *Mind*, LXVII (1958), pp. 502–13.

[30] ". . . words may have a meaning and so, in a different though related sense, may a speaker mean something by the words he uses. But this latter kind of meaning would be impossible if the words used did not already mean something in the first sense . . . something which the speaker did not himself *make* them mean . . . Of course words may be defined arbitrarily for a special purpose, but only in terms of other words with an established common meaning or of commonly understood techniques such as ostensive definition. Nobody can make his words mean something simply by willing that they should." P. Winch, "Nature and Convention," p. 245.

reason, one is not limited to circumstantial *ad hominem* arguments in moral philosophy as one so clearly is in matters of taste. It may not be true to say that "a Chinese gentleman of the fifth century B.C., an Athenian citizen of the same period, a medieval monk and a contemporary citizen of Ealing or Ninji-Novgorod, can . . . settle down and reach agreed and valid conclusions as to the duties of any man in well-defined moral situations."[31] But this does not mean that agreement between these men on the criteria of rational choice among ways of life is impossible, or that one could not expect to find agreement between men scattered in time and place on a question of moral goodness, as seen *in terms of* a rationally preferable way of life.[32]

When one shows that way of life *A* is rationally preferable to way of life *B*, he has not shown that *A* is the absolutely-best way of life. This could be shown only if all possible ways of life could be compared. As Bernard Mayo rightly remarks, it is not necessary that someone have access to an absolute standard before he can rightly say that one way of life is better than another.[33] Whether there is or must be a best possible way of life, one need not know it in order to make a rational choice between ways of life. Just as in physical science the absolute truth about the universe may be inaccessible, so in moral theory the absolute truth about ways of life may be inaccessible to philosophy. Nevertheless, one can have good reasons for preferring one way of life

---

[31] W. B. Gallie, "Liberal Morality and Socialist Morality," *Philosophy, Politics and Society* (London: Oxford University Press, 1956), p. 117.

[32] Suppose one objects that even if the conditions of rational choice are correctly stated, the demands imposed on one who attempts to fulfil these conditions are such that no purely rational choices among ways of life could ever be made. Thus, if no one is ever in a position to claim to have made such a choice, no one is ever in a position to claim that any of his value judgments is ultimately justified.

It must first be admitted that the criteria for rational choice are somewhat like counsels of perfection. But though no one may be able legitimately to claim to have met the criteria perfectly, knowing and acting on them is none the less useful. Surely it is true that one will make a choice among competing makes of automobiles that is the more rational the more it is free, informed, and unbiased. We are capable of some degree of self-knowledge with respect to our own freedom, knowledge, and bias; we are aware that our choices between some goods are more rational than our choices between others; we are also aware that improvement in meeting the criteria of rationality is possible. Thus, on this analysis, whenever we find that an act, rule, principle, or obligation that is unjustifiable in terms of one way of life is justifiable in terms of another, and that the latter way of life is rationally justifiable by comparison with the former, then we are given the necessary and sufficient grounds for choosing the latter way of life.

[33] *Ethics and the Moral Life* (London: The Macmillan Company, 1958), p. 42.

to another, just as one can have good reasons for preferring one hypothesis to another in physical science, or soft-cooked potatoes to half-raw ones without any reference to an Ideal Food.

In sum, when a man says he is (or is said to be) a relativist in morals, one wants to know: A. Is he a cultural relativist, does he believe that there are fundamental moral differences between people? or does he believe that moral differences are superficial because rooted in theoretical (theological, philosophical, scientific, etc.) differences? B. Is he an ethical relativist, that is, if he does believe that there are fundamental differences between people, does he believe that there is no rational way of ultimately deciding, in terms of a way of life, who is right?

INTRINSICALLY WRONG ACTS

A major point of disagreement between situationists and their opponents concerns the denial by some situationists that there are kinds of acts that are always wrong no matter what the circumstances. Analytic philosophers today are much concerned with a whole range of associated questions: How can human actions properly be described? Are several alternative descriptions possible, and if so, is just one of these uniquely satisfactory for moral evaluation? Can one, and if so on what grounds, draw a plausible line between action, circumstance, and consequence? If one can, but need not necessarily include consequences in our description of an action, then one might say either "this kind of act (which includes consequences in its 'fuller' description) is wrong" or, equivalently, "this act (not including consequences in its description) is wrong because of its consequences." But then the utilitarian-formalist and the intrinsicalist-extrinsicalist distinctions break down.[34] In the space available here little can be done even to make clear the importance of these questions. However, the following may prove helpful in supplying background for the articles of Bennett, Kolnai, Fletcher, and McCabe.[35]

[34] Cf. Ruth Macklin, "Actions, Consequences and Ethical Theory," *The Journal of Value Inquiry*, I (1967), 72–80, for an outline of some dimensions of these issues and a good bibliography.

[35] Cf. J. Milhaven, S.J., "Towards an Epistemology of Ethics," *Theological Studies*, XXVII (1966), pp. 228–41, which studies "the axiom that the essential purpose of a particular act suffices to determine its moral and immoral use" and makes a plea for "recognizing more extensively the empirical evidence of moral judgments." Also see

One can distinguish two sorts of descriptions or definitions of acts, naturalistic and moralistic. A naturalistic (or morally neutral) description of an act includes only properties known empirically, while a moralistic (or morally evaluative) description includes terms of moral evaluation. Thus one might describe an act by saying "Jones spanked his son" or by saying "Jones cruelly hit his son," the former being a brief naturalistic description, the latter a brief moralistic description. Note that unanimous agreement as to the applicability of the first description to what Jones did would be probable, but possibly not on whether Jones was wrong in so acting. There would probably be unanimous agreement as to whether the act as moralistically described was wrong ("cruelty is wrong" is tautological), but possibly not on whether that description was applicable. Thus if one gives a naturalistic description of an act, there is little or no problem about knowing whether the description applies; yet there is a serious problem about knowing whether such an act is always right or always wrong no matter what the attendant circumstances are. On the other hand, if one gives a moralistic description of an act, there is little or no problem about knowing whether such an act is always morally wrong no matter what the attendant circumstances; but there is a serious problem, it would appear, about knowing whether that description applies to the case in hand.[36]

In the light of this distinction, one now wants to know: is there a kind of act that can be both naturalistically defined and also be known to be always wrong? Can one find an act, call it x, such that x is both

Thomas A. Wassmer, S.J., "A Re-examination of Situation Ethics," *Catholic Lawyer*, V (1959) pp. 106–12; "Morality and Intrinsic Evil," *Catholic Lawyer*, XI (1965), pp. 180–83, and 236; "Is Intrinsic Evil a Viable Term?", *Chicago Studies*, V (1966), pp. 307–14.

[36] To take another example, consider the two following definitions of "theft". The first is that given by Eric D'Arcy in his *Human Acts* (London: Oxford University Press, 1963): "The theft of B's x is ascribed to A if, and only if, (1) A took x; (2) x did not belong to him, but to B; (3) he did not return it to B, but consumed, sold, or destroyed it; (4) B had not given A leave for the action," (p. 62). The second definition is that given by Austin Fagothey in his *Right and Reason* (St. Louis: C. V. Mosby Co., 1967): "For an act to be theft . . . four elements are required and sufficient: (1) That the act be an act of taking. (2) That the thing be another's property. (3) That the owner be unwilling to let me have it. (4) That his unwillingness be reasonable" (p. 93). The first definition is naturalistic; but is every theft as therein defined *wrong*? The second definition is moralistic (since it refers to "*reasonable* unwillingness"); but how does one *tell* whether an act is theft?

naturalistically described and is also part of the rule "It is never right to do x, no matter what the circumstances or consequences are likely to be?" Will, for example, any of the following do? x is breaking a promise? x is telling a lie? x is getting a divorce? x is committing adultery? x is torturing your wife to death while making her believe you hate her? Breaking a promise, telling a lie, getting a divorce, etc. can be naturalistically described, but can they be known to be always wrong? [37]

The difficulty with the outlandish examples like that of torturing one's wife or the Southern sheriff's hanging a Negro he knows to be innocent as a sop to a white mob intent on lynching six other innocent Negroes [38], is to determine their moral relevance. Is consideration of such unlikely situations, hardly found even in fiction or science fiction, helpful in discussing kinds of acts? One might say: "If I knew that I could save two billion people on earth from an immediate and painful death by torturing my wife, etc., then I morally ought to torture her." But in what sort of strange world could one ever know this antecedent condition sufficiently well to act on it? Do situationists and act-utilitarians deny intrinsic morality because they have in mind examples which their opponents refuse to consider morally relevant when speaking of intrinsically wrong acts? How much difference is there between one who refuses to consider outlandish cases and says "x is always wrong, no matter what the circumstances," and one who says "x is not always wrong," and then offers an outlandish case as a counter-example to the intrinsicalist thesis?

At least occasionally therefore, those who assert that no acts are

---

[37] In *Christian Morals Today* (Philadelphia: Westminster Press, 1964), p. 16, Bishop Robinson writes: "There are some things of which one may say that it is so inconceivable that they could ever be an expression of love—like cruelty to children or rape—that one might say without much fear of contradiction that they are for Christians always wrong." ("Cruelty to children," one might note, is moralistically referred to; and whether "rape" is understood naturalistically or moralistically is not clear, e.g., could one rape one's own wife? would such an act ever be justifiable?). Cf. Helmet Thielicke, *Theological Ethics*, Volume 1: Foundations (Philadelphia: Fortress Press, 1966), pp. 643–47 for a defence of the position that although "from the standpoint of justification all things are possible, . . . certain limits . . . cannot be transgressed."

[38] Cf. the discussion in J. J. C. Smart's *An Outline of a System of Utilitarian Ethics* (Victoria: Melbourne University Press, 1961); Smart's "The Methods of Ethics and the Methods of Science," *Journal of Philosophy*, LXII (1965), pp. 344–49; and Kenneth Stern, "Testing Ethical Theories," *Journal of Philosophy*, LXIII (1966), pp. 234–38.

intrinsically wrong have in mind naturalistic descriptions, while those who deny this have in mind moralistic descriptions. Further, the acceptability or non-acceptability of unlikely examples may possibly influence a man's adoption or rejection of the intrinsicalist thesis.

CHRISTIAN ETHICS

Despite the fact that many of those who are situationists are Christian theologians, we will in these pages continue to shy away from strictly theological dimensions and presuppositions on the ground that, in the space available, understanding will be maximized by concentration on the philosophical themes and counterparts of situationism. This will mean that no direct (though, it is to be hoped, considerable indirect) light will be shed on the much discussed question: is situationism a rejection of Christian morality or its fulfilment in contemporary terms? [39]

It is obvious even to casual observation that Christian ethics is in a state of flux and possibly of radical change.

Item (1): in the past there was virtually unanimous consent among Christians about the morality of certain "kinds of acts," but such a consensus no longer exists on a great variety of issues such as sexual and marital ethics, capital punishment, and the conditions or possibility of "just war." Once this occurs, it becomes necessary to take a new look at traditional arguments for traditional moral conclusions; this implies a rigorous investigation of the conditions and nature of moral justification.

Item (2): a changing understanding of the Bible has raised questions for both Protestant Christian Ethics and for Catholic moral theology, though it is clear that the Bible was never as important a source of moral doctrine for Catholics as it was for Protestants. One can no longer use the Bible to proof-test moral arguments in quite the same way as formerly. As D. E. Nineham has written:

If the thesis put forward . . . is sound . . . the gospels must be treated in the first instance as so many *formulations of the early church's growing tradition*

[39] Christian morality may be described as the position according to which: (*a*) Christian belief and experience are crucial in giving a man the psychological (or "existential") capacity (or motivation) for acting morally; (*b*) the moral ideal has been revealed in Jesus Christ and in his teachings; (*c*) no ethical theory which is not conceived in Judaeo-Christian supernatural terms can be adequate in practice.

about the ministry of Jesus . . . A question mark is clearly set against . . . the practice, which still largely governs the life of the Churches, of quoting individual sayings and incidents from the gospels as precedents.[40]

Item (3): the growing adoption of situationism by Christians has eliminated the radical division between Christian and the recent Anglo-American philosophical moralities on the intrinsic wrongness of certain kinds of acts. In 1958, G. E. M. Anscombe wrote that "the differences between the well-known English writers on moral philosophy from Sidgwick to the present day are of little importance." The reason offered is that:

> . . . every one of the best known English academic moral philosophers has put out a doctrine according to which, e.g., it is not possible to hold that it cannot be right to kill the innocent as a means to any end whatsoever and that someone who thinks otherwise is in error. . . . Now this is quite a significant thing: for it means that all these philosophies are quite incompatible with the Hebrew-Christian ethic. For it has been characteristic of that ethic to teach that there are certain things forbidden whatever *consequences* threaten, such as: choosing to kill the innocent for any purpose, however good; treachery; . . . The prohibition of certain things simply in virtue of their description as such-and-such identifiable kinds of action, regardless of any further consequences, is certainly not the whole of the Hebrew-Christian ethic; but it is a noteworthy feature of it . . .[41]

If situationism does ally itself to analytic moral philosophy on this issue of intrinsic morality, one might legitimately wonder why most analysts have paid, and, it can be expected, will pay so little attention to situationist ethics. The answer is simple: situationism is a species of religious ethics, and religious ethics is thought to be philosophically indefensible because of its presupposition that ethics is a heteronomous discipline, somehow depending on God for its foundations. It may prove helpful to examine some of the reasons for the influential

---

[40] "Eyewitness Testimony and the Gospel Tradition," *Journal of Theological Studies*, XI (1960), pp. 254–56 (my italics). Because of the centrality of natural law theory in traditional Catholic moral theology, discussion often took place there at a recognizably more philosophical level than among Protestant moralists, where Biblical language and justification has a more important role to play; but given the questioning spirit in which many Catholic moral theologians now view natural law, the relation of philosophy to theology is being re-evaluated.

[41] "Modern Moral Philosophy," *Philosophy*, XXXVIII (1958), pp. 9–10. Cf. A Boyce Gibson, "Morality, Religious and Secular," *Journal of Theological Studies*, XIII (1962), pp. 1–13.

contemporary analytic view, though one not shared by all analysts, that God is dead in ethics.

The traditional view can be found expressed in a recent textbook:

If there were no God and no future life, the conclusion would be reasonable enough that man ought to get as much pleasure and as little pain out of his brief span as possible. But if there is a God and a future life, no such conclusion follows; man may provide for his temporal welfare to the fullest, yet miss his last end and slide into eternal ruin.[42]

Or in the words of T. S. Eliot:

If you remove from the word 'human' all that belief in the supernatural has given to man, you can view him finally as no more than an extremely clever, adaptable and mischievous little animal.

Or as Orestes says in Sartre's *The Flies*:

There is nothing left in heaven, neither good nor evil, nor anybody to give me order. For I am a human being, Jupiter, and every human being must invent his way.[43]

---

[42] Austin Fagothey, S.J., *Right and Reason* (St. Louis: C. V. Mosby Co., 1967), pp. 176–77. Richard Robinson somewhere relates the anecdotes of the "Papist Priest" who says to a pair of well-behaved atheists: "I can't understand you boys— If I didn't believe in God, I should be having a high old time." Miss Anscombe has claimed ("Modern Moral Philosophy" *Philosophy*, XXXIII (1958), pp. 1–19), that moral uses of "ought" or obligation statements, have no reasonable sense outside a divine-law conception of ethics. Thus for an atheist to say one morally ought to do something is to make a statement in which the expression "morally ought" has only a mere mesmeric force. Unless "ought" is used in a theistic context, it has no genuine use, for only if God be accepted as a law-giver can we come to believe that there is anything a man is categorically bound to do on pain of being a bad man. The concept of obligation becomes, without God, a Holmesless Watson.

But Miss Anscombe has also argued that while the motives, spirit, meaning and purpose of the moral life of Christians depends on revelation, the content of the moral law (actions which are good and just) is not essentially a matter of revelation. Moral truths may be *per accidens* revealed (one may find out from an authority something he could have thought out for himself; or some of the facts about what is the case may be revealed); but "there does not seem to be room for . . . moral truths which are *per se* revealed." "Authority in Morals," *Problems of Authority*, ed. John Murray Todd (Baltimore, Md.: Helicon Press. 1962), pp. 170–88, esp. pp. 186–88. Cf. Toulmin, 14.8, "Ethics provides the reasons for choosing the 'right' course: religion helps us put our *hearts* into it;" and also R. N. Smart, "Gods, Bliss and Morality," *Proceedings of the Aristotelian Society*, LVII (1957–1958), pp. 59–78.

[43] (New York: Vintage Press, 1955).

The contrasting contemporary view, written with reference to the existentialist emphasis on the relevance of God to ethics, is expressed by Mary Mothersill:

Unless one can sympathize with the extremely peculiar notion that God's non-existence somehow blurs the distinction between right and wrong, the existentialist lesson will seem not only meager but pointless.[44]

Ian Ramsey, the Anglican Bishop of Durham, who is himself an analytical philosopher of religion, writes of the relation between morals and religion:

. . . it seems to many nowadays that any distinctive association of morality with religion will be disastrous not so much for religion as for morality. Here is a new turn in religious controversy. Far from religion claiming, as in the eighteenth century, to afford new sanction for old duties, far from religion being the acknowledged basis of all true morality, there are many amongst us, and they number amongst them believers, as well as unbelievers, who find insuperable, and from a practical point of view disastrous, difficulties in the traditional under-pinning of morality by religion.[45]

Given this radical opposition between the traditional and the majority analytic views, and on the assumption that the reasons for the traditional view are fairly well known, we might do well here to concentrate on the answer to this question: why does the analyst believe that the theist will not be better able than the atheist to know what is wrong, good or bad? Clarity demands a careful staking out of the ground. (a) We are not discussing the question whether or not a Christian, or any other religious person who accepts propositions as true because held to be divinely revealed, knows better than an atheist what is right or good. (b) Nor are we speaking to the question whether a theist will, or is more likely to do what is right or good than is an atheist. Perhaps the theist will have more incentive or motive; perhaps he can more easily avoid moral pride and complacency; perhaps seeing an act as the fulfillment of God's will does give a kind of additional

[44] *Ethics* (New York: The Macmillan Company, 1965), p. 18.

[45] *Christian Ethics* . . . , pp. 10–11. Ramsey follows with a passage quoted from an unpublished lecture by R. M. Hare: "Once people realise that they can have a rational morality without the orthodox God, and cannot have one with him, one of his chief props—indeed, perhaps, his only surviving prop that had any strength—will have disappeared. And it is this situation for which Christians ought to be preparing."

nobility to the moral act and a kind of ignobility to the immoral act. Perhaps the theist who takes God to be his and every other man's Creator or Father will be more inclined actually to treat other men as his brothers; but one may want to insist that the father-brothers relationship does not tell a man *how* his brothers are to be treated or what is good for them given the extension of "brother" to all men. (c) Nor need one deny that a theist has a significantly different cosmic view or *Weltansicht*—only that it is significantly different as regards knowledge of *what* is right or good. (d) Finally, it is, of course, true that the theist's answer to the question: what is the ultimate source of morality? will differ importantly from that of the atheist; obviously every ultimate-source question receives importantly different answers from the two.

Most analysts believe that with the possible exception of knowledge of duties to worship God, there is no reason to believe that a theist has any advantage over an atheist. Put more concretely: if Brown is today a theist, and tomorrow becomes an atheist, his knowledge of what is right or good will not have changed except, possibly, with regard to duties of worshipping God; and if Jones is today an atheist, and tomorrow becomes a theist, his knowledge of what is right or good will not have changed except, possibly, with regard to duties of worshipping God.[46]

The analyst might explain his own position in the following way:

1. "If one were to insist that knowledge of God's existence and attributes, e.g., of God as 'Goodness Itself' is necessary to know at least some goods or right acts, a response might be made in a manner similar to that of Aristotle to Plato's claim that knowledge of Ideal or Universal Good is necessary to know particular goods: there is no good reason

---

[46] The reason one can say it is only possible that a theist may be aware of special duties to God derives from the difficulty of seeing the point of formal worship: as Socrates asked in Plato's *Euthyphro*, how can we benefit God by worshipping Him or offend Him by not worshipping Him? It might be added that the appropriateness of extending the notion of worship to include all good acts, and by consequence, of regarding moral blemishes and inadequacies not merely as failings but as sins or offences against God, is closely bound up with giving a satisfactory answer to Socrates' question. One might, of course, follow either the John Baillie line: having a morality is equivalent to having a religion; or the R. B. Braithwaite line: religious statements are used only as moral assertions. But then for Baillie there are no atheists, and for Braithwaite there are no theists. Cf. Baillie's *Our Knowledge of God* (London: Oxford University Press, 1939); and Braithwaite's "An Empiricist's View of Religious Belief," Eddington Memorial Lecture (London: Oxford University Press, 1955).

to think so. No scientist or craftsman acts as if knowledge of Ideal Good is helpful. One cannot even find a plausible reason for thinking such knowledge might be helpful:

> ... it is not easy to see *how* knowing some Ideal Good will help a weaver or a carpenter in the practice of his own craft, or how anybody will be a better physician or general for having contemplated the absolute Idea. (*Nicomachean Ethics*, I, ch. 6.)

2. "Is there any reason to believe that a theist can be sure some sorts of action and omission are always wrong, while an atheist cannot? Can a theist know which kinds of acts are intrinsically evil, or even that any are by some method not open to the atheist? To get the conclusion, '*x* is intrinsically evil, is always wrong to do,' the theist would need an argument containing a premise rejected by the atheist—but which premise? It is not easy to think of a single plausible candidate.

3. "If there were any reason to believe that the theist somehow derives from theism, moral insights which leave behind some of the doubts and uncertainties of moral situations, or principles as absolute and ultimate as their divine source, then the theist would have made his case. Failing this, he may be accused of implicity arguing: God is absolute and ultimate, and since moral principles come from God, moral principles are absolute and ultimate. (The missing premise: 'whatever comes from God is absolute and ultimate' is seldom asserted.)

4. "A defender of the theist's alleged ethical superiority might argue as follows: every man needs either to believe in God or in a substitute-God; but as the only likely substitute-god is oneself, the atheist must make of himself a god and adopt an egoist ethics. However, it would appear that even if, *pace* Satan, an egoist could consistently adopt only an atheist stance, the converse, that an atheist could consistently adopt only an egoist stance, does not follow. There is considerable evidence to the contrary. One cannot, furthermore, successfuly make the case that it is especially reasonable or rational for an atheist to be an egoist; again the evidence to the contrary is too strong.

5. "The standard argument for the independence of morality from religion, which still persuades most analytically oriented philosophers,

though not all,[47] might be put as follows: Suppose there is a God who issues commands: 'Do *x*,' or 'Do *y*.' Before one morally ought to obey, he must come to believe that x and y are good; obeying out of fear of punishment or promise of reward is not to act morally. Since 'God commanded *x*' and '*x* is morally good' are not equivalent, indeed neither entails the other, the two must be known to be true independently. Even if one were to affirm 'Whatever God commands is good,' the establishing of this proposition calls for an independent criterion of goodness: we must use our own moral awareness and sensitivity to judge God's commands to be good, and as ones which morally ought to be obeyed. The only way of escaping this conclusion is to assert, following Ockham, that what makes an act commanded by God good is only the fact that it is commanded by God; but this would make the classification of acts as right or wrong purely arbitrary and contingent matter—a matter of divine whim."

Such is the challenge the analyst offers those who affirm the dependence of ethics on knowledge of God's existence (and perhaps on other "metaphysical presuppositions" such as the immortality of the soul).

For further background to situationism, it might be well to include a sketch of the usual lines of criticism taken by opponents of Christian ethics as a form of religious ethics. Christian ethics, it is alleged is: (a) excessively conservative and resistant to change; (b) legalistic; (c) vague about the role of "love" or "agapé."

(a) Since revelation, though given, calls for interpretation, it implies authority. However, divine-right or authoritative institutions tend to become entrenched power-structures and are notoriously impervious to change and criticism from below. Further, the organizing structure of religious morality is a coherent set of parables or fables, and there

---

[47] For challenges to the "traditional view," see D. A. Rees, "The Ethics of Divine Commands," *Proceedings of the Aristotelian Society*, *LVII* (1956–1957), pp. 83–106; G. E. M. Anscombe's "Modern Moral Philosophy," *Philosophy*, *XXXIII* (1958); Patterson Brown's "Religious Morality," *Mind*, *LXXII* (1963), pp. 235–44; and the articles by R. N. Smart, Ian T. Ramsey, I. M. Crombie in *Christian Ethics and Contemporary Philosophy*. For the "traditional" view, see Kai Nielsen, "Some Remarks on the Independence of Morality from Religion," *Mind*, LXX (1961), pp. 175–86, and Patrick H. Nowell-Smith, "Religion and Morality," *Encyclopedia of Philosophy*, ed. Paul Edwards (New York: The Macmillan Company, 1967), with appended bibliography, VII, pp. 150–58.

is pressure not to violate the unified pattern. Hence change is far harder than for the man who needs only to reject a principle about whose soundness he has doubts, and to substitute another.

(b) Those who believe that morality requires a belief in God take a formalist or deontological view of morality. They tend to think of its structure as akin to a legal system with a divine lawgiver who makes uncompromisingly stringent demands on his subjects. In this view, non-theists are moral outlaws, deaf to the moral imperative. Being brought up to emphasize discipline and overcoming temptation makes one sympathetic to the view that morality is a matter of obeying rules and that the solution of a moral problem can be always found by appealing to the appropriate rule.

(c) "Love" is taken to be "the summary of biblical ethics," but the nature and role of love is notoriously unclear. Is love a disposition, a a principle, a property, a method, a goal, a motive, an ideal, a ruling norm, or the sum of all the virtues? If one is not given detailed rules about how to go about loving God, one's neighbor and one's enemies, being told to "do the loving thing," to "do whatever love demands" is to be given an unconscionably vague instruction. Specifications like "turn the other cheek," if taken seriously, demand an impossible heroism.

Another important line of criticism would question the rationality of religious ethics by looking to the relation between ethical norms and religious belief. If religious belief rests on faith, and thus cannot be rationally established or justified, and if moral norms depend logically or existentially on religious belief, these norms participate in the non-justifiability by reason of religious belief. Religious morality, then, on its own view of itself, is non-justifiable rationally. By contrast, at least some systems of philosophical ethics do claim to be rationally justifiable.

UTILITARIANISM vs. FORMALISM

Many of the moves and countermoves made by situationists and their opponents can be underlined conveniently by examining the analogous moves and countermoves made by utilitarians and their opponents, the formalists, for in both instances the issues are much the same. Furthermore, once one has seen the great variety of theoretical options which can all be classified as utilitarian, one will more easily see how theorists who differ importantly from one another can nonetheless be rightly identified as situationists.

A. Ethics: normative ethics and metaethics
B. Normative ethics: utilitarianism and formalism
C. Utilitarianism
   1. Act/rule utilitarianism: the distinction
   2. Act-utilitarianism: the argument
   3. Rule-utilitarianism: the argument
   4. Normative/descriptive utilitarianism
D. Formalism
   1. Act-formalism
   2. Rule-formalism

Ethics: normative ethics and metaethics

Philosophical ethics, sometimes termed "moral philosophy," "ethical theory," or simply "ethics," can be divided into normative ethics, which deals with general questions concerning what is good or right, and metaethics, which deals with the meanings of ethical terms and justification of ethical judgments.[48] Normative ethics guides us in the making of moral judgments about our own or others' actions; metaethics helps us determine how best to analyze ethical sentences and to justify normative judgments. (The discussion of ethical relativism above deals with a crucial metaethical issue.)

Ethicians have usually argued that the most obvious candidate for a standard of moral judgment—the prevailing code of morality—is not satisfactory. The moral rule and standards of a society are never very precise, admit of exceptions, and may sometimes be successfully attacked as imperfect or even immoral; sets of moral rules may vary from society to society and those who live within a single society may have different and conflicting codes, each of which is claimed to be the best. As a result, ethicians have offered a variety of moral standards.

Normative ethics: utilitarianism and formalism

Two of the most widely defended normative theories are utilitarianism and formalism. The former is a type of teleological or goal-directed

---

[48] Cf. William K. Frankena, *Ethics* (Englewood Cliffs, N. J.: Prentice-Hall, Inc., 1963), Ch. 1; and for a more elaborate treatment, see my "Can Metaethics Advance Ethics?", *Philosophy in an Age of Christian Renewal* (Notre Dame, Ind.: University of Notre Dame Press, 1968).

theory which makes "good" the central ethical term. Formalism is a type of deontological or ought-directed theory which makes "right" the central ethical term. Both offer an answer to the question: how does one tell what he morally should do? Utilitarians and other teleologists say: choose the act which produces a maximum of good. The formalist disagrees and holds that sometimes one should choose the act which does not produce a maximum of good, e.g. sometimes one should not tell a lie even if lying in a particular case would maximize good.

Teleologists differ among themselves both on what the good is, considering it to be coextensive with "pleasure," or with "happiness," or with "human welfare," etc., and on *whose* good should be maximized. The ethical egoist believes that the agent should maximize his own good; the utilitarian (ethical universalist) believes that the agent should maximize the good of all concerned or influenced by the action.[49] Since situationists are not ethical egoists, we shall first examine the utilitarian options, and then turn for a briefer look at formalist options.

Utilitarianism

Utilitarianism can be defined as the doctrine that the rightness and wrongness of actions is determined by the goodness and badness of their consequences for all concerned. It answers the question: which of

---

[49] It is generally assumed that what is best for one man is not always likely to be best for all concerned, and consequently that the way of life of the egoist will differ from that of the utilitarian. Whether it is logically and/or practically possible for there to be a coincidence between the two, is open to dispute. One might argue, as Aristotle appears to have done, on the basis of natural sanctions only, and Aquinas appears to have done, on the basis of both natural and supernatural sanctions, that what is good for one person in the long run is good for everyone else in the long run, that there is at least a practical coincidence between actions indicated as desirable on the basis of concern for the interests of all and actions which promote the long-run interests of the agent. One might say, as Aristotle might be interpreted to have said, that it is to one's long-run interest to develop "habits" or dispositions or attitudes which lead one to concern himself mainly with the welfare of others, even though one recognizes that having and acting from these habits lead occasionally to acting against one's own interests: for on balance one can best achieve his own welfare by acting to further the welfare of others. A recent development of a somewhat similar view, "attitude utilitarianism," can be found in Michael Scriven's *Primary Philosophy* (New York: McGraw-Hill, Inc., 1966), Ch. VII, p. 238, where he argues that "it proves possible to show that reasons *can* be given to the selfish man that show it is in his interest to abandon the selfish point of view in favor of an unselfish one, just because this is *not* the same as giving a selfish man reasons for acting unselfishly here and now."

the alternative courses of action should I choose? by replying: choose that action which promises to maximize the balance of good over evil for all concerned.

1. *Act/rule utilitarianism: the distinction.* A number of terms in this definition of utilitarianism are vague or ambiguous. One example is the term "actions" in "the rightness and wrongness of *actions* is determined by . . ." If "actions" is taken to mean particular and separate actions, the position is that of the act-utilitarian according to whom each individual action is to be judged right or wrong according to its consequences, independently of whether similar actions generally maximize welfare. Thus, if in a given situation the relevant options are lying, telling the truth, and remaining silent, the act-utilitarian will choose that option which promises to have the best consequences in this particular case.

On the other hand, if by "actions" is understood kinds, types, or sorts of actions, the position is that of the rule-utilitarian. According to this interpretation one should first determine which kinds of actions, e.g. lying, telling the truth, or remaining silent, generally promotes human welfare; then one adopts that kind of action as an inviolable rule because it promises to maximize human welfare.

Briefly, the act-utilitarian strives toward the greatest realization of human welfare by applying the test of good/bad consequences directly and immediately to each individual act, though he does so in the light of rules as distillations of experience. The rule-utilitarian strives toward the greatest realization of human welfare by applying the test of good/bad consequences immediately to kinds of acts, and only mediately to individual acts.

2. *Act-utilitarianism: the argument.* A typical act-utilitarian line of defense might be phrased as follows: "It would be wrong not to do the act which on balance leaves the world a better place. To choose to follow a rule when in a particular case this would not maximize welfare is rule-worship. Rules of thumb are useful and following them will generally, though not always, maximize welfare. Nevertheless one should always be willing to break any rule at all whenever it will contribute to the achievement of the greatest welfare. Welfare is the goal of morality generally and of moral rules in particular. If breaking a rule in a given set of circumstances will make for a better world, then this is what should be done."

A typical line of attack on act-utilitarianism has been put as follows:

Suppose everyone followed the act-utilitarian principle in behavior. This would mean that every time one answered a question, even under oath, one must think it one's duty to answer falsely if one thinks so doing will serve the public (including one's own) good . . .

(Act-utilitarianism) implies that if you have employed a boy to mow your lawn and he asks for his pay, you should pay him what you promised only if you cannot find a better use for your money. It implies that when you bring home your monthly pay-check you should use it to support your family and yourself only if it cannot be used more effectively to supply the needs of others. It implies that if your father is ill and has no prospect of good in his life, and maintaining him is a drain on the energy and enjoyments of others, then, if you can end his life without provoking any public scandal or setting a bad example, it is your positive duty to take matters into your own hand and bring his life to a close . . .

But if people really thought and acted in this way, no one could have any assurance about what might happen on important occasions in the future. Institutions would be undermined (Take marriage: a man would feel it his duty to commit adultery, if the net expectable utility — assuming it can be kept secret — would exceed that of refraining!). A great number of people, if not everyone, would feel insecure.

If the act-utilitarian, then, criticizes the formalist on the ground that the formalist cannot explain *why* we should do certain things like keep promises, and so on, when doing so does more harm than good, one reply the formalist might make is that at least the practice of following his principles will secure the long-range public good, whereas the practice of everybody following the act-utilitarian principle will lead to harm and injustice.[50]

For many, the preceding line of criticism leads to rejection of act-utilitarianism. Today most utilitarians have adopted some form of rule-utilitarianism because it seems to embody the best of both worlds, utilitarianism and formalism.

3. *Rule-utilitarianism: the argument.* A rule-utilitarian might explain the way rules of morality are determined and applied as being somewhat analogous to the way rules of a sport such as professional football are determined and applied. (That "rule" need not be taken in this way is made clear by the subtle and elaborate analysis of "rule" developed in the article by B. J. Diggs below.) The rules of professional football

---

[50] Richard B. Brandt, "Towards a Credible Form of Utilitarianism," *Morality and the Language of Conduct*, ed. Hector-Neri Castanada and George Nakhnikian (Detroit, Mich.: Wayne State University Press, 1965), pp. 109–10; and Brandt's *Ethical Theory* (Englewood Cliffs, N. J.: Prentice-Hall, Inc., 1959), pp. 390–91.

are re-evaluated periodically and slight modifications often are introduced. The criterion for determining which of two proposed and opposite modifications is to be chosen is a utilitarian one: the welfare of those concerned. Will rule A or rule B make professional football a better game, attract larger audiences, reduce the number of injuries, make for a more exciting game by better balancing disparities between teams, etc.? Once a rule is chosen on utilitarian grounds, the rule must be observed to the letter. No exceptions are permitted and an appeal to break the rule in a particular game, even if ignoring the rule would make *this* game far more exciting, would be considered absurd. Similarly, moral rules are far more than rules of thumb; they are inviolable once they have been justified on utilitarian grounds. Such a view, it might be said, appears to give due weight to rules and consequences; it conforms to ordinary notions of what it means to act morally.

A division of rule-utilitarianisms might be made on the basis of whether 'rule' means the best possible rule of the rule actually operating in society. When it is the former, the right thing to do is to determine and follow the best possible rules, regardless of the actual rules of the society in which one lives. This position leads to a set of rules very much like those of Kant, for whom the right act is that which conforms to the right maxim or rule, and the right maxim is that which conforms to the super-rule or: "Act only on that maxim through which you can at the same time will that it should become a universal law." If justifying acts by maxims and maxims by the categorical imperative would give a welfare-maximizing set of maxims or rules—an interpretation that is not surely contraindicated by the examples Kant chooses in his *Foundation of the Metaphysics of Morals*[51]—then the similarity between a crucial part of Kant's position and best-possible-rule utilitarianism is striking. If however, Kant's set of maxims would not be welfare-maximizing if followed, then he would be more properly-classified, as is usual, as a formalist whose concern with welfare is quite indirect.

Interpreting "rule," on the other hand, as actual rule or rule conventionally operative in a society, gives a form of rule-utilitarianism defended recently by Stephen Toulmin.[52] For Toulmin, acting morally is acting according to the actual rules of the society in which one lives.

[51] (New York: Liberal Arts Press, 1959).
[52] Cf. *Reason in Ethics* (London: Cambridge University Press, 1960), pp. 140–43.

Such rules are meant and believed to maximize welfare and to minimize illfare. In areas of growing understanding and in times of changing institutions, one should act according to modified rules which are at once both within the grasp of the members of the society and more closely approach the ideal of minimizing preventable suffering than do prevailing rules. While agreeing with Kant on the need for following rules, Toulmin would plant his feet more firmly in the existing rules, and only gradually move on from there to rules more effectively promoting welfare. Kant would ignore existing rules and urge each man to live rationally according to the one set of ideal rules.

A major difficulty with at least some forms of rule-utilitarianism is that the problem of stating rules with all the wanted exceptions leads to the collapse of rule-utilitarianism into act-utilitarianism. This is a problem that formalists also must face. As Paul W. Taylor puts it:

It may be the case that the moral rule that imposes the obligation to keep promises is justified on grounds of utility, but this leaves open the question whether the obligation to keep a promise *in every particular case* always outweighs the utility of breaking a promise *in every particular case.* Suppose, for example, that A has borrowed some money from B and has promised to pay it back on a certain date. Suppose further that A's child has meanwhile come down with a grave illness that requires many months of hospital care, so that if A repays his debt to B he will not be able to afford this hospital care. Does the obligation to keep his promise outweigh all consideration of the consequences of his doing so? . . . Now if we make a legitimate exception to the rule in those cases where our keeping a promise would have *extremely* bad consequences, it would seem that the act-utilitarians could reply: Why do the consequences have to be *extremely* bad for there to be a legitimate exception? If consequences are relevant in justifying the breaking of a promise, why shouldn't we be doing what is morally right when we (truly) think that the consequences of breaking our promise will be better, *however slightly better*, than the consequences of our keeping it? And if this is granted, rule-utilitarianism collapses into act-utilitarianism. Any act is right when its consequences are better than those of any alternative, and we need not consider whether the act conforms to or violates a rule.[53]

Another objection (which may easily be modified to tell against act-utilitarianism also) is raised by William Frankena:

[53] P. W. Taylor, ed., *Problems of Moral Philosophy* (Belmont, Calif.: Dickenson Publishing Co., 1967), pp. 224–25.

Suppose we have two rules, R_1 and R_2, which cannot both be made a part of our morality. Suppose further that in the case of each rule we know the results of everyone's always acting in appropriate occasions on that rule . . . and that . . . we find the score even—in both cases we obtain the same balance of good over evil in the long run for the universe as a whole . . . It may still be that [R_1 and R_2] distribute the amount of good realized in different ways: acting on R_1 may give all of the good to a relatively small group of people . . . while acting on R_2 may spread the good more equally over a larger part of the population. In this case, it seems to me that we must hold and would say that R_1 is an unjust rule and that R_2 is morally preferable. If this is so, we must give up rule-utilitarianism.[54]

4. *Normative/descriptive utilitarianism.* Among the other possible divisions and subdivisions of utilitarianism one deserves a brief mention, the distinction between normative and descriptive utilitarianism. Normative utilitarianism is defended as a system of normative ethics, a systematic proposal about how we ought to think about moral issues; descriptive utilitarianism is defended as a system of descriptive ethics, an analysis of how we do think about conduct. J. J. C. Smart argues that this distinction is important because often objections are taken as objections directly against utilitarianism when they are rather objections to descriptive utilitarianism and do not apply to normative utilitarianism. In effect, objections that people do not really think that way or say that kind of thing when they are thinking or speaking morally, do not constitute objections to the normative utilitarian, for he can respond, that they *should* think and speak as utilitarians even though they do not.[55] People may think and speak and act as though certain beliefs about natural phenomena are true when they are in fact false; the criterion of a good scientific theory is not the closeness of its match with people's beliefs, but its correspondence with natural reality. Similarly, the normative utilitarian would insist, the criterion of the truth of an ethical theory is not the closeness of its match with people's moral beliefs, but its correspondence with moral reality.

Formalism: act-formalism and rule-formalism
Formalists hold that a particular action or kind of action can be known always to be right or wrong regardless of the consequences. Some formalists adopt Kant's position, according to which one can know

---

[54] Frankena, p. 33.
[55] "Utilitarianism," *Encyclopedia of Philosophy* (New York: The Macmillan Company, 1967), vol. VIII, p. 207.

what is right or wrong by the application of the categorical imperative, but formalists usually say that one knows right and wrong by a sort of intuition or insight into the act or kind of act.

Those holding that what is known to be right or wrong are purely particular judgments like "In this situation I ought to pay the debt," might be called act-formalists. Rule-formalists, on the other hand, attend to general judgments like "One should always pay his debts."

1. *Act-formalism.* For act-formalists each situation is different. After direct knowledge, perhaps by intuition, one must somehow decide what to do. This decision must be made without appeal to rules or balancing good over evil. General rules for the act-formalist can at best serve as summaries of past experience and in no sense are determinative of what is right to do. One looks at the situation and sees what to do.

Most existentialists might usefully be classified as act-formalists, with an emphasis on "decision" rather than on "intuition," and on the uncertainty or "fear and trembling" that moral decisions arouse. Some situationists, too, might be best classified as holding a position akin to act-formalism inasmuch as they oppose general-rule morality in favor of being moved by love or agapé. They accord no important role to evaluation of consequences because they believe, along with most formalists, either that no useful calculus of consequences is available or that consequences are not determinative of morality.

The main argument for act-formalism, according to Frankena, is that since each situation is unique, no general rules can possibly be of help in deciding the right thing to do. But, one might argue, though each situation is in some respects different from each other, it does not follow that it is different in all respects or even in morally relevant respects. Science deals with phenomena each one of which differs in some respects from any other, but nonetheless true general statements are usefully made. And if science finds general rules and laws useful in dealing with phenomena, each one of which is unique, is there any good reason for thinking that general statements and rules will not prove useful in dealing with unique moral situations?

Frankena continues:

For the [act-formalist] "this is what X ought to do in situation Y" does not entail anything about what X or anyone else should do in similar situations. Suppose that I go to Jones for advice about what to do in situation Y, and he tells me that I morally ought to do Z. Suppose also that I recall that the day before he had maintained that W was the right thing for Smith to do in a situation of the same kind. I shall then certainly point this out to Jones and ask him if he is not being inconsistent. Now suppose Jones does not do anything to show that the two cases are different, but simply says, "No, there is no connection between the two cases. Sure. They are alike, but one was yesterday and involved Smith. Now it's today and you are involved." Surely this would strike us as an odd response from anyone who purports to be taking the moral point of view. The fact is that when one makes a moral judgment in a particular situation, one implicitly commits himself to making the same judgment in any similar situation, even if the second situation occurs at a different time or place or involves another agent.[56]

2. *Rule-formalism.* Rule formalists maintain that the standard of right and wrong consists of general rules. As these are not derived from particular cases they are not mere rules of thumb, but are valid independently of whether or not they maximize welfare. Usually the rules are taken to be rather specific, like ones about keeping promises, telling the truth, and avoiding adultery. Rule-formalists are liable to charges of rule-worship from act-utilitarians and act-formalists. They are challenged by the difficulty of formulating rules which adequately include all the desirable exceptions and are rationally hierarchized to avoid conflicts of rules.

One objection raised against those who rely on intuition to know what is right or wrong, and particularly telling against rule-formalists, has been stated by W. H. Hudson:

In most cases where a moral decision has to be made, it is not simply a matter of seeing how one principle applies in that case, but which of a number of principles is to take precedence. In such situations, how is one to decide what one ought to do? The answer which intuitionists give is apparently that one 'feels' or 'sees' what one ought to do. This is plainly intended to mean something more than simply that one decides what to do. But can we make it mean more? The given situation may be familiar or novel. If familiar, then it may make sense to say that the instantiated principles come with certain 'weights', if by that we mean that they come to us graded in accordance with past decisions which we have made in similar situations. But what all this talk of 'weight' amounts to is that, in the past, we have decided to act in one way rather than another. If the situation is novel, when does one know which obligation 'feels' heavier? Surely when one has decided what one ought to do! As J-P. Sartre wrote of this 'feeling', in discussing the pupil who asked whether he ought to stay with his mother or join the Free French in England, feeling is formed by the deeds that one does; therefore I cannot consult it as a guide

---

[56] Frankena, pp. 21–22.

to action. To the question 'how am I to decide which of conflicting obligations to fulfil?' the answer 'By weighing them against each other' is really no answer. All it comes to is the triviality, 'Decide by deciding.' [57]

DEWEY'S PRAGMATISM

Many American situationists, most notably Fletcher, pay tribute to Dewey's pragmatism as important in developing their own insights. Structurally there are striking similarities between the two, though the key-concepts are far from identical.[58] One might summarize by saying that science plays a role in Dewey's thought similar to that played by Christian love in the thought of the situationist. For neither does the past bind the present. For neither is ethics autonomous. Dewey would contend that it is impossible adequately to analyze ethical statements without using the social sciences, especially psychology and sociology; the situationist would make Christian love crucial to practical ethics in a quite analogous fashion.[59] Dewey proposes to reconstruct ethics and value theory along empirical, even experimentalist lines; the situationist does so along theological lines. For the one, not only does science provide the tool of ethical analysis, but the very values that make a

[57] *Ethical Institutionism* (New York: St. Martin's Press, 1967), p. 52.

[58] On Dewey's pragmatic ethics, see his *Reconstruction in Philosophy* (New York: Mentor Books, 1950), Ch. VII, and John Dewey and James H. Tufts, *Ethics* (New York: Henry Holt & Co., 1932); W. K. Frankena, "Ethical Theory," *Philosophy* (Englewood Cliffs, N. J., 1964), pp. 377–92; John E. Smith, *The Spirit of American Philosophy* (New York: Oxford University Press, 1966), Ch. IV; Richard J. Bernstein, Introduction to Dewey's *On Experience, Nature and Freedom* (New York: Library of Liberal Arts, 1960); Stanley Cavell and Alexander Sesonske, "Logical Empiricism and Pragmatism in Ethics," *Pragmatic Philosophy* (Garden City, N. J.: Doubleday & Co., 1966), pp. 382–95.

[59] Cf. Douglas A. Rhymes "The 'New' Morality," *Religion in Life*, XXXV (1966), p. 173. ". . . the approach made by a Christian to problems of ethical decision must have the following characteristics: 1. the goodness of an action will be determined . . . by what is the relevant action for that individual in order that he may live his life in its wholeness and secure the maximum welfare of all concerned in the situation. This will mean that for the Christian the only absolute recognized will be the absolute of love, and in any given situation it will be a case of working out and training people to work out what is the maximum response of love within that situation . . . The constant element will be the search for the maximum of love, but the embodiment of this will differ with every century and with every individual.

2. There will be the need to find the common moral ground between the believer and the nonbeliever, between the Christian and the humanist . . . For me the essential difference between the Christian and the non-Christian does not lie so much in the manner by which moral decisions are made but rather in the spiritual strength available to the Christian in living through the grace of prayer and sacrament."

man a good scientist, such as devotion to truth, impartiality, tolerance, sense of dignity, integrity, etc., are taken to be those which make a man a good man; for the situationist Christian faith and love play analogous roles. Both stress doing the right thing in relation to what is occurring in the "context": Dewey in relation to a scientific reading of the context; the situationist in relation to a theological reading of the context or "what God is doing." [60] The two have been subjected to somewhat parallel lines of criticism: Dewey, for what Sidney Hook calls his "systematic over-optimism about human *willingness* to follow the lead of intelligence"; the situationist, for his allegedly over-optimistic trust in love as sufficient to give the right answer; Dewey, for his naturalistic breaking down of the distinction between the empirical "is" and the evaluative "ought"; the situationist, for his breaking down the distinction between reason and faith; and both pragmatism and situationism are sometimes criticized as ethics of expediency and appeasement.

Neither Dewey nor the situationist is in danger of "rule worship." Since each situation is unique, one can be armed only with what will help to analyze this situation more adequately. There are no ultimate and definitive contexts. Unlike the existentialists, both look to the situation for the *resolution* of the problem, and Dewey emphasizes the rationality of the solution. Stephen Pepper summarizes Dewey's approach:

[Dewey] pointed out something so much on the very doorstep of our actions that we have walked right over it every day of our lives without noticing it. For we all do take for granted that there is a moral situation whenever we find we have got into one. But for generations men have never looked at the situation itself in which a man finds himself. A problematic situation, when carefully analyzed, furnishes its own criterion for the solution of the problem contained in it. [61]

There is a similarity, too, in the way Dewey and the situationist would deal with the badly handled past situation. Both would say that it is useless to mourn past mistakes whether one's own or others'. The badly handled past situation has presented us with a new situation, and this now calls for analysis.

[60] Cf. Paul Lehmann, *Ethics in a Christian Context* (New York: Harper and Row, 1963): "The primary question is not 'What does God command?' The primary question is 'What does God do?'" (p. 100).
[61] *Ethics* (New York: Appleton-Century-Crofts, 1960), p. 139. Cf. pp. 140–52 for an extended Deweyite realistic analysis of a moral problem.

How is the satisfactory solution to the moral problem defined? The situationist answers: do what love commands. Dewey answers: reduce to the minimum the set of tensions inherent in the situation, detect the ills that need remedy in the special case, and use intelligence to formulate plans and methods for dealing with them; search out the melioristic solution, for one can always make the situation *better*.

Finally, both Dewey and some situationists would agree with the utilitarian that the goal of morality is to increase human welfare as much as possible. Dewey, however, finds in traditional utilitarianism an unacceptable fixity and finality of ends: if the end, e.g. "pleasure," is given once for all, the task of finding the solution to a moral problem is turned into the technical exercise, of searching for means to the given end.[62] For Dewey both ends and means are the object of a rational search and, in the light of the problematic context, one must constantly redefine in what the goodness and badness of consequences consist. For some situationists, similarly, because God is seen to be somehow actively involved in the situation, the solution cannot be found by the application of a utilitarian calculus.

NATURAL LAW

Traditional natural law moral theory is roughly interpreted as the theory that man is intelligent, reality is intelligible, and man can come to know what he ought to do by coming to know reality. Situationists and some of their opponents[63] indict traditional theory as being excessively legalistic, giving a set of practical "precepts"[64] which are, as a matter of fact, not universal but are rather precipitates of medieval social and religious conditions. However, it is not clear that all forms of natural law theory are closed to situationist ways of thinking and an attempt will be made here to give an interpretation which may be compatible with some situationist insights. This may help to supplement

[62] Cf. Dewey's evaluation of utilitarianism in *Reconstruction in Philosophy*, pp. 143–45.

[63] Cf. Paul Ramsey, *Basic Christian Ethics* (New York: Scribner's, 1950); for Ramsey's attacks on Robinson, Lehmann, and Fletcher, see his *Deeds and Rules in Christian Ethics* (New York: Scribner's, 1967).

[64] These precepts have been estimated to be forty in number, at least according to Aquinas: cf. appendix to Vernon J. Bourke's "Natural Law and the Contemporary Mind," *Teaching Thomism Today* (Washington, D.C.: Catholic University Press, 1964).

the articles by DeKoninck and Fried below, both of whom defend natural law positions.[65]

The only full-fledged natural law theory which receives much attention and has many defenders today is that of Thomas Aquinas, and it is this theory we shall view through situationist lenses. We might begin with a passage taken from the heart of Aquinas' treatment of natural law, in his *Summa theologiae*, I–II, q. 94, a.4: "Whether the natural law is the same for all men?" After answering the question with a qualified "yes" (the general principles are the same for all, but not all specific principles), he continues:

. . . it is right and true for all to act according to reason, and from this principle it follows, as a practical conclusion, that goods entrusted to another should be restored to their owner. Now this is true for the majority of cases. But it may happen in a particular case that it would be *injurious, and therefore unreasonable*, to restore goods held in trust; for instance if they are claimed for the purpose of fighting against one's country. And this principle [i.e. goods entrusted to another should be restored to their owner] will be found to fail the more, according as we descend further towards the particular, e.g., if one were to say that goods held in trust should be restored with such and such a guarantee, or in such and such a way; because the greater the number of conditions added, the greater the number of ways in which the principle may fail, so that it be not right to restore or not to restore [italics mine].

Aquinas seems to be making the anti-legalistic point that a moral rule should not be observed when human welfare would be damaged by its observance. Further, there is no way to reformulate the rule by adding qualifications, exceptions, etc., so as to make it a rule-always-to-be-observed.

There is thus a set of rules which should be treated only as rules of thumb and which should be broken whenever breaking a rule promises better to serve human welfare than observing it. How wide is this class

---

[65] Cf. Peter Knauer, S.J., "La determination du bien et du mal moral par le principle du double effet," *Nouvelle Revue Theologique*, LXXXVII (1965), pp. 356–76 (summarized in *Theology Digest*, XV (1967), pp. 100–104), for a discussion which distinguishes extrinsic from intrinsic evil, and indirect from direct evil effect, on the basis of "proportionate reason." If there is a proportionate reason for doing an act, the act is not intrinsically evil and the evil effect is not "directly intended." "On peut admettre un mal, ontologique dans la mesure où il est justifié par une raison *proportionnée:* dans ce cas, il n'est qu'indirectement volontaire . . . agir avec une raison proportionnée (terme-clé de toute la morale) revient à avoir un 'finis operis' simplement bon . . ." The similarity of this position to act-utilitarianism is hard to miss.

of rules? As wide as is the class observance-of-which-always would sometimes be injurious and therefore unreasonable; the complementary class is that set of rules the observance-of-which-always would never be injurious.

Aquinas then goes on to speak of the rule "theft is wrong," the observance of which is never injurious but is violated by some whose reason is "perverted by passion, or evil habit, or an evil disposition of nature:"

Thus at one time theft, although it is expressly contrary to the natural law, was not considered wrong among the Germans, as Julius Caesar relates.

It seems likely that Aquinas was misled, that stealing (*latrocinium*) for him and for "the Germans" did not contextually mean the same thing, much as parricide did not mean the same thing to the Romans and to some primitive tribes, and lying does not mean the same thing to us and to the Ba-Ila.[66] (Aquinas does, as is well known, permit "theft" in cases of "evident and urgent necessity.") [67]

Are all moral rules for Aquinas like the rules concerning loans and stealing, good rules of thumb, applying *ut in pluribus*, in many or most cases? Apparently not. It would appear he believed there are rules like "never commit adultery," rules which should never be broken on one's own authority. (As he would consider adultery to be all right if commanded by God, who would then take immediate responsibility for seeing that long-run human welfare is thereby served, this position is not wholly unlike that of the situationists, with their "do what divine

---

[66] The Ba-Ila are a Bantu tribe in Northern Rhodesia who neither regard truth as a virtue nor lying as a vice: "They lie in the most barefaced and strenuous manner . . . without the least shame. They lie often when it is to their advantage to tell the truth" (Edwin W. Smith and Andrew M. Dale, *The Ila-speaking Peoples of Northern Rhodesia* (London: Macmillan, 1920), p. 379, quoted by Alexander Macbeath, *Experiments in Living* (London: The Macmillan Company, 1952), pp. 370–72. Macbeath offers an explanation: "The real explanation of the difference of attitude to truth-telling is, I think, to be found in the important part which the belief in black magic or sorcery plays in the life of the Bantu . . . If a man believes, as the Bantu does, that any of his neighbors may be, and that some of them in fact are, endowed with supernatural powers which may be used to do him or his neighbors harm; and if he further believes that giving them information provides them with the means of using these powers, we have a state of affairs in which not mutual trust and confidence but mutual fear and suspicion are likely to flourish. In such circumstances, truth-telling is not likely to be regarded as a virtue."

[67] Cf. *Summa theologiae*, II–II, q. 66 a. 7.

love commands.") The goal of the observance of any rules apart from those dealing directly with God is the promotion of human welfare,[68] and Aquinas, in effect, believed that human welfare would never be served by adultery. It might be that he took the rule: adultery is always wrong, to be equivalent to the rule: never sleep with another's spouse out of lust, when the only relevant good consequence would be the satisfaction of sexual passion. Adultery on this interpretation has been moralistically described, and forbidding adultery means forbidding the satisfaction of sexual passion in a way that entails injustice to one's spouse. If no other circumstances or consequences are known to be relevant, this, all would admit, is always wrong.

In a stable society, words like "adultery" have relatively stable situational meanings, calling to mind standard situations and applications, and presupposing a standard set of consequences. In such a society one can formulate a large number of rules; a violation of any rule would "naturally" be thought of as having bad consequences; and the rules would therefore elicit everyone's rational assent and might even be alleged to be self-evident or intuitively evident.[69] The explicit statement of the rule would carry with it, implicitly, a whole theoretical and practical situational context of understood circumstances and consequences. Such a rule would never be rationally violable, given the whole context. Other rules, e.g. concerning "goods entrusted to another," which are understood to be sometimes violable, have a more open context and refer to acts naturalistically rather than moralistically described. Both sorts of rules are presumably valuable; as R. M. Hare has argued,[70] without formulated principles and rules, the teaching of morality is impossible.

In sum then, Aquinas lived in a stable society where it was easy to believe that the situational meanings of certain sorts of acts was more

---

[68] "We do not offend God except by doing something contrary to our own good," *Summa contra gentiles*, III, 112.

[69] "Practical principles, if they are accepted sufficiently long and unquestioningly, come to have the force of intuition. Thus our ultimate moral principles can become so completely accepted by us, that we treat them, not as universal imperatives, but as matters of fact; they have the same obstinate indubitability." R. M. Hare, *The Language of Morals* (New York: Oxford University Press, 1964), 11.2; Cf. Bruno Schuller, "La théologie moral peut-elle se passer du droit naturel?", *Nouvelle Revue Theologique*, LXXXVIII (1966), pp. 455–56: "le noyau de toute connaissance des valeurs présente quelque analogie avec celle des couleurs."

[70] *The Language of Morals*, 4.3 ff.

stable over time than they actually proved to be. The standard counter-examples today are usury and contraception, whose "meanings" have not remained constant.[71] He was, of course, right in believing that when tied to their situational meanings acts are morally constant; but he failed to make it crystal-clear that acts apart from their situational meanings are morally inconstant, that acts naturalistically described do not have the moral constancy of acts moralistically described.

Finally, the term "natural law" is somewhat unfortunate, for it seems to have been easy to believe that "natural law" is somehow given ("the ought-to-be is based on what is"[72]) in a way independent of man's understanding or belief about, not knowledge of, reality (the ought-to-be is based on what is understood-to-be). Although natural law is man-discovered-law, the term "law" tends to lead one to think that moral laws or "precepts" can somehow be "read off" nature and are subject to interpretation by authorities. The temptation to stretch the similarities between the paradigm or "first-analogue," civil law, and the secondary meaning, natural law, too far, has not always been resisted with sufficient vigor.

THE READINGS

For one unfamiliar with situationism the place to begin is the Fletcher–McCabe Debate. Here one can find the main theses of situationism vigorously laid out by a challenging American exponent of situationism, Joseph Fletcher, and a forceful attack on some of these theses by a moralist familiar with both the philosophical and theological dimensions of situationism, Herbert McCabe.

The next to last article below, Aurel Kolnai's, might well be the place to begin for one who is already familiar with situationism and is looking for a searching and detailed critical analysis written from the viewpoint of an intrinsicalist. Kolnai directs his attention mainly to Fletcher's

---

[71] John Noonan, *Contraception; A History of Its Treatment by its Catholic Theologians and Canonists* (Cambridge: Harvard University Press, 1965); *The Scholastic Analysis of Usury* (Cambridge: Harvard University Press, 1957).

[72] "Le devoir-être se fonde dans l'être . . . Puisque le devoir-être est fondé sur l'être, l'homme sera soumis à des lois morales qui vont se diversifier au fur et à mesure, des changements que lui-même va connaître au fil des temps," Schuller, "La théologie morale . . . ," p. 464. And see Schuller's sound interpretation of the force of St. Paul's "Wives, obey your husbands" and "Nature itself teaches that it is shameful for a man to wear his hair long," p. 456, and pp. 468–69.

version of situationism, and Fletcher, in the last article below, responds directly to Kolnai's critique.

Louis Dupré's article furnishes an overview of the opposition between situationists and their opponents, and suggests that the opposition need not be so fierce as sometimes appears.

The other articles develop philosophically relevant themes, but themes of narrower scope than that of the situationist vs. the legalist or intrinsicalist. Renford Bambrough argues against moral skepticism and relativism. Jonathan Bennett explores the concept of intrinsically wrong acts. A. C. Ewing and B. J. Digg discuss utilitarianism, one of the main pregenitors of situationism. Eugene Fontinell develops a version of pragmatic ethics, and Charles DeKoninck and Charles Fried develop versions of natural law, which contrast interestingly with and illuminate the situational option.

II. Readings

A. The Fletcher-McCabe Debate

Joseph Fletcher

> Dr. Joseph Fletcher is a professor at the Episcopal Theological School in Cambridge, Mass. He is the author of *Morals and Medicine* (1954), *Situation Ethics* (1966) and *Moral Responsibility* (1967).

Herbert McCabe

> Father Herbert McCabe, O.P., is a former editor of the *New Blackfriars*, and the author of *What is Ethics All about?* (1969).

For Professor Joseph Fletcher there are three possible approaches one can take to moral decision-making. (a) One possibility is the *antinomian* or extemporist approach of, for example, a Sartre, an approach which repudiates not only rules but even general principles of morality. (b) At the other extreme are the *legalists*, for whom some moral rules are absolute and inviolable no matter what the circumstances. (c) Somewhere in the middle are the *situationists* who, like the antinomians, reject all absolute moral rules, but who nonetheless, like the legalists, find general moral principles to be helpful.

Fletcher then develops the contrasts between the legalistic "old" morality and the situationist "new" morality. These include the differences between intrinsicalist and extrinsicalist, between Thomist and Occamist, between realist and nominalist, and between absolutist and relativist.

The sense in which the situationist follows Kant's principle, "Treat people as ends and never as means," is given considerable attention. "Moral wrong" or "sin" might even be defined as treating persons as means, or more simply, as using persons. There is but one intrinsic good, love, and but one intrinsic evil, hate; all else is situation-dependent. Thus since no kinds of acts are intrinsically good, when one refers to an act as good or as evil, one is not referring to a property of the act, a characteristic every act of that sort has, but to a predicate of the act, a characteristic some acts of that sort have contingently, incidentally, or "accidentally" (in the Porphyrian sense). Thus, for example, if a transient extra-marital or adulterous sex liaison is full of loving concern for the other, it is better than conjugal sex which is unloving, and in which the other is treated as a means. Personal commitment, though transient, and good motivation are far more important than institutional forms.

Love is the only measure*
by Joseph Fletcher

The new morality, so called, is taking a long, hard second look at some of our assumptions. It does not oversimplify the issues at stake, even though some of its professed advocates do, yet it most certainly poses the essential questions. It might be said to be a revolt against what Henry Miller, the paper tiger of the sex rebels, calls "the immorality of morality" (in *Stand Still Like the Hummingbird*).

Any serious discussion of the new morality should begin with philosophical candor. Let it be understood, then, that the new morality is a form of ethical relativism. A *locus classicus* might be Paul Tillich's blunt statement, "The truth of ethical relativism lies in the moral law's inability to give commandments which are unambiguous both in their general form and in their concrete applications. Every moral law is abstract in relation to the unique and totally concrete situation. This is true of what has been called natural law and of what has been called revealed law."

An old joke can serve to pose the problem. When a rich old man asked a lovely young woman if she would sleep the night with him she said, indignantly, "No." He then asked if she would do it for $100,000? She said, "Yes!" She even agreed to $10,000, but when he came down to $500 she exclaimed, "What do you think I am?" He replied, "We have already established that. Now we are haggling over the price." Is any girl who has "relations" (a debased way to use the word) outside marriage *ipso facto* a prostitute or loose woman, guilty of sin or wrong? Or, as the new moralist would say, does it all depend upon the situation?

* This and the following article by Herbert McCabe, O.P., together with responses by each, are reprinted with permission from *Commonweal*, January 14, 1966, pp. 427–440.

There are at bottom just three lines of approach to moral decision-making. One of them, perhaps the least followed but having at least some following, is the antinomian or law-less (non-principled) method. It operates with spontaneous decisions. Christian antinomians or extemporists, such as those St. Paul opposed in Corinth, often claim to be above any moral law (since they are "saved" or guided directly by the Holy Spirit). In any case they repudiate not only all rules of morality but even general principles. Non-Christian antinomians, such as Jean-Paul Sartre, make their moral decisions with "autonomy" and "instantaneity," i.e., without help from general maxims, unpredictably, wholly within the situation, in the belief that one "moment" of existence is entirely discontinuous from others—so that we cannot generalize about our decision-making.

For example, even if you described in the most complete detail all of the facts involved and all of the considerations *pro* and *con* for joining a labor union where the antinomian works, or whether he should respond to a plea for a loan from a good family man or from a hopeless wastrel, he could not possibly say how he might decide until he was there, then, led by God's spirit or his own. Spontaneity is the key to his method.

At the opposite end of the spectrum of approaches is legalism. In this ethical strategy the "situational variables" are taken into consideration, but the circumstances are always subordinated to pre-determined general "laws" of morality. Legalistic ethics treats many of its rules idolatrously by making them into absolutes. Classical Christian ethics and moral theology ("seminary" or "manualistic" ethics and casuistry), like the conventional wisdom, has been mainly of this kind. Not all legalism is cruelly rigid or callous about sticking to the letter even if the spirit is ignored but too much of it is guilty on that score. The scriptural law of Protestant morality and the natural law of Catholic morality, each in its own way, have treated principles as rules rather than maxims. In this kind of morality, properly labeled as legalism or law ethics, obedience to prefabricated "rules of conduct" is more important than freedom to make responsible decisions.

For example, if you were a Roman Catholic husband and found that, for whatever reason, the only method of family limitation which worked was contraception, you would either have to go on begetting unwanted children beyond a responsible number or cease the unitive lovemaking which is a vital part of a good marriage. This would be because contraception is declared (at least as of this writing) by your Church to be always "against nature." If you were a Jehovah's Witness you would refuse a blood transfusion to save your life, or even your child's, because "the Bible says we must abstain from blood" (which it does, however differently you might exegete the "texts" cited).

The third method of approach is that of the "new" morality. This is situation ethics. In this moral strategy the governing consideration is the situation, with all of its contingencies and exigencies. The situationist enters into every decision-making situation armed with principles, just as the legalist does. But the all-important difference is that his moral principles are *maxims* of general or frequent validity; their validity always depends upon the situation. The situationist is prepared in any concrete case to suspend, ignore or violate any principle if by doing so he can effect more good than by following it. As Dietrich Bonhoeffer said in his prison-written *Ethics*, after conspiring to assassinate Hitler, "Principles are only tools in the hand of God, soon to be thrown away as unserviceable."

Adultery, for instance, is ordinarily wrong, not in itself but because the emotional, legal and spiritual entailments are such that the over-all effects are evil and hurtful rather than helpful—at least in our present-day Western society. But there is always the outside case, the unusual situation, what Karl Barth calls the *ultima ratio*, in which adultery could be the right and good thing. This writer knows of such a case, in which committing adultery foreseeably brought about the release of a whole family from a very unjust but entirely legal exploitation of their labor on a small farm which was both their pride and their prison. Still another situation could be cited in which a German mother gained her release from a Soviet prison-farm and reunion with her family by means of an adulterous pregnancy. These actions would have the situationist's solemn but ready approval.

HOW IS ONE TO JUDGE?

With these three ethical perspectives in mind, how are we to "judge" the Puerto Rican woman in Bruce Kendrick's story about the East Harlem Protestant Parish, *Come Out the Wilderness*. She was proud of her son and told the minister how she had "made friends" with a married man, praying God she'd have a son, and eventually she bore one. The minster, dear silly man that he is, told her it was okay if she was repentant, and she replied, "Repent? I ain't repentin'. I asked the Lord for my boy. He's a gift from God." She is *right* (which, by the way, does *not* mean a situationist approves in the abstract of the absence of any husband in so many disadvantaged Negro and Puerto Rican families).

It is necessary and important to note this: that situation ethics or the "new morality" is *not* the existentialists' or antinomians' method. Unfortunately the waters of debate have been badly muddied since the second world war because some observers, both Catholic and Protestant, have got the two all mixed up and confused. Future historians of modern ethics may fix the start of this confusion in the advice of Roman Catholic moral theologians, which led to an allocution by Pope Pius XII on April 18, 1952. He used the terms "existential" and "situational" as synonymous. On February 2, 1956, situation ethics in another papal utterance was called "the new morality," and ever since then the debate has been at sixes and sevens. The *situationism* of the "new" morality is definitely *not* existential, in the sense that secular and atheist exponents of it use the term.

There are three, not just two, alternatives open to honest people who want to choose their moral course, whether they happen to be Christians or not. We don't have to be either legalists who absolutize ethical principles, or extemporists who make decisions without any principles at all. We can choose (and I would urge it) to be situationists, acknowledging our heritage of canonical and civil principles of right and wrong but remaining free to decide for ourselves responsibility in all situations which principles are to be followed, or in some cases to decide that the "relevant" principles are to be rejected because they would result in more evil than good.

What, then, is good? Asking this question drives home the basic fact that the "new" morality, situationism, is a moral strategy or procedural doctrine which has to be seen in tandem or partnership with a substantive companion-doctrine—personalism. And "personalism" here means the ethical view that the highest good, the *summum bonum* or first-order value, is human welfare and happiness (but not, necessarily, pleasure). Good is first and foremost the good of *people*. Christians call it "love," meaning neighbor-concern or *agapé*. This love means, of course, a social attitude, not the romantic emotion that the word has come to connote in popular literature. The Great Commandment orders Christians to love, i.e., to seek the well-being of people—not to love principles. Non-Christians may call it something else, for example, "justice" or "altruism" or "humanism" or the like, but whatever label they use, it is a personalist devotion to people, not to things or abstractions such as "laws" or general principles. Personal interests come first, before the natural or scriptural or theoretical or general or logical or anything else.

SEXUAL ETHICS

When we think about the conflict between the old or classical morality, the law ethic, and the new morality, the love ethic, we can see that the nub of it is the choice between the notion that a thing is right or wrong inherently and intrinsically, given in the nature of the thing (maybe because God created it "to be what it is"), as legalists or absolutizers would say, or only contingently and extrinsically right or wrong, depending on the circumstances, as situationists or relativists would say. It goes back, in intellectual history, to such controversies as the realist-nominalist debate. The intrinsic idea of moral quality is Thomist, the extrinsic idea is Occamist. The situation ethic is extrinsicalist; it claims that moral quality is nominal, not real. Practical men may not recognize that this kind of philosophical issue is at stake, but it is.

It all depends on the situation, say the extrinsicalists. In some situations unmarried love could be infinitely more moral than married unlove. Lying could be more Christian than telling the truth. Stealing could be better than respecting private property. No action is good or right in itself. It depends on whether it hurts or helps people, whether or not it serves love's purpose—understanding love to be personal concern—*in the situation.*

The situational-personal ethic, in short, subordinates principles to circumstances and the general to the particular, as well as making the "natural" and the biblical and the theoretical give way to the personal and the actual.

For the sake of a clear and striking illustration we might turn to sex relations and the ethics of reproduction. And, furthermore, let us address the subject in terms of the *Christian* version of situation ethics. (We could use truth telling, or buying and selling, or diplomacy and national defense, or something else. The same considerations would come into play whatever the area or "field" of decision-making might be.)

Alas, the very word "morals" in popular use means sex conduct, as we can see in newspaper headlines about a "morals charge." (This ridiculous reduction of morality to sexuality probably got its start in English translations of references in the Bible to fornication, as when I Thess. 4.3 is rendered "abstain from immorality." The Greek and Latin texts without pruriency or evasion say *fornication.*) Actually, the "new morality" is a wide-ranging ethical theory of far more varied bearing than sex, but that is what it is focused upon in the street debates. So be it. Suppose we look at sex, to give our discussion a specific set of operational terms.

Sexual intercourse may or may not be an act of love. Love, as understood in the Christian situation ethic, is an attitude of concern and not an emotion of desire. A *Playboy* cartoon went to the heart of the matter by showing a rumpled young male saying to a rumpled young female in his arms, "Why speak of love at a time like this?" The point is that, Christianly speaking, sex which does not have love as its partner, its *senior* partner, is wrong. If there is no responsible concern for the *other* one, for the partner as a subject rather than a mere object, as a person and not a *thing*, the act is immoral.

The new morality, therefore, requires its practitioners to be who-askers (who will be helped or hurt?)—not, as with legalistic morality, what-askers (what does the law prescribe?). Immanuel Kant, even though he was a legalist himself, was nevertheless right about his maxim: treat persons as ends, never as means. This is essentially the personalism of the Summary of the Law in the gospels: love God and neighbor, with nothing about following a code of law or a set of abstract, before-the-fact rules.

It comes down to this: people are to be loved and things are to be used. "Things" include material objects and general principles. Immorality occurs when things are loved and people are used. When anybody "sticks to the rules," even though people suffer as a consequence, that is immoral. Even if we grant, for example, that generally or commonly it is wrong or bad or undesirable to interrupt a pregnancy, it would nevertheless be right to do so to a conceptus following rape or incest, at least if the victim wanted an abortion. (Legalism of the Protestant, "scriptural law" variety has no biblical prohibition of abortion, and like Jewish opinion approves of therapeutic abortions and is divided over the morality of non-therapeutic reasons for it.)

The Christian situationist says to all men, to all who care about others, whether they are Christians or not: "Your love is like mine, like everybody's. It is the Holy Spirit. Love is not the work of the Holy Spirit, it *is* the Holy Spirit—working in us. God *is* love, he doesn't merely 'have' it or 'give' it; he gives himself, to all men of all sorts and conditions: to believers and non-believers, high degree and low, dark and pale, learned and ignorant, Marxists and Christians and Hottentots."

Long ago St. Chrysostom said the essence of sin is in the substitution of means for ends. Modern social analysts are saying the same thing when they speak of "the error of substituting instrumental for terminal values!" Chrysostom meant that sin treats means as if they were ends in themselves. But in the Christian ethic (at least in its situational version) things are means only, and only persons are ends. We could restate it by the assertion that sin is the exploitation or use of persons. This is precisely what prostitution is. Therefore in a familiar phrase, the prostitute is far more sinned against than sinning. She is infinitely closer to righteousness than are her customers. In the same way, on the same logical base, we can say that the classical capitalist commodity theory of labor, largely a dead letter now due to trade unionism's struggles, is or was a sinful, evil principle.

In teenage social life if a boy seduces a girl in order to appear in his own eyes or his friends' as a Big Man, he is using her; he is guilty of sin or "moral evil." If a girl seduces a boy out of curiosity or some such motive, she is committing the same wrong; if she seduces him in order to lure him into marriage she is committing a far greater sin than simple fornication ever could possibly be, even if they are married to make it legal. Such married sex is legal prostitution and a case of sinning not only formally and materially but also with malice! Even if she lured him into marriage *without* fornication the guilt lies just the same. What is more despicable than a technical virgin, male or female? The new morality weighs motive heavily in its scales, along with means and ends. The new morality is not *soft* morality.

As we have noted, Karl Barth, the Swiss theologian, who speaks of "law" a great deal, nevertheless allows for what he calls the *ultima ratio*, the outside chance that in a particular situation what the law forbids can be excused. In this way Barth, like many Catholic moral theologians, is prepared out of mercy and compassion to excuse an act of fornication or a loveless marriage *in the situation*, in the rare case. But it would be a matter of excusing an evil (because unlawful) act. For Barth and Catholic metaphysics, the evil is "real"—objectively given *de rerum natura* in such categories as fornication, adultery, homosexual acts, contraception, abortion, sterilization, and the like.

IS ANYTHING INHERENTLY GOOD OR EVIL?

This is not the situationist's view. For him nothing is inherently good or evil, except love (personal concern) and its opposite, indifference or actual malice. Anything else, no matter what it is, may be good or evil, right or wrong, according to the situation. Goodness is what *happens* to a human act, it is not *in* the act itself. This is, in a way, a "nominalistic" doctrine. Like the situationists, Emil Brunner, another Swiss theologian, is more plainly in the camp of such a morality. To use language not his own but in keeping with his thought, he sees that *goodness or rightness is a predicate of actions, not a property of them!*

A clarion statement of this position is William Temple's: "The rightness of an act, then, nearly always and perhaps always, depends on the way in which the act is related to circumstances; this is what is meant by calling it relatively right; but this does not in the least imply that it is only doubtfully right. It may be, in the circumstances, certainly and absolutely right." This is, the action even if unlawful, even if it violates a moral maxim or rule, will be positively right; not merely an excusable wrong!

Bishop Pike of California, following the situational method in large part, has turned in his ethical treatise (*Doing the Truth*) to the story of how Judith used her sex to save Israel from Holofernes' army. The Bible obviously approves and applauds her action, her deliberate sexual seduction. (They wrote the story in such a way as to leave her technically chaste by getting away before Holofernes got her into bed with him, thus illustrating the ethical dishonesty of legalism, as well as its willingness to accept the lesser of evils. But this is what the notion of intrinsic evil always degenerates into!) A situationist would also applaud Judith's action, but wouldn't be driven by the theory to extricate her from the logic of her seduction. In any case, the Biblical Judith is a model for governments which use a woman's sex to entrap enemy espionage agents in blackmail, to inactivate them. Is the girl who gives her chastity for her country's sake any less approvable than the boy who gives his leg or his life? No!

True chastity is a matter of personal integrity, of sincerity and purity of heart. It is not sexual. Righteousness or virtue is willing the good of the neighbor. Von Hugel said that "caring is the greatest thing, caring matters most." Not all legalists and not all relativists are agreed about sexual promiscuity, of course, but the chances are that the Christians among them look upon promiscuity as irresponsible, careless, insincere, even as indifference. They (we) believe that promiscuity ignores and flouts the value and integrity of persons, turning casual sexual partners from true subjects into what some psychologists significantly call "love *objects*". It turns them into things. In the same way that sex is right or wrong according to its treatment of persons, so with the so-called "obscene." Frankness about sex is not wrong. As somebody said recently, obscenity is the word "nigger" on the lips of a Bull Connor type cop.

Even a transient sex liaison, if it has the elements of caring, of tenderness and selfless concern, of mutual offering, is better than a mechanical, egocentric exercise of conjugal "rights" between two uncaring or possibly antagonistic marriage partners. Sexual intercourse is not right or good just because it is legal (by civil or canonical law), nor is it wrong just because it is outside the law. So-called common-law marriages recognize this.

The personal commitment, not the county clerk, sanctifies sex. A man or wife who hates the partner is living in sin. A couple who cannot marry legally or permanently but live together faithfully and honorably and responsibly, are living in virtue—in Christian love. In this kind of Christian sex ethic the essential ingredients are caring and commitment. Given these factors, the only reason for disapproving sexual relations would be situational, not legal or principled. It would because the circumstances, realistically and imaginatively weighed, with a responsible eye on remote as well as immediate consequences, balance out against the liaison rather than for it. There is nothing against extramarital sex as such, in this ethic, and in *some* cases it is good.

As an example of the fact-weighing problem (situationism is *very* data conscious) we can cite a recent proposal by a Unitarian-Universalist minister in Michigan. He recommends that teenagers be prepared for sexual maturity in temporary trial marriages of limited duration and with parental consent. From a Christian perspective, most situationists (if not all) would hold that the teenagers would simply be practicing on each other, and the mere fact that their using each other would be *mutual* would only compound the evil, not justify it. The scheme seems unbelievably naïve on the score of emotional and cultural risks.

Advocates of Hugh Heffner's *Playboy* doctrine of promiscuity, arguing that sex is just "fun," are backing a naturalistic hedonism which is poles apart from the Christian ethic. Their argument is that anything sexual is all right if it does not hurt anybody. A lot hangs on that big word "hurt." But Christians say that nothing is right unless it *helps* somebody. Here lies the true issue of sex ethics—not moral maxims nor sentimentality nor romanticism nor antisexual fears. We do not praise a technical virgin whose petting practices are sexually unrestrained, nor do we condemn a loving transgressor of the law who is emotionally honest although technically unchaste.

If a defensive manoeuver can be forgiven here, suppose we hear Msgr. Pietro Palazzini, a Catholic moralist and Secretary of the Sacred Congregation of the Council, in his article about situation ethics in the *Dictionary of Moral Theology*. He says that situation ethics "must not be understood as an escape from the heavy burden of moral integrity. For, though its advocates truly deny the absolute value of universal norms, some are motivated by the belief that in this manner they are better safeguarding the eminent sovereignty of God."

One last word. The *Christian* criteria for sex relations are positive: sex is a matter of certain ideals of relationship. These ideals are based upon a certain faith: about God, Christ, the Church, who man is, and his destiny. Therefore, if people do not embrace that faith (and most don't), there is no reason why they should live by it. And most do not! It is time we faced up to this. Nowadays in the "secular city" it is easier and easier to see who are committed Christians and who are not. On any serious view of the matter, sex is not the decisive thing. Character shapes sex, sex does not shape character. Virtue never goes out of style but styles change. If true chastity means a marital monopoly, then let those who believe in it recommend it by reason and example. Nothing is gained by condemning the unbeliever. Indeed, to condemn him is more unjust (immoral) than a sexual escapade!

The fact is that all along churchmen have relied on *prudential* arguments against sexual freedom—the triple terrors of conception, infection and detection—not upon Christian sanctions. But modern medicine and urban anonymity have made sex relatively safe. The danger-argument is almost old hat. It is true, of course, that coital adventures may bring on delayed emotional reactions, but the same is true of petting. And in any case, these feelings are largely guilt feelings which changing cultural norms are making archaic or even antediluvian. The guilt is going. If Christians honestly and seriously believe that there are matters of *principle* at stake, as distinct from situational factors, they had better make them clear. And whatever they come up with, they aren't going to make a good case for absolute, universal, and unexceptionable ethical negatives. Or positives. The new morality is a better morality than that—than the old morality.

McCabe's Statement

Herbert McCabe, O.P., rejects situationism because it is an inadequate account of human moral behavior. More specifically, it gives the wrong answer to the question: are there some things one must never under any circumstances do? The right answer is, yes.

McCabe rejects "legalism," the position that conformity to law is the necessary and sufficient condition of good action: if an act is to be good, then it must conform to law, and if an act conforms to law, then it must be good. The truth is that conformity to law is a necessary but not a sufficient condition of goodness: every good act conforms to law, but not every act that conforms to law is good; good acts must in addition be done out of love. Now there are some kinds of acts that cannot be done out of love, and so are always wrong, killing an innocent man, for example, or, more strikingly, killing a baby by roasting it alive. Part of what is implicitly transmitted in both these descriptions of human action is a moral evaluation, ". . . and this killing is morally wrong." In effect there is no significant difference between "Fred killed a baby by burning it alive" and "Fred killed a baby by burning it alive, and that was wrong."

The situationists are wrong in saying that human acts receive all their moral import from the motive or intention with which they are done. Some acts are rightly judged to be morally bad or good before anything is said about motivation. Just as words have meaning before one uses them in a certain context to express a certain idea, so acts have meaning before one uses them in a certain situation with a certain motive.

Ethics says, do the loving thing. But one cannot do the loving thing unless he can distinguish loving things from unloving things. And if this is possible, it implies that one can identify and describe some kinds of bodily behavior as unloving. And if one can so identify some acts, then since the command to do the loving thing is absolute, one ought to prohibit unloving behavior absolutely by moral rule or law.

Situationism is intelligible only if one accepts a certain dualistic view of man according to which all bodily acts are morally neutral and none is more, or less, apt to carry or express moral goodness, or badness; meaning comes rather, and exclusively, from the interior intention with which the bodily act is performed. This is unacceptable, for on such a position the situationist cannot offer a satisfactory answer to the challenge: if there are no public criteria by which we may recognize at least lack of love, how do you recognize it in yourself?

McCabe's last major criticism is that situationists take too narrow and too limited a view of what "situation" comprehends. A human act relates a man not only to his immediate neighbors but to all mankind, and so calls for something more than the pedestrian, bourgeois view which sees in the moral hero or "man of principle" only a man with his nose stuck deep in a moral rule-book.

The Validity of Absolutes
by Herbert McCabe

For the New Moralists there are two sorts of ethics, one based on law the other on love. They contend that Christian moral teaching, which began as an anti-legalist ethics of love, has degenerated down the centuries into one of law. There is clearly a good deal of truth in this; moral theology, particularly in the Roman Catholic Church, has become legalistic and this does represent a departure from the authentic Christian tradition. The British catechism, now happily abandoned, on which I was brought up, had a section allegedly about charity. It began with a couple of questions about our obligation to love God (no mention, I need hardly say, of God's love for us) and then the third answer went: "We show that we love God by keeping his commandments, for Christ says, 'If you love me keep my commandments.' " From then on the compiler obviously felt more at home: "How many commandments are there?" "Say the ten commandments," etc. Nowhere was there any reference to Christ's words "A new commandment I give you, that you love one another."

This kind of thing really can be called legalistic and an appalling distortion of the Gospel message. It was, however, simply a popular reflection of the contemporary works of moral theology which were in fact manuals for confessors and devoted themselves to the demarcation and classification of sins. Such works have not yet been replaced. The Church is in desperate need of a new moral theology and there is as yet hardly any sign of it. We have a few scattered essays and the gallant but, I think, finally unsuccessful, attempt of Father Bernard Häring, and that is all.

I do not believe that the New Morality is what we are looking for. I think it presupposes a view of man and of society that is no longer acceptable in the twentieth century. The New Moralists seem not to have taken sufficiently seriously either Ludwig Wittgenstein or Karl Marx. I do not, of course, want to suggest that what they have to say is without value. On the contrary, the campaign against legalism, the attempt to appreciate the concrete predicaments of men, has been useful and necessary. The stress on the value of the human person is extremely welcome even though, as I shall suggest, the concept of the person that they have at their disposal seems to me a limited and bourgeois one. I take it, however, that I am not invited to speak of the vast area over which we should agree, but of that small but crucial area in which I believe they are mistaken. This concerns the validity of absolute moral principles.

To put it more simply, the question is: Are there some things that you must never under any circumstances do? I think it is possible to formulate such prohibitions, the New Moralists do not. They think that no law can be unconditionally binding because in every concrete situation law is subject to the over-riding consideration of love.

Let us be clear that this is not an argument about legalism. I mean by a legalist one who holds that good behavior consists precisely in obeying laws. He holds that conformity to law is not only a necessary but a *sufficient* condition for morally good action. Of course legalism is not usually an articulate theory; it is rather a disposition which shows more in what a man says than something he explicitly maintains. A man infected with legalism shows it by giving only perfunctory attention to any element in the moral life other than that of law. He believes, more or less consciously, that so long as a man obeys the law he is safe: conformity to the rules will get you by.

Now a man may reject such legalism because he holds that conformity to law is insufficient for good action, even if he thinks it is necessary. This was the position of, for example, Thomas Aquinas who in some 300 Questions of the *Summa Theologica* concerning morality has just 18 of them on law (and only one, incidentally, on "natural law"). I do not mention Aquinas because I think his moral theology sufficient for our time but because he is a good example of a man who rejects both legalism and the New Moralists' view of law. For Aquinas, love is the soul or life ("*forma*") of every virtue. By this he means almost the exact opposite of what a transliteration might lead one to expect. He means that every genuine virtue is just a form of love. Chastity without love is, for him, not true chastity at all but its corpse; and for an Aristotelian such as he was, a dead body is not even a body, it is a heap of chemicals which happens to be easily mistaken for a body. Moreover, he held that chastity without love would in a fairly short time cease even to resemble true chastity; like a corpse it would soon fall to pieces and begin to smell.

This is evidently not a legalist position and yet Aquinas certainly thought that some prohibitions were unconditionally binding; he thought, in fact that it is possible to describe a piece of human behavior which would always be wrong, which *could* not be an expression of love. Of course it is possible to do this tautologically by introducing some reference to wickedness or lack of love into your description of the behavior. You can safely say "Cruelty will always, under all circumstances, be wrong," because you are not prepared to count anything as cruelty unless it is loveless. But this would be trivial. Aquinas would maintain, and I think rightly, that it is possible to give a description of some piece of behavior which does not smuggle in any value terms and then to say that such behavior will always be wrong. For example, it would always be wrong to kill a baby by roasting it alive—and in case you think this is a fantastic example, remember that this is what napalm bombs and nuclear weapons do. (One exponent of the New Morality has, in fact, recently claimed that it could be an act of love to kill 100,000 people with an atomic bomb.)

The reason why a great many moralists reject this idea is that there seems to be a movement from a description of certain physical events (i.e., a description in physicists' language) to one in terms of value, and they cannot see how the jump is made. They cannot see how you can deduce from a mere description of a state of affairs, that it ought or ought not to be the case. I think this puzzle begins to dissolve once we realize that a description of human behavior, such as "killing a baby by roasting it alive," is not couched in physicists' language but in the language of inter-personal communication. A physicist, as such, knows nothing of killing, but only of movements of particles or whatever in space-time; killing is not, as such, a physicists' event, it is a human event. This does not mean, as the old dualist view of man would suggest, that a killing is a combination of two events, one a physicists' in the public world and the other a mental event (an act of "intention") in the private world. It was, I think, the greatest achievement of Wittgenstein to show that the mental world is not private. To have a mind is not essentially to have a means of withdrawing from the public world into a secret world of your own, it is to have a special way of belonging to the public world, it is to belong to a community.

CAN VALUES BE DEDUCED FROM FACTS?

What characterizes human beings is their special way of being together: their relations with each other are not just those of things with things, but of persons with persons. Their interactions are communication; descriptions of human behavior precisely as human are descriptions of what goes on in this world of communication. It is these descriptions (in which the significance of the behavior is part of *what* the behavior is) that are relevant to the formulation of moral laws. To say "Fred is killing an innocent man" is neither to speak in physicists' language nor is it to speak of what goes on privately in Fred's head—what he may be saying to himself silently while he is acting. It is to describe something as human behavior, as having a place in the system of communications that *constitutes* the existence of human beings. (Language, the use of signs, constitutes the human community, as sacraments constitute the ecclesial community: but *all* human activity is "significant," just as all of the Christian life is "sacramental.") It is a valid objection to the old Roman Catholic anti-contraceptive arguments that they were based on a physiologists' description of sexual activity rather than on a description of it as human behavior, as an activity of communication, an activity with significance and not merely with effects.

Human action has significance in itself prior to any significance that may be given to it by what a man may have in mind when he does it—though this, of course, is also an important element in morals. Significance pertains in the first place to the community as a whole. I am saying this: Human acts have significance not the way stones have temperature but the way words have meaning. I cannot change the temperature of the stone just by taking thought, but neither can I change the meaning of a word just by taking thought, for it belongs to the language not to me. Nor can I change the value of my behavior by taking thought, for its value is its meaning in the total system of communications which is the human world.

I must say a little more about the "non-subjectivity" of meaning. A word does not have meaning because there is something that it stands for, not even a "mental thing," a concept in my mind. It has meaning because it has a certain function in communication. When we know how a word is used in a certain community we know its meaning; this *is* its meaning. It follows that I cannot endow a word with meaning privately. I can no more create private meaning than I can issue private money. Money is what it is and has its value by playing a part in the system of financial communication. (Money is just a particular kind of language.) I do not confer meaning on my words by the ideas I have in my head when I use them. Meaning is thus, in a certain sense, "objective," though not in the way that the height of a tree or the speed of a train is an objective fact; meaning, again, is "subjective," though not in the way that a dream or a preference for kippers is subjective. Meaning belongs to the world of "inter-subjectivity," the world in which persons are present to each other not as object to subject but as co-subjects.

Language is the use of *sheer* signs; linguistic activity is simply for the sake of its significance and not for any physical effect. Other things we do for the sake of the effect they achieve but these activities too, in so far as they are human activities, have significance. When we extend the notion of meaning from the area of sheer signs (the use of which is merely one department of human behavior) to the total field of human inter-relations we speak of the *moral* significance of behavior. My words have meaning as playing a part in linguistic communication, my speech (or any other activity of mine) has moral significance as playing a part in the total system of communications that constitutes the human community.

The human body is the source of significant behavior. The human body is not, like a knife or a word, significant because it is used in a certain way; the body is not used, it uses these other things. The dualistic view of man, which has been such a constant temptation to Western philosophy, pictures a self inside the body and using it rather as an announcer inside a radio station uses the mechanism at his command to deliver messages to the outside world. The analogy is bound to fail fairly quickly not only because you have to be a body first of all in order to be *inside* anything, but more importantly because you have to be a body to *use* a medium of communication.

The human body is not, therefore, a medium but a source of significance, and this distinguishes it radically (substantially) from other things. Other things may be human by participation in bodily life—and everything that man touches he humanizes in this way. It is the purpose of human work to make the world man's clothing—but the body *is* humanly alive. As the Thomist said, human life is the substantial form of the body, that which makes it *what* it is; or, as Wittgenstein put it,

"The best picture of the soul is the body." It is because there are human bodies that there is a world of communication and it is by my bodiliness that I belong to this world. Without a body I am absent—this is what happens to the dead. (The bodily resurrection of Christ asserts that He is present.)

MORALITY AS BODILY ACTIVITY

The sphere of morality, then, is the sphere of bodily activity, not the activity of physical objects as such but of human bodies. Of course not every piece of human behavior we characterize as loving or wicked is itself a piece of overt bodily activity or inactivity. A man may have love or hatred in his heart without this being expressed in some single bodily activity. But in the first place such secret thoughts are defined by reference to some bodily activity and, secondly, they derive their moral value from the value of such bodily behavior. Thus I may have secret thoughts which are not expressed in words, not even perhaps in words that I imagine myself speaking inaudibly. But *what* I have been thinking is what I would say if I *did* express it in signs (and therefore with my body).

There is such a thing as simply having a wicked intention which is never realized. Thus the maintenance of the nuclear deterrent requires that large numbers of people should be ready under given circumstances to murder a great many innocent people. This intention exists even if the murder never actually takes place. Such an intention is not of course normally hidden; it is presumably the business of the Security Services to weed out of key positions people who have not got it, so it must be detectable in some kind of overt behavior. But the essential point is that the intention itself is only wicked because the act itself of using nuclear weapons on cities is wicked.

The human body is definitive of love. I mean by this that in order to explain the meaning of "love" you have to describe some bodily activities: feeding the hungry, visiting the imprisoned, etc. It is true that we speak of God as loving although He is not a body, but when we say this we take a word whose meaning we understand in a bodily context and extend it into a realm which we do not understand. When we say that God is loving, as when we say anything else about God, we don't know what we mean; we are using words to try to mean something. Moreover: "In this the love of God was made manifest amongst us, that God sent His only Son into the world that we might live through Him."

We only know the love of God in the bodily life of Christ, and primarily, of course, through our sacramental sharing in the bodily life of the risen Christ.

"Love," then, has meaning by reference to human bodies in their various complex relations of communication, and ethics is the analysis of love. I am not maintaining a behaviorist view that love is a particular set of bodily activities; if this were so we could prescribe love by prescribing the "correct" activity in each situation: this would be a legalist position. On the contrary, loving, like thinking, is an open-ended concept which is exemplified in an indefinite number of ways. There are methods of calculating but there is no method of thinking; similarly, there is no method of loving.

This half of the truth is well recognized by the New Moralists. What needs to be seen too, however, is that if "love" is to have any meaning at all, there must be pieces of behavior which count as unloving, just as there are pieces of behavior which count as muddled thinking. If we can describe such pieces of behavior then we can lay down absolute prohibitions, for even the New Moralists recognize that the command to love is absolute.

Let me try to make that a little clearer. There is no single bodily activity which is playing football. When we imagine a man playing we think of him running about a field kicking a ball, but of course a man can be engaged in playing football while standing perfectly still or while performing some maneuver that has never been seen or imagined before. Playing football does not consist in following out a choreographer's script mechanically, it is a creative activity—only human beings can play football. But if we were told that absolutely *any* activity could count as playing football, we should begin to feel that the word had lost its descriptive content and that while it might have significance as, say, an incantation, it was of no use for differentiating between various human activities. A recommendation never to stop playing football would then be a cheerful noise rather than a useful directive.

THE DUALISM OF THE " NEW MORALITY"

Now the New Moralists seem to hold that "loving" can be used to differentiate between kinds of behavior, and is therefore descriptive, but also that there is no possible piece of behavior which might not be called "loving." I think it is possible for them to hold this only because they believe that the adjective "loving" is descriptive not of bodily behavior as such but of something else that accompanies it. I think, in fact, that the New Morality only becomes plausible on a dualistic view of man according to which moral values attach to events in an "interior" invisible life which runs alongside a man's public physical life. Activities in the public visible world are in themselves morally neutral. We speak of them as virtuous or wicked according to whether they are accompanied or not by an act of loving in the interior life. The two lives are not intrinsically connected; we can make rough empirical generalizations about which public acts are usually accompanied by love, but such rules of thumb have no sort of necessity.

"One cannot," says the Bishop of Woolwich, "start from the proposition that sex relations before marriage or divorce are wrong or sinful in themselves. They may be in 99 or even 100 cases out of 100, but they are not intrinsically so, for the only intrinsic evil is lack of love." Here we have an admirably clear statement that love does not consist in actual behavior but in something else which may accompany behavior. It follows from this, that moral laws which must, of course, be about bodily activity (or inactivity) cannot be about what morality is about, for morality is certainly about love. The most we can say is that it is extremely probable that if a man deliberately burns a child to death this will turn out not to have been an act of love, just as it is extremely probable that a man who has voted conservative all his life will do so again. Such generalizations are a useful guide but no more. We cannot make sure predictions about what behavior in a given situation would be unloving; we can only enter the situation, at least imaginatively, and see what happens.

The question I would put to the New Moralist, then, is the one that the post-Wittgenstein critic would put to any philosophical dualist: If there are no public criteria by which we may recognize at least *lack* of love, how do you recognize it yourself? If the word "love" does not have a meaning in the public language (which implies at least criteria of its *mis*-application) how can it have meaning to you, how do you know that what you are doing is loving?

The second of my criticisms of the New Moralists concerns their use of the word "situation." They maintain that we should approach each moral situation with an innocent eye, we should be sensitive to its complexity; we should not seek merely to classify it according to preconceived categories. We should not say simply: "Here we have a clear case of adultery, it must stop," but "Here we have these particular people in these particular relationships in this place at this time: what now is the best for them in terms of their personal integrity and fulfillment, how can they best be brought to maturity in Christ in and through this situation?" The first attitude is characteristic of the civil law. What the court wants to know is whether or not you were exceeding the speed-limit, whether or not you deliberately shot this man, it is not concerned with the whole of your human situation but simply with one aspect of your life, where it impinges in a fairly crude way on the lives of others. It is doubtless an excellent thing that magistrates and policemen should have these limits on their range of legitimate interest, but it makes them a poor model for the moralist whose subject matter should be human life as such.

It would be hard to find anyone to disagree with platitudes of this kind. What is new about the New Morality is the rather limited view it takes of the human situation in which a man lives. It deals, it seems to me, essentially with Suburban Man and supposes that his situation is his suburb. A man's context is thought of as the people next door, the men he does business with, the enemies and friends he makes, the people he would mention in his autobiography. That is why I have described their notion of the personal as bourgeois.

Let us by all means jettison the "natural law" view of man, according to which Fred is of a certain nature with a certain function rather like a hammer or a lawn-mower. Once we understand what man is "for" we can tell what would be appropriate and what inappropriate behavior. Let us say instead that Fred exists in his world, in his dynamic personal relations with others, that the activity which is authentically *his* is to be discovered not by contemplating any static essence of man but by considering the existence of Fred in his context. Let us do this; but then the question arises insistently: What is my context? Or, to put it another way: Who is my neighbor? The parable of the Good Samaritan is notoriously easy to misinterpret. We say "When I meet someone beaten up by the roadside, *that* is my neighbor." But we are inclined to place the emphasis on the meeting instead of on the need for help. This is a tendency I detect in the New Morality.

The Varied Contexts of Life

I exist, in fact, in many contexts and the problem of morality—the problem of really being myself—is not simply to do justice to one selected context but to get the priorities right. Do I at the deepest level exist amongst the people I meet or amongst mankind? Do I have a personal relationship only with those I meet or with all who share a common life—and ultimately this means all men? Is my basic situation that of a man amongst the three or four people obviously involved in my marriage problem, or is it that of a man amongst my fellow men? As soon as we recognize that there are many overlapping situations and that there are priorities among them, we recognize the possibility of moral tragedy—that what is best for these people in their ultimate situation may not be what is best for them in this obvious context.

As I write this we have a clear illustration of it in Southern Rhodesia: First there is the doctrinaire classifier, the man who has never really looked at the details of the Rhodesian situation at all. He says: "Here we have a clear case of racial discrimination, it must stop." He does not know any Rhodesians, black or white, he does not know the complex personal relations between them; he simply applies a crude moral code. Next we have the white Rhodesian, or more likely, his friend who has visited him. He will come back and tell you how humane and decent the whites really are. If you actually lived there, he says, if you knew the people involved, you would realize how absurd the doctrinaire picture is. These people have built a real civilization; there is no brutality, no lynching; a Negro is legally entitled to enter the best hotel in Salisbury. The whites are not tyrants and slave-owners desperately trying to retain their power. They are just ordinary decent chaps who understand the native and are genuinely seeking in the given concrete situation to do the best for all the people involved. God knows what would happen to everyone if the Communists had their way and every African had a vote . . . and so on.

If we disagree with this apologist it is not because we prefer the abstract doctrinaire position, it is because we think him not sufficiently aware of the concrete situation in which the white Rhodesian actually lives. He has seen only the narrow circle of people white or black, whom he "personally" knows. He has missed the full range of the situation which extends in fact to the limits of mankind. A man is not only with the people he meets but with all men and he is part of a stage in human history. The demands of this total situation may mean the destruction of much that was valuable in the narrower context.

The industrial revolution destroyed a traditional way of life the value of which was obvious in its own context and the defects of which were only apparent in a much wider setting. This culture collapsed because its capacity for valid personal relationships was restricted to too narrow an area. The ethic of the "situation" takes no account of the need for this kind of revolution and I think it is just this that commends it to western liberalism. Revolution means a questioning of the situation, it means that we are not content to do the best we can in the given circumstances but that we change them. Both attitudes are exemplified in the early church. St. Paul was situational about slavery; he tried to show how a man may exercise Christian love within this setting. On the other hand the early Church was revolutionary about marriage: the idea of monogamous divorceless marriage, of total sexual commitment of a man and woman was no reformist attempt to get the best out of the marriage situation. It was a radical re-statement of what marriage is, it set sexual relations in a new and wider context, the context of redemption as St. Paul shows in Ephesians. The full implications of the Christian view of sex have not yet been worked out by the Church but at the very start the proclamation of "One man, one wife" was at least as subversive and "impractical" as the African demand for "One man, one vote."

When therefore we come across a "man of principle," someone who rigidly or ruthlessly abides by a course of action at the expense of what seem to be the obvious demands of kindness in a situation, we need to ask: Has he got his nose buried in the rule-book so that he can't see what is in front of him, or is it that he sees more than what is in front of his nose? What we call "absolute" moral demands are just the demands of the total human situation as far as we can seen them—and I believe it is part of the fact of divine revelation that we are helped to see them. Such demands may conflict with the demands of a smaller situation into which we have entered, but the absolutist morality is based on the priority of the situation into which we enter by being born.

Nothing takes precedence over the demands of the personal relationships in which I am involved by simply belonging to mankind. To exist at all is to be involved with others: "Social activity and social mind by no means exist only in the form of activity or mind that is *manifestly* social . . . even when I carry out scientific work—an activity which I can seldom conduct in direct association with other men—I perform a social, because a *human* act. It is not only the material of my activity—like the language itself which the thinker uses—which is given to me as a social product. My *own* existence *is* a social activity" (KARL MARX).

Joseph Fletcher Rejoinder to McCabe.

Fletcher was challenged to say how, in the alleged absence of public criteria, he could distinguish loving from unloving behavior. He answers that love is active concern for human welfare, a predicate of human acts, and is contextual; but it does not follow that in a given situation any act at all would express love, for the right act is the one that is measured by and blends both motive and situation.

To the charge that situationists use "situation" too narrowly, Fletcher answers that the situationist is concerned not only with short-run but also with long-run consequences, like other utilitarians, and takes as his specific goal the expression of the greatest amount of love for the greatest number of neighbors possible.

Agreement and Disagreement
by Joseph Fletcher

There are lots of reasons for welcoming Herbert McCabe's position paper—for its freshness among other things. It is when the ecumenical dialogue with Roman Catholics is driven down from the formalistic level of theological doctrine to the dynamic level of theological ethics, where the real believing is shown by the behaving, that an encounter in depth takes place.

Father McCabe is not prepared to go as far as Father Louis Monden, the Belgian Jesuit moralist, who says (in his *Sin, Liberty and Law*) that "we must clearly affirm with the great classical authors that Catholic morality is, in fact, a *situation ethics*" (his italics). All the same he *is* ready to confess that he does not regard Aquinas' ethics as "sufficient for our time," and with that we are ready and able to talk! There is, I might say, hardly a trace in what he has written of the "peccametry" or slide-rule-for-sins approach so prominent in the old morality.

Up to this point neither of us has taken adequate note of how old the "new" morality is, at least in the history of Christian ethics. The situation ethic is the one that Jesus endorsed. Indeed, the conflict between Jesus and Pharisaic Judaism was entirely an ethical one, not doctrinal. Jesus was, after all, in Wellhausen's famous phrase, a Jew. When St. Paul took up the cudgels on behalf of Jesus' challenge of the Torah law ethics, he added to his task an additional conflict, a doctrinal one—the incarnational faith about who this Jesus was, who dared to recommend that a hungry man ignore the sacral laws and break open the tabernacle to eat the reserved sacrament, the "shew bread." Paul like Jesus taught that whatever is *expedient* in the situation is good, if it serves love's purposes. It was an ethic of responsible freedom (grace), over against an ethic of obedience to laws. And

79

almost overnight, of course, legalism regained its control; the old morality built new and "Christian" systems of canonical and moral laws. (Re-read Ivan's legend of the Grand Inquisitor in Dostoyevsky's novel, *The Brothers Karamazov*!)

There are two complaints against the new morality in Father McCabe's treatment. In one he goes to the heart of the matter, the issue as between intrinsic and extrinsic views of morality, by trying to defend the old morality's claim that there are "some things that you must never under any circumstances do." His second complaint is against what he suspects to be a "bourgeois" narrowness or myopia in the new moralists' comprehension of situations. Let's take each complaint up for a brief rejoinder, in his order.

The first one is far and away the more important and the more solidly based. That is to say, Father McCabe puts his finger quite correctly on a real issue. The disagreement here is not based on any misunderstanding; he appears to oppose the new morality because he understands it only too well! He follows St. Thomas' realism, finding the locus of value in certain human acts, where as I as a nominalistic ethicist take a relativistic and pragmatic view, seeing right or wrong as predicates but not as properties.

The personalism in his ethics, or what Gordon Allport has called "interpersonalism," strikes an answering chord in the new morality. But as a new ontological basis for the old morality's realistic idea of the good it proves to be far less than convincing. Even though he repudiates "the old Roman Catholic" physicalism, his attempt to objectify value in a semi-behaviorist description of goodness as intrinsic ends up as almost a mystique of a sort: no sale. (This is no quarrel necessarily with his treatment of the *communication* side of "meaning" in linguistic analysis, or what he calls its "intersubjectivity." My challenge is to his opaque treatment of *what* he "means" to communicate!)

I entirely agree with Father McCabe that we can state action-propositions without smuggling value terms or moral judgments into them. Indeed, I would go farther: I would say that for critical ethical purposes it is necessary to outlaw value factors, whether explicit or implicit. But therefore I must protest his doing so in spite of what he says. He goes on, in spite of it, to imply that nuclear deterrent armament "embodies" an intention to *murder* people. As a pacifist he is, of course, pre-committed in principle or moral "law" (here is the doctrinaire rub) to treating nuclear weaponry as intrinsically unjust killing. As a realist or intrinsicalist he is, in doing so, only adhering to the logic of his value-theory.

(At another time we could discuss—not, perhaps disagreeing as much as we do in this exchange—what is entailed in Father McCabe's profoundly true and curiously Lutheran assertion of the *deus absconditus* "When we say that God is loving, as when we say anything else about God, we don't know what we mean; we are using words to try to mean something.")

THE CHARGE OF DUALISM

As a major part of his reasoning Father McCabe holds that the new morality is somehow dualistic, but he has not succeeded in showing that it is. Unless, of course, the very concept of ethical antimony—of good and evil or right and wrong—is itself dualistic! But that would be a sloppy use of the term and Father McCabe does not so use it. His point is, apparently, that the situationist or "new" moralist is dualistic if his intention to act lovingly (his "interior, invisible life") does not always coincide with his actions (his "public, physical life"). To dispose of this forced assertion we need, I suggest, merely to recall his earlier remark when supporting his own legalist-pacifist judgment on nuclear warfare: "There is such a thing as simply having an intention which is never realized." Exactly!

McCabe asks the situationist, "If there are no public criteria (he means, surely, *objective* criteria, to be non-Wittgensteinian for a moment!) by which we may recognize at least *lack* of love, how do you recognize it yourself?" The reply is: "The lack of love is indifference, not hate, and the work of love is the active will to contribute to the neighbor's wellbeing; what these will be in practice will vary according to the situation." Father McCabe wants me to say that the presence or absence of love is in the action itself (telling the truth, shooting a man, feeding a child, fornicating, alms giving); he cannot free himself from the realist assumption that love is a property.

But human love cannot be reified. It is to be predicated of human acts, it does not "infuse" them. It is something that *happens* to be true of an action rather than residing *in* it. Love is contextual, not phenomenal. Theologically expressed, only with God is love a property. With finite men it is relative and imperfect and contingent, depending for its measure upon the interplay of motive or intention and the *Gestalt* or configuration of situational factors.

TAKING ACCOUNT OF CONSEQUENCES

Father McCabe's second complaint comes down to a charge that, to use the language of ethical analysis, the situationist new morality only takes immediate consequences into account and *fails* to weigh seriously the remote consequences at stake in moral decision-making. In short, he suspects us of dealing with artificially delimited situations or contexts. This he calls suburban and bourgeois.

God forbid that we should be guilty of such things! But McCabe really does not show that we are. Indeed, he only claims he finds "a tendency" which he only "detects" at that. His illustration, the struggle for justice in Southern Rhodesia, hardly serves his purpose since situationists could, and do, add all of the situation's elements up to a balance in favor of Britain's and the black Rhodesians' reject of white supremacy (*this* situationist does, for example!). At the same time, doctrinaire advocates of white supremacy "in principle" can and do characteristically favor the Ian Smith forces in the struggle, just as doctrinaire advocates of black liberation "in principle" favor Wilson's policy.

Nevertheless, even though reference to Rhodesia settles nothing either way as to the validity of the old and new moralities (Father McCabe at least clearly favors *reform* of the old morality), the discussion has helped to remind us that the social complex is involved in moral choices. Or, to put it a bit differently, every personal decision lies within a total context of social policy and social welfare. Surely, to use a familiar label, the situationist must be sophisticated enough to be *utilitarian*: he is to try responsibly to decide his course with due regard to the greatest amount of love for the greatest number of neighbors possible. Contrary to Tolstoy's opinion, love cannot wear blinders, seeing only one or two neighbors at a time.

I had already remarked that *personalism* is on the new morality's team, and that Father McCabe approves of at least that much. Now we may add utilitarian *distributism*, which he rightly thinks is required by any serious ethic.

In conclusion, then, the new morality is a three-part package: it is situationist in its strategy, personalist in its norm and first-order value, and distributist in its range and outreach. It cannot cut its cloth according to any code or system of prefabricated laws, no matter how illuminating they may often be, and regardless of whether they are claimed to be natural and/or scriptural. Nothing but love is good in and of itself, and love is, in fact, only an imperative, not a property. It is what we serve, not something we are or have. God may be love, as St. John believed, but we human beings are only commanded to act lovingly—according to the situation.

Herbert McCabe Rejoinder to Fletcher

McCabe takes Fletcher to be saying that one evaluates the right thing to do in a situation both (a) by seeing how one's caring for others can best be expressed, and (b) by taking consequences into account. But how do we recognize this "caring" or loving concern for others? If it is not the case that some kinds of acts better express this caring more than others do, it would appear that we know which acts are accompanied by caring through some sort of intuition, through "just knowing", and this reduces situationism to antinomian spontaneism.

Situationist utilitarianism can meet the standard objections to utilitarianism no better than can other forms of utilitarianism. How do we set a limit to the consequences to be taken into account? In a sense, an act has an infinity of consequences. And if *acts* are not intrinsically good or bad, what grounds are there for saying, as utilitarians implicitly do, that consequences are intrinsically good or bad?

It is, finally, urgent practically to abandon situationism, for situationists tacitly accept and so implicitly underwrite an institutional environment which ought to be radially and profoundly changed.

The Total Context
by Herbert McCabe

I find it interesting that each of us was so anxious to repudiate his own end of the spectrum. I took elaborate pains not to be labelled a legalist while Professor Fletcher tried equally hard to show that he was not an "existentialist" or antinomian. He half convinces me of this. This is because he is antinomian only half the time, the rest of the time he is a good old-fashioned consequentialist—one who believes that human acts are good or bad simply according to the goodness or badness of their consequences.

The ordinary existentialist believes that you can't make any moral judgments until you are *in* the situation of decision. Professor Fletcher believes merely that you can't make valid judgments unless you take account of the whole situation of decision: there is no such thing for him as deciding that there are, for example, things men must not do to each other whatever the circumstances. Taking the situation into account, however, means for him different things at different times: sometimes it means evaluating the effects of your action, sometimes it means taking into account something called "caring," the presence of which is the hallmark of a good act. This caring which is distinct both from the act itself and its effects, seems to be some kind of psychological state. Neither of these positions seems to me plausible.

Let us begin with "caring." This seems to be much the same as "loving" and it is something that may or may not *accompany* actions. It is not itself displayed or exercised in ordinary activity. Professor Fletcher, for example, does not believe in sexual love; for him sex and love are, or can be, *partners*. He does not say this unthinkingly, he is fully aware of the implications of his position. Thus he says quite explicitly that chastity is not sexual. This is because, as he says, "it is a

84

matter of personal integrity, of sincerity and purity of heart" and for him, evidently, sex can never be any of these things, it can only be accompanied or partnered by them. Professor Fletcher does not tell us how we are to recognize caring or loving or purity of heart in ourselves. I suspect he believes that we "just know" when we care for somebody or love somebody, and in that case he is in a very similar position to the old antinomian who "just knew" what the Holy Spirit was guiding him to do. Most Christians think that we can tell whether we love by considering our behavior (and in particular our misbehavior): "Love is not arrogant or rude. Love does not insist on its own way; it is not irritable or resentful . . . (1 Cor. 13)."

Not only does Prof. Fletcher not tell us what caring is like, he also omits to explain for whom we ought to care. If the proper object of care is an individual—and he does seem to suggest this—why should I care for this individual instead of that? Almost all moral decisions of the slightest interest involve choosing the person who is to be hurt. To be told to care isn't any help here. On the other hand, if we take the view that the person exists in his communal relationships and that the primary object of care is the community or field of communication that makes personality possible, then we are going to find that sometimes, in extreme cases, the "caring" act is one that doesn't obviously benefit any nearby individual and may indeed harm nearly everyone in sight.

SETTING LIMITS

The other side of Professor Fletcher is a consequentialist and I shall not delay over the objections to this which are as old as the theory itself. In the first place how do we set a limit to the "consequences" of an act? Does an action change in moral value as history brings forth ever new consequences? This is a fine position for a historian but not much use to someone who has to make a decision. In the second place, if we may not say that acts are good or bad in themselves, how can we say this about consequences. If bombing Vietnamese peasants is neither good or bad in itself but becomes good because its consequence is to save men from Communism, how do we decide that it is good to save men from Communism? Of course consequences must make a difference to moral judgments but consideration of them can't be what judging *means*. However this is a stale debate; the new morality should offer us something fresher than that.

Two passages in Professor Fletcher's paper illustrate why it is *urgent* to stop playing the new morality game. "In any case, the Biblical Judith is a model for governments which use a woman's sex to entrap enemy espionage agents in blackmail, to inactivate them. Is the girl who gives her chastity for her country's sake any less approvable than the boy who gives his leg or his life? No." Quite apart from the breathtaking implications of "gives her chastity"—as though chastity were some kind of individual possession like a limb instead of a loving relationship with others (Stalin gave up mercy and love for his country's sake, is he any less approvable . . . etc.)—the really disturbing thing about this is its underwriting of a political set-up in which such practices are accepted as "realistic" and normal.

An even more revealing statement is this one, after the story of the woman in East Harlem: "She is right (which by the way does *not* mean a situationist approves in the abstract of the absence of any husband in so many disadvantaged Negro and Puerto Rican families.)" No, not in the abstract, just in the concrete. "She is right" is a betrayal of the revolution that is required in East Harlem. Of course such a woman caught up and lost in the jungle of the acquisitive society may be blameless, may be a saint, and of course the first thing that matters is to understand and sympathize with her immediate position; but she is *wrong*. To say she is right is to accept, as she does, the social situation in which she lives. A genuine moral judgment cuts deeper than that; it questions such a "situation" in terms of something greater. When we say "You can't apply the same high moral standards to slaves as you do to us" we accept slavery as an institution. Of course to punish or condemn the slave for lying or stealing is to hit the wrong target; it is the masters who bear the blame, but the blame is for the slave's wrong action.

I find it significant that, with all their disclaimers about morality having a much wider field, situationists do in fact incessantly talk about sex. I think the reason for this is that in the moral problems that arise concerning sex it is easy to believe that only a few people are really involved. It is relatively easy to forget that this activity, like all human activity, takes place in the total human context and has implications for all mankind. It is because my membership of the human race has implications for all I do that situationism, the new morality, is an inadequate account of human behavior.

B. Themes and Issues in Situationism

Louis Dupre

> Louis Dupré is professor of philosophy at Georgetown University, and the author of the influential *Contraception and Catholics: A New Appraisal* (1964).

Renford Bambrough

> Renford Bambrough teaches at St. John's College, Cambridge, and is the editor of the recent *New Essays on Plato and Aristotle* (1965).

Jonathan Bennett

> Professor Jonathan F. Bennett, formerly of Cambridge University, is presently Chairman of the Department of Philosophy, Simon Fraser University, British Columbia. His most recent book is *Kant's Analytic* (1966).

Alfred C. Ewing

> Alfred C. Ewing taught philosophy at Cambridge University for many years and is the author of a number of books on ethical theory, including *The Definition of Good* (1947), *Ethics* (1953), and *Second Thoughts on Moral Philosophy* (1959).

B. J. Diggs

> Professor B. J. Diggs is Chairman of the Department of Philosophy at the University of Illinois.

Eugene Fontinell

> Professor Eugene Fontinell is chairman of the philosophy department at Queens College of the City University of New York.

Charles DeKoninck

> The late Professor Charles DeKoninck was for many years Dean of the Faculty of Philosophy at Laval University and was the author of numerous works in philosophy and theology, including the influential *De la primauté du bien commun contre les personnalistes* (1943).

Charles Fried

> Charles Fried is Professor of Law at Harvard University.

Introduction to Louis Dupré

Professor Dupré distinguishes two sorts of situationist opposition to objective morality. One of these takes a philosophical approach and rejects *any* standard as an absolute criterion of morality; the other takes a theological approach and rejects any *human* standard as an absolute criterion of morality, while admitting a God-given standard.

The philosopher-situationist positively emphasizes human creativity and the priority of intention over act; he rejects any reliance on rules of good and evil. Dupré agrees that a static concept of human nature must be rejected, but sees the situationist as going too far, as going all the way to a purely subjective concept of human nature. The situationist also goes too far in rejecting any and all binding moral norms, for without norms the alternatives are perplexed inactivity or emotion-based acts. The situationist is right in thinking that an act, a lie, for example, which in one situation is right, is wrong in a different situation. But it is a mistake to say that there is no principle which together with an objective evaluation of the situation determines the rightness or wrongness of acts in all cases. The universal and objective principle which determines the morality of lying, for example, is this: never use language in any way which jeopardizes man's life in a community. There are, in addition to such universal principles, even some negative concrete moral rules which always obtain, such as "Never commit adultery." To the situationist objection that it may be necessary to commit adultery if this is the lesser of two evils, Dupré responds that it is never the case that one is faced with such a choice, and that since adultery is always destructive of essential human values, adultery is never right.

The theologian-situationist is one who carries to its limit the traditionally Protestant tendency to mistrust fallen human nature as a source of moral light for a Christian; perhaps there is a natural moral law, but it is insufficient to express man's personal relationship with God. Catholics have traditionally tended to underemphasize the subjective, the creative, and the impulse of God in favor of what is really an exaggerated emphasis on the objective and the rational.

Dupré concludes with a call for a balanced theory, one which gives proper attention both to the claims of a dynamic concept of human nature and to those of absolute moral objectivity, being at the same time open to the demands of a personal relationship to God.

Situation Ethics and Objective Morality*
by Louis Dupré

It has been said that the term "situation ethics" or its equivalent "contextualism" has become too large to be meaningful. In an article in the *Harvard Theological Review*, James Gustafson convincingly shows how the term covers moral systems which significantly differ from each other. He even maintains: "The debate between context and principles ... forces an unfair polarization upon a diversity of opinion that makes it both academically unjust, and increasingly morally fruitless. Persons assigned to either pole are there for very different reasons, and work under the respective umbrellas in very different ways."[1]

Gustafson is obviously right in asserting that men come to contextualism from different starting points and that "the place from which they start sets the pattern for what considerations are most important in the delineation of Christian ethics."[2] It is equally certain that "moralists of principles" differ considerably from each other. But the assertion that the distinction itself between situation ethics and ethics of principles has become too vague to be a fruitful topic of discussion is true only if the meaning of the term "ethics of principles" is extended beyond that of "objective morality." Such is obviously the case for Gustafson, who includes under ethics of principles several authors whom objective moralists would definitely characterize as situationist (in fact, all the moralists whom he discusses with the exception of Paul Ramsey). From an "objective" point of view, Gustafson's distinction is a distinction *within* situationism.

* Reprinted with permission from *Theological Studies*, XXVIII, (June, 1967), pp. 245–257.
[1] James F. Gustafson, "Context versus Principles: A Misplaced Debate in Christian Ethics," *Harvard Theological Review*, LVIII (1965), p. 192.
[2] *Ibid.*, p. 185.

It is the thesis of the present article that the distinction between objective morality and situation ethics remains relevant and even necessary to a fruitful discussion. Both objectivists and situationists complain that the other party misrepresents their position. This confusion indicates that the distinction between the two trends of thinking is not clearly defined. To clarify this distinction situationism must be divided into two entirely different moral approaches.[3]

One asserts that objective norms can never be absolute. The other rejects *any* immanently human standard (subjective or objective) as an absolute criterion of morality. The former approach, which is primarily philosophical, has both secular and religious adherents. It is an emphatic assertion of the irreducibly subjective character of human freedom against any moral system which subjects this freedom to the norms of its own objective expressions. The latter approach is theologically inspired: its followers are mainly Protestants who wish to develop a moral theory that is more consistently in accord with the Christian revelation of sin and redemption than a morality based upon the natural law.

We will discuss both approaches successively, even though they cannot always be kept distinct. Those who favor the philosophical line of thought often introduce theological elements into the argument. Similarly, all "theological" situationists at times borrow from a philosophy of the subject. Still, the two standpoints are so basically different that they must be treated separately.

THE PHILOSOPHICAL APPROACH

A common objection leveled against situation ethics is that it has no absolute principles. Nothing could be more false. For the situationist, the human person is an absolute value that cannot be subordinated to anything else. It is precisely because of its absolute character that he refuses to subjugate the original, subjective impulse of freedom to principles arising out of the objective expression of this freedom.

The situationist agrees with the objective moralist that human nature is an absolute norm of action. But he basically disagrees on the definition of this nature. For him, the nature of a free being is exactly the opposite of an objective, given datum: it is subjective creativity.

---

[3] This is not meant to deny further distinctions within situationism, but only to limit the discussion to what is absolutely essential from an objective point of view.

Whatever promotes creative freedom is moral; whatever hampers it is immoral. True, this rule provides no ready-made solution for every possible moral problem. But the crucial question in morality is not whether the ethical rule prescribes a universal line of action for each particular situation, but whether it provides man with *certain* guidance in each situation for bringing his behavior in conformity with his true (primarily subjective) being. And this, the situationist claims, his principles do.

The situationist refuses to accept objective rules of good and evil as absolutely valid because the moral intention cannot be determined exclusively by the objective structure of an act (even if this structure is correctly evaluated). Good and evil belong to the interior realm of freedom *before* belonging to the objective expressions of freedom. Of course, the situationist is well aware that subjectivity is not pure inwardness; the human subject necessarily expresses itself in objective forms. For that reason, man must also lay down objective rules for conduct. Situation ethics must not be confused with Kantian ethics, in which the morality of an act is determined *entirely* by the intention, independently of the object as such. Yet, objective rules alone are insufficient to determine morality, since freedom always retains an absolutely unique element of subjectivity which cannot be circumscribed objectively.

The insufficiency of objective norms as absolute criteria of morality was first worked into a moral theory by Søren Kierkegaard. According to the Danish thinker, inwardness is the essence of man as free being. It also is his ultimate end, attainable only in a confrontation with the transcendent Ground of his freedom. In striving toward inwardness, freedom leaves behind all its objective expressions as essentially inadequate. No objective moral standards, then, can properly measure the inward movement of the spirit. Nevertheless, Kierkegaard emphasizes, the moral law is important as an indispensable stepping-stone toward the religious stage of life. Only he can transcend the law who has seriously tried to live up to its demands. Even *within* the religious life the moral law remains important (at least in Kierkegaard's later writings), since it now becomes reincorporated into man's relation to the transcendent: the fulfilment of the law becomes an act of religious love.

I am not sure that situationists today would follow their great precursor on this last point. For them, the creativity of freedom commences forever anew and the objective norms that guided man's behavior in the past can never be more than empirical guidelines, assisting him but not compelling him in the present realization of his freedom. If people think that objective norms are absolute, this is only because until recently man's general state remained relatively stable. Walter Dirks, a Catholic situationist, writes:

A peasant's son, held by the regulations of his milieu to be a peasant, and growing up in a world penetrated with the duties of his state in life, was far less in a position than his counterpart today not to know what God wanted from him. What God expected from him was that he become a good peasant, and that meant doing in his place and time everything that a good peasant had always done; he had only to ask his elders and to do what they all did. The simpler and the more solid are the rules of the social order in which the possibilities of the human being are firmly and clearly articulated, the more is good realized in acceptance and submission.[4]

However, as the human condition has undergone a succession of rapid changes and placed us in entirely new situations, the rules of the past appear to be less universal. Situation ethics brings out the often-neglected element of creativity which should weigh heaviest in any moral theory.

Yet, the objective moralist cannot but wonder whether this isolation of the subjective aspect of freedom from its objective expression must not become self-destructive in the end. As Father Herbert McCabe pointed out in *Commonweal*,[5] without objective norms the situationist is not able to define, much less to apply, his own criterion of morality, namely, love or respect for the human person. Even to evaluate the "situation" itself, he must recur to objective norms. Who in a conflict situation should have the priority of my love? What is the most moral expression of love, for example, toward someone who seems to need the love of a person whom he or she is unable to marry? To leave such questions to one's creative subjectivity can only result in utter perplexity, or in a self-deceiving rationalization of emotional inclinations. Freedom is subjective, but it realizes itself in an objective world.

The situationist will retort that the attitude of the objective moralist

[4] Walter Dirks, "How Can I Know What God Wants of Me?" *Cross Currents*, V (1954), p. 81.
[5] Herbert McCabe, "The Validity of Absolutes," *Commonweal*, LXXXIII (1965–1966), p. 436.

is not so very different from his own. To certain acts he applies principles which he does not apply to similar acts in different situations. Of what avail are objective, general rules when, in the final analysis, the situation alone determines whether we will apply them or not? Is the objective moralist not deceiving himself in maintaining universal principles?

Here it is the objective moralist's turn to complain that his position is misunderstood. True enough, an identical act can be good in one situation and bad in another. No general precept of veracity binds the prisoner of war interrogated by the enemy about military secrets of his country. But does this mean that no universal precept applies to this case? Not at all, for one and the same universal principle may very well have two opposite applications. In this case the universal precept is not "to speak the truth under any circumstances" but "never to use language in a way which jeopardizes man's life in a community." This precept both obliges man to speak the truth to whoever has a right to it, and forbids him to reveal a truth that could seriously endanger the safety of his legitimate society (even though he would have to mislead those who seek its destruction). In the latter case, speaking the truth would destroy the very value which the precept of veracity is supposed to protect. What we have, then, is a truly universal and objective principle that must be applied in different and sometimes contrary ways depending upon the situation. Yet, it is never the situation itself nor my subjective impulse which ought to determine the course of action. To be moral, a decision must synthesize a *universal* moral principle with an *objective* evaluation of the present situation.

The situationist is quite right in pointing out that some concrete precepts exclude the application of others. But the objective moralist rejects his conclusion that *therefore* no moral principles are universal. The questions to ask are: "Which essential values of human nature are at stake?" and "How can I do justice to *all* these values without excluding any one of them in the present situation?" In trying to answer the second question, I may discover that a concrete maxim used in similar circumstances to promote a value may in a particular case jeopardize another equally essential value. The only conclusion which follows from such a discovery is that *this particular way of pursuing* the value is inadequate and should be rejected, for no essential value may be pursued to the exclusion of all others.

Here the situationist will object that it is impossible to do justice to

all essential human values involved in a particular situation and therefore one must at times choose one value while deliberately excluding
another. However, this statement reveals a pessimism concerning
human nature which the objective moralist is unable to share. To
settle for the lesser of two evils may seem necessary to the situationist.
To the objective moralist it is immoral, because human nature cannot
contradict itself to the point where every possible course of action in a
particular situation becomes destructive of an essential human value.
The whole discussion, then, turns upon two opposite concepts of human
nature. Now this opposition may well be caused by different theological
positions. But just as often the situationist's stand is simply a reaction
against an outdated, static concept of human nature. This concept is
seldom explicitly stated, but it becomes painfully evident in the way
the moralist handles casuistics. The assumption underlying most
casuistic ingenuity is that, *since human nature remains always the same,*
moral science can work out enough "cases" over a period of time to
protect all essential human values in all possible situations. The casuist,
then, attempts to foresee every eventuality so that even the most concrete precept becomes provided with some sort of absolute universality.
Wherever *that* situation occurs, *this* solution applies. Of course, the
casuist is the first to admit, moral textbooks have to be updated, but
this is mainly a matter of addition and subtraction: the new editor's
task consists in integrating into the existing system the situations
created by recent technological inventions, and in eliminating those
situations which have become obsolete.

Many situationists, though feeling the inadequacy of this solution,
still unquestioningly accept the premise of a static human nature. They
have resigned themselves to the contradiction and see no other way to
evade it than by a retreat into the purely subjective.[6] Such an attitude
is unsatisfactory from a theoretical viewpoint. Still, it deserves credit
for implying at least on a practical level that human nature is not the
immutable, given entity which the traditional casuist all too frequently
assumes. Freedom excludes the possibility of drawing up a set of
definitive concrete moral rules. Man's cultural and moral evolution
requires much more from the moralist than a mere adaptation of his

---

[6] Let it be noted that the position described here is primarily a Catholic one. The
Protestant situationist deduces his conclusions mostly from theological premises
which we will discuss later.

long-established solutions to the present state of technological progress. To use one example, the basic question in the current problem of birth control is not whether the newly-invented steroids must be termed "sterilizing" or not, as if that could decide the entire moral issue. The real problem is whether a temporary sterilization (or whatever one calls a deliberate interruption of the ovulatory process) which was considered to be illicit in the past, is still immoral when the total human situation with respect to procreation has become basically different.

The objective moralist is undeniably right in assuming that human nature remains *basically* identical and, consequently, that its most *fundamental* principles are absolutely universal. But these principles are to be specified in a number of particular precepts, and if the moral law is the law of a dynamic, self-creating being, most of its particular precepts cannot be fixed once and forever. The distinction between absolutely universal principles and their less universal specifications is not a new invention in objective morality; it was already made by St. Thomas Aquinas in the *Summa theologiae*:

We must say that the natural law as to the first common principles is the same for all both as to rectitude and as to knowledge. But as to certain more particular aspects, which are conclusions, as it were, of those common principles, it is the same for all in the majority of cases, both as to rectitude and as to knowledge, and yet in some few cases it may fail both as to rectitude, by reason of certain obstacles . . . and as to knowledge.[7]

Even more explicit is a seldom-quoted text of *De malo*:

The just and the good . . . are formally and everywhere the same, because the principles of right in natural reason do not change . . . Taken in the material sense, they are not the same everywhere and for all men, and this is so *by reason of the mutability of man's nature and the diverse conditions in which men and things find themselves in different environments and times.*[8]

This essential distinction between an absolute and a relative element in the moral law receives hardly more than lip service from many objective moralists. That is precisely the reason why situationists tend to go to the opposite extreme and deny the existence of any universal objective principles. But in doing so, they seem to adopt the thesis of the most rigid natural-law moralists, namely, that any relativization

[7] *Summa theologica*, 1–2, q. 94, a. 4.
[8] *De malo*, c. 2, a. 4, d. 13 (italics added).

of the concrete moral precepts jeopardizes the universality of *all* objective moral principles. This, however, is a false assumption; for the distinction between universal principles and less universal applications of these principles by no means implies that all concrete moral precepts allow of exceptions. Some acts are always and under any circumstances destructive of an essential human value. An act of adultery, for instance, cannot but violate the universal precept of justice and is therefore always wrong. The biblical example of Judith is often cited as a proof to the contrary. But if Judith's intention was to seduce Holofernes to adultery (which is not altogether clear from the text), even the most flexible objective moralist will find no better explanation for her action, I am afraid, than the primitive character of Judith's (or the author's) moral consciousness. That the narrator commends her for her patriotism is quite irrelevant. The books of the Bible reflect the moral mentality of their authors' time and environment. They reveal the religious meaning of man at a particular stage of his moral development, but by no means do they indicate that this stage has attained the highest ideal of moral refinement.

THE THEOLOGICAL APPROACH

So far we have interpreted situation ethics merely as a reaction against a rationalist and ahistorical moral-law theory. For Protestant moralists, however, situation ethics is obviously more than that. The basic reason for their disagreement with natural-law theory is not, as is sometimes said, a misunderstanding of the theory due to the shabby and inaccurate manner in which it is set forth in some standard texts, but rather a different theological concept of human nature. Any ethical theory which neglects the difference between man's situation before and after the Fall must look *a priori* suspect to the Protestant. Only in the original state of innocence could human nature provide an absolute norm of morality. After the Fall this original nature became an unattainable ideal rather than a realistic moral norm. The notion of an absolute natural law that continues to rule in man's present condition is, for the Protestant situationist, an unsuccessful attempt to maintain identical moral norms despite drastic changes in man's moral condition. The distinction between invariable, universal principles and the variable precepts through which these principles are to be applied has, in his eyes, no other function than to "adapt" the law of man's innocence to a situation in which this law can no longer be fully observed. Rather than camouflage the relativity of any moral law in the fallen state of man by a contrived and ineffective absolute law, the situationist openly admits that since the Fall human nature can no longer be an absolute norm of morality.

The natural-law moralist will undoubtedly reply that this is a misinterpretation of his concept of "relative" precepts. The moral law was already relative before the Fall; the relativity does not result from any concessions to the corruption of human nature, but from the necessity of applying the absolute to a variety of situations.

The answer is correct, and many Protestant situationists would undoubtedly do better to study first the basic meaning of the concepts which they reject. Yet, I fear, a better understanding of the terms will still not convert them to the natural-law position; for the essential question remains whether human nature after the Fall is still able to provide an absolute norm for action. The answer of Reformed theology to this question has been traditionally negative and would, therefore, seem to be irreconcilably opposed to a natural-law morality.

Still, modern theologians engaged in rethinking the historical element of the original sin seem to become increasingly reluctant to found the relativity of all natural law upon historical change of which we know nothing. Perhaps we may therefrom conclude that man's sinfulness no longer provides as strong a basis for rejecting a natural-law theory as it used to do.

More emphasized today is the different way in which Reformed theology conceives of God's relation to man. By its subjective, strictly personal character, this relation eschews the dominion of objective rules. While Catholics usually think of grace as an objective, common state provided through the Church and the sacraments, salvation for most Protestants means a unique and strictly personal call of God in Christ. But if the call is personal, so are the obligations. What God expects from His elect does not necessarily coincide with the immanent laws of human nature. Abraham's sacrifice is there to illustrate this. Any immanent determination of God's relation to man jeopardizes its transcendent character and is an assault on His absolute supremacy. Of course, insofar as the world is a coherent totality, it is intrinsically bound to certain objective rules which God Himself must respect. To break these rules constantly could only lead to chaos and destruction. But there is no reason why the divine election of an individual person must be subjected to similar restrictions.

The usual Catholic objection to this attitude is that God must be consistent with Himself. If He has created man in accordance with certain laws, He owes it to Himself to respect these laws. As Josef Fuchs, S.J., puts it: "God's personality and freedom do not exclude but presuppose that his own essence is 'given before' all personal and free volition. It therefore constitutes the 'measure' of everything. God, precisely because He is God, cannot deny or give up His own essence. Likewise, He cannot deny or give up the image of His essence which is man."[9]

But is this objection really responsive to the Protestant position? If God's demands in the order of salvation would constantly be in conflict with the objective requirements of human nature, they would obviously jeopardize His creation. But the Protestant situationist does not hold such a position. He does not even deny the existence of some sort of objective moral law. He merely says that this law is insufficient to express man's personal relationship with God in Christ. Objective moral laws promote man's *immanent* development. But they must not restrict man's obedience to transcendent divine orders, even if those orders occasionally conflict with these laws. God's commands can no longer be called transcendent if they are entirely subjected to the rule of man's immanent laws. Moreover, the Protestant situationist may turn the tables upon his opponent by pointing out that too much insistence on the necessity of a strict conformity between the transcendent and the objective immanent order could have results which the Catholic would be most reluctant to accept. It would, namely, exclude all miracles as arbitrary interferences of God with the universal rules of His own creation. Finally, references to the image of God such as the one in the above-quoted text are preposterous as long as we have not defined to what extent this image is preserved in man's sinful nature. Can we call objective morality a pure reflection of God's own essence? This question must be settled before the objective moralist can ever hope to convert the situationist to his position.

A third and perhaps even more basic Protestant objection to the natural-law theory is shared by many secular moralists. We mentioned it in the beginning of this article. An objective ethical system cannot do justice to the creative element in morality. Man must *seek* what is right for him, and this search will never be finished. Right and wrong

---

[9] Josef Fuchs, *Natural Law* (New York: Sheed and Ward, 1965), p. 129.

are not simply given. Even to say that he "discovers" moral values is not sufficient if it implies that values pre-exist to his finding them. Moral values are never simply there; they are created in the moral act itself. What goodness is becomes clear only in good acts. Moral goodness exists only to the extent that people are actually good. Men of heroic virtue, therefore, are much more than examples; they are authentic creators of moral virtue.

If one agrees with this position, the only relevant question with respect to the present discussion is whether man's moral creativity is better preserved in situation ethics than in an objective moral system. Many objective moralists would deny this. The absolute "obedience" to God's Word which some situationists advocate is hardly more creative than the most rigid natural-law theory (e.g., Emil Brunner in *Das Gebot und die Ordnungen*). Whether it is God's Word that orders me or an "immutable law of nature" makes little difference. Many situationists have broken through the legalism of "nature," only to fall victim to an equally rigid legalism of the Word of God. Their morality still consists in fulfilling obligations that remain extrinsic to personal freedom. What is needed is not another extrinsic source of moral obligation, but a more dynamic concept of human nature. Such a concept can be worked out within an objective moral system as well as in situation ethics.

But that is not all; for the objective moralist will object that in denying the absolutely normative character of all objective rules, the situationist, instead of liberating the creative aspect of freedom, merely ends up with an aimless impulse. It is true enough that no fixed norms can adequately determine the course of human freedom. Since freedom is an inventive and creative forward surge, human nature—that is, what is given originally and what has been acquired through past decisions—can never provide a definitive rule of action. But this does not mean that freedom determines itself in a vacuum. Freedom can exercise itself only *within* the objectivity of nature. Unless it respects the objective, given part of the self, the creative impulse becomes destructive.

CONCLUSION

The preceding confrontation between objective morality and situation ethics calls for a theory that combines the subjective-creative with the objective-rational element of freedom. No moral system in the past has done full justice to both these elements. Nor does the concept of natural law, with its heavy hereditary taint of objectivism and rationalism, seem particularly apt to reconcile both views. Nevertheless, some absolute objective and immanent standard appears to be indispensable.

The main problem is whether such a standard would be acceptable to both Protestant and Catholic theologians. Catholics have traditionally maintained an objective moral theory. But usually it was done in such a rigid and inflexible fashion that the dynamic aspect of human nature completely disappeared. In principle, however, Catholic theology does not object to a more dynamic moral theory as long as the notion of an objective moral law is preserved.

Nor would an objective basis of morality conflict with Reformed theology. Few Protestants would deny that human freedom implies some intrinsic norms independent of any revelation. We do not need the gospel to recognize that mass murders in concentration camps basically conflict with the dignity of man. Some may perhaps argue that without Christ's redemption human nature cannot avoid committing such crimes. But everyone will admit that non-Christians are able to *recognize* these acts as essentially immoral and that they do not indulge in them any more than Christians do. Protestant situationists may object that natural law cannot be a *sufficient* norm for Christian ethics. We wholeheartedly agree with them: nature can provide only general norms and some negative concrete precepts. But at least one must admit that there is some basic standard of morality which can be known without the aid of the revelation. It is important to stress this at a time when all men must co-operate to prevent certain criminal actions of recent history from ever being repeated.

Nor does the acceptance of man's nature as an absolute moral norm interfere with the strictly personal aspect of his relation to God. This relation is not made less personal by the fact that all men participate in the same incarnated freedom. Objective guidance in the exercise of freedom does not eliminate the ineffable character of the choice. Each man's vocation, therefore, remains unique and incomprehensible to others, even though it shares with others the same objective rules for the preservation of a common nature.

Protestants justifiably refuse to accept every single law that Catholic moralists, at one time or other, have presented as "natural law." In fact, none but the most general (and, I think, negative) precepts can ever be safely said to belong to the moral law of nature. However, the purpose of this discussion is not to discover a set of unchangeable concrete precepts. The position here presented has nothing in common with that of the objective moralist who overlooks the dynamic, personal aspect of human nature and simply attempts to present all rules that were indispensable at one time as eternal laws of God. My point is rather that a dynamic concept of nature and a personal relation to God are not incompatible with absolute moral objectivity. Indeed, without such objectivity man's moral activity is bound to operate in a vacuum. Not even a nominalist philosophy in which God's free decision alone makes good and evil could prevent such a position from being ultimately self-destructive.

Introduction to Renford Bambrough

In the following article, Bambrough argues that those who follow Moore in relying on common sense to ground belief in the objectivity of the external world, or who use the linguistic method to the same effect, are inconsistent to reject common sense or common language to ground belief in the objectivity of morals. Just as common sense and common language lead us to reject the scepticism of the senses, so do they lead us by exactly analogous arguments to reject moral scepticism. It would be paradoxical for anyone to deny either that the external world exists or that stealing is wrong, for surely any grounds or reasons we might have for such a denial are weaker than the proposition denied.

There are, to be sure, arguments offered by those who would reject the common sense account of moral knowledge, and the greater part of Bambrough's paper is devoted to elaborating and answering these. Such arguments come, basically, to a comparison of moral discourse with other sorts of discourse, to the serious disadvantage of moral discourse. Surely, we are told, values differ from facts: look at the wider range and greater persistence of moral than of factual disagreement, for example. Moreover, moral, but not scientific, beliefs are a function of our environment and training. Then too, morals are more a matter of feeling than are other sorts of knowledge; if this were not so, moral arguments could be settled on rational grounds and would not need to be abandoned, beyond a certain point, as hopeless. And does not the opposite view, objectivism, lead to authoritarianism, to religious persecution and the like?

In the last part of his paper, Bambrough asks why the common sense and common language account of moral enquiry is so vigorously attacked by those who pride themselves on fidelity to common sense and common language. He answers that some deny that we know moral truth, in order to emphasize the relative inferiority of moral knowledge relative to others, such as mathematical or scientific knowledge, or even to our knowledge that there is an external world: the most emphatic way of saying that a sort of knowledge is not of high quality, not worth bothering about, is to say that it is not really *knowledge*. On this reading, what the moral sceptic *says* is wrong, but what he *means* may be, and is, correct. Nonetheless this is a poor way of proceeding, for it consists in taking as a standard of comparison a sort of knowledge which has no more right to be taken as a standard than that with which it is compared.

Proof of the Objectivity of Morals
by Renford Bambrough

It is well known that recent British philosophy, under the leadership of G. E. Moore and Ludwig Wittgenstein, has defended common sense and common language against what seem to many contemporary philosophers to be the paradoxes, the obscurities and the mystifications of earlier metaphysical philosophers. The spirit in which this work is carried on is well indicated by the titles of two of the most famous of Moore's own papers: "A Defence of Common Sense" and "Proof of an External World." It can be more fully but still briefly described by saying something about Moore's defence of the common sense belief that there are external material objects. His proof of an external world consists essentially in holding up his hands and saying, "Here are two hands; therefore there are at least two material objects." He argues that no proposition that could plausibly be alleged as a reason in favor of doubting the truth of the proposition that I have two hands can possibly be more certainly true than that proposition itself. If a philosopher produces an argument against my claim to *know* that I have two hands, I can therefore be sure in advance that *either* at least one of the premises of his argument is false, *or* there is a mistake in the reasoning by which he purports to derive from his premises the conclusion that I do not know that I have two hands.

Moore himself speaks largely in terms of knowledge and belief and truth and falsehood rather than of the language in which we make our common sense claims and the language in which the sceptic or metaphysician attacks them, but his procedures, and still more the *effects* of his work, are similar to those of other and later philosophers who have treated the same topic in terms of adherence to or departure from common language. A so-called linguistic philosopher would say of the sceptic that he was using words in unusual senses, and that when he said that we do not know anything about the external world he was using the word "know" so differently from the way in which we ordinarily use it that this claim was not in conflict with the claim that we make when we say that we *do* know something about the external world.

It is easy to see the kinship between Moore's method and the linguistic method, so easy that many more recent writers have failed to see that Moore's method is distinct from the linguistic method. Moore takes the words of the sceptic literally, and shows that what he says is literally false. The linguistic philosopher recognizes that what the sceptic says is literally false, and goes on to conclude that the sceptic, who must be as well aware as we are that what he says is literally false, is not speaking literally. Both Moore and the linguistic philosopher maintain with all possible emphasis (Moore is famous for his *emphasis*) that we literally *do* know of some propositions about the external world that they are true; they both hold fast to common sense and common language.

It is also well known that most contemporary British philosophers reject intuitionist and objectivist accounts of the nature of moral reasoning. The most famous and fashionable of contemporary British moral philosophers, while they differ substantially in the detail of their accounts of moral judgments and moral reasoning, agree in drawing a sharp contrast between moral reasoning on one hand, and mathematical, logical, factual, and scientific reasoning on the other hand. They sharply contrast *fact* with *value*. They attach great importance to Hume's doctrine, or what they believe to have been Hume's doctrine, that *is* never entails *ought*, that from no amount of factual evidence does any evaluative proposition logically follow; that no set of premises about what is the case, unless they are combined with at least one premise about what is good or what ought to be the case, can yield any conclusion about what is good or what ought to be the case. While simple and extreme subjectivism is seldom explicitly defended nowadays, simple and extreme objectivism is almost never defended. Most of the fashionable doctrines, with the great stress that they lay on the emotive, prescriptive and imperative functions of moral propositions, lean so far towards the subjectivist end of the scale that they are sometimes, and naturally, lumped together under the title of "the new subjectivism." We are repeatedly told that there are no moral *truths*, that there is no moral *knowledge*, that in morals and politics all that we can ultimately do is to *commit* ourselves, to declare where we stand, to try by persuasion and rhetoric to bring others to share our point of view.

A speaker at the Cambridge Moral Sciences Club not many years ago began a paper on moral philosophy by saying that he would assume that we all agreed that all forms of objectivism must be rejected, and he was so used to swimming with a full tide that he was obviously and sincerely surprised, not to say *shocked*, to find that there were some people present who would not allow him to take this agreement for granted.

What is apparently not very well known is that there is a conflict between the fashionable allegiance to common sense and common language and the fashionable rejection of intuitionism and objectivism in moral philosophy.

I have no doubt that the philosopher I have just referred to, and most of those who agree with him about moral philosophy, would accept Moore's argument, or something closely akin to it, as a conclusive argument in favor of the claim that we have knowledge of the external world.

Most contemporary British philosophers accept Moore's proof of an external world. Most contemporary British philosophers reject the claim that we have moral knowledge. Therefore there are some contemporary British philosophers who both accept Moore's proof of an external world and reject the claim that we have moral knowledge. The position of these philosophers is self-contradictory. If we can show by Moore's argument that there is an external world, then we can show *by parity of reasoning*, by an exactly analogous argument that we have moral knowledge, that there are some propositions of morals which are *certainly* true, and which we *know* to be true.

My proof that we have moral knowledge consists essentially in saying, "We know that this child, who is about to undergo what would otherwise be painful surgery, should be given an anaesthetic before the operation. Therefore we know at least one moral proposition to be true." I argue that no proposition that could plausibly be alleged as a reason in favour of doubting the truth of the proposition that the child should be given an anaesthetic can possibly be more certainly true than that proposition itself. If a philosopher produces an argument against my claim to *know* that the child should be given an anaesthetic, I can therefore be sure in advance that *either* at least one of the premises of his argument is false, *or* there is a mistake in the reasoning by which he purports to derive from his premises the conclusion that I do not know that the child should be given an anaesthetic.

When Moore proves that there is an external world he is defending a common sense belief. When I prove that we have moral knowledge I am defending a common sense belief. The contemporary philosophers who both accept Moore's proof of an external world and reject the claim that we have moral knowledge defend common sense in one field and attack common sense in another field. They hold fast to common sense when they speak of our knowledge of the external world, and depart from common sense when they speak of morality.

When they speak of our knowledge of the external world they not only do not give reasons for confining their respect for common sense to their treatment of that single topic but assume and imply that their respect for common sense is *in general* justified. When they go on to speak of morality they not only do not give reasons for abandoning the respect for common sense that they showed when they spoke of our knowledge of the external world, but assume and imply that they are still showing the same respect for common sense. But this is just what they are *not* doing.

The common sense view is that we *know* that stealing is wrong, that promise-keeping is right, that unselfishness is good, that cruelty is bad. Common language uses in moral contexts the whole range of expressions that it also uses in non-moral contexts when it is concerned with knowledge and ignorance, truth and falsehood, reason and unreason, questions and answers. We speak as naturally of a child's not knowing the difference between right and wrong as we do of his not knowing the difference between right and left. We say that we do not know what to do as naturally as we say that we do not know what is the case. We say that a man's moral views are unreasonable as naturally as we say that his views on a matter of fact are unreasonable. In moral contexts, just as naturally as in non-moral contexts, we speak of thinking, wondering, asking; of beliefs, opinions, convictions, arguments, conclusions; of dilemmas, problems, solutions; of perplexity, confusion, consistency and inconsistency, of errors and mistakes, of teaching, learning, training, showing, proving, finding out, understanding, realising, recognising and coming to see.

I am not now saying that we are right to speak of all these things as naturally in one type of context as in another, though that is what I do in fact believe. Still less am I saying that the fact that we speak in a particular way is itself a sufficient justification for speaking in that particular way. What I am saying now is that a philosopher who defends common sense when he is talking about our knowledge of the external world must *either* defend common sense when he talks about morality (that is to say, he must admit that we have moral knowledge) *or* give us reasons why in the one case common sense is to be defended, while in the other case it is *not* to be defended. If he does neither of these things we shall be entitled to accuse him of inconsistency.

I *do* accuse such philosophers of inconsistency.

Moore did not expect the sceptic of the senses to be satisfied with his proof of an external world, and I do not expect the moral sceptic to be satisfied with my proof of the objectivity of morals. Even somebody who is not a sceptic of the senses may be dissatisfied with Moore's proof, and even somebody who is not a moral sceptic may be dissatisfied with my proof. In fact, somebody who regards either proof as a strictly valid and conclusive argument for its conclusion may nevertheless be dissatisfied with the proof. He may reasonably wish to be given not only a conclusive demonstration of the truth of the conclusion, but also a detailed answer to the most popular or plausible arguments against the conclusion.

Those who reject the common sense account of moral knowledge, like those who reject the common sense account of our knowledge of the external world, do of course offer arguments in favour of their rejection. In both cases those who reject the common sense account offer very much the same arguments whether they recognise or fail to recognise that the account they are rejecting is in fact the common sense account. If we now look at the arguments that can be offered against the common sense account of moral knowledge we shall be able to see whether they are sufficiently similar to the arguments that can be offered against the common sense account of our knowledge of the external world to enable us to sustain our charge of inconsistency against a philosopher who attacks common sense in one field and defends it in the other. (We may note in passing that many philosophers in the past have committed the converse form of the same *prima facie* inconsistency: they have rejected the common sense account of our knowledge of the external world but have accepted the common sense account of moral knowledge.)

It will be impossible in a small space to give a full treatment of any one argument, and it will also be impossible to refer to all the arguments that have been offered by moral philosophers who are consciously or unconsciously in conflict with common sense. I shall refer briefly to the most familiar and most plausible arguments, and I shall give to each of them the outline of what I believe to be an adequate answer in defence of the common sense account.

"*Moral disagreement is more widespread, more radical and more persistent than disagreement about matters of fact.*"

I have two main comments to make on this suggestion: the first is that it is almost certainly untrue, and the second is that it is quite certainly irrelevant.

The objection loses much of its plausibility as soon as we insist on comparing the comparable. We are usually invited to contrast our admirably close agreement that there is a glass of water on the table with the depth, vigour and tenacity of our disagreements about capital punishment, abortion, birth control and nuclear disarmament. But this is a game that may be played by two or more players. A sufficient reply in kind is to contrast our general agreement that this child should have an anaesthetic with the strength and warmth of the disagreements between cosmologists and radio astronomers about the interpretation of certain radio-astronomical observations. If the moral sceptic then reminds us of Christian Science we can offer him in exchange the Flat Earth Society.

But this is a side issue. Even if it is true that moral disagreement is more acute and more persistent than other forms of disagreement, it does not follow that moral knowledge is impossible. However long and violent a dispute may be, and however few or many heads may be counted on this side or on that, it remains possible that one party to the dispute is right and the others wrong. Galileo was right when he contradicted the Cardinals: and so was Wilberforce when he rebuked the slave-owners.

There is a more direct and decisive way of showing the irrelevance of the argument from persistent disagreement. The question of whether a given type of enquiry is objective is the question whether it is *logically capable* of reaching knowledge, and is therefore an *a priori*, logical question. The question of how much agreement or disagreement there is between those who actually engage in that enquiry is a question of psychological or sociological fact. It follows that the question about the actual extent of agreement or disagreement has no bearing on the question of the objectivity of the enquiry. If this were not so, the objectivity of every enquiry might wax and wane through the centuries as men became more or less disputatious or more or less proficient in the arts of persuasion.

"*Our moral opinions are conditioned by our environment and upbringing.*"

It is under this heading that we are reminded of the variegated customs and beliefs of Hottentots, Eskimos, Polynesians and American Indians, which do indeed differ widely from each other and from our own. But this objection is really a special case of the general argument from disagreement, and it can be answered on the same lines. The beliefs of the Hottentots and the Polynesians about straightforwardly factual matters differs widely from our own, but that does not tempt us to say that science is subjective.

It is true that most of those who are born and bred in the stately homes of England have a different outlook on life from that of the Welsh miner or the Highland crofter, but it is also true that all these classes of people differ widely in their factual beliefs, and not least in their factual beliefs about themselves and each other.

Let us consider some of the moral sceptic's favourite examples, which are often presented as though they settled the issue beyond further argument.

(1) Herodotus reports that within the Persian Empire there were some tribes who buried their dead and some who burned them. Each group thought that the other's practice was barbarous. But (a) they agreed that respect must be shown to the dead; (b) they lived under very different climatic conditions; (c) we can now see that they were guilty of moral myopia in setting such store by what happened, for good or bad reasons, to be their own particular practice. Moral progress in this field has consisted in coming to recognise that burying-*verus*-burning is not an issue on which it is necessary for the whole of mankind to have a single, fixed, universal standpoint, regardless of variations of conditions in time and place.

(2) Some societies practise polygamous marriage. Others favour monogamy. Here again there need be no absolute and unvarying rule. In societies where women heavily outnumber men, institutions may be appropriate which would be out of place in societies where the numbers of men and women are roughly equal. The moralist who insists that monogamy is right regardless of circumstances, is like the inhabitant of the northern hemisphere who insists that it is always and everywhere

cold at Christmas, or the inhabitant of the southern hemisphere who cannot believe that it is ever or anywhere cold at Christmas.

(3) Some societies do not disapprove of what we condemn as "stealing." In such societies, anybody may take from anybody else's house anything he may need or want. This case serves further to illustrate that circumstances objectively alter cases, the relative is not only compatible with, but actually required by, the objective and rational determination of questions of right and wrong. I can maintain with all possible force that Bill Sykes is a rogue, and that prudence requires me to lock all my doors and windows against him, without being committed to holding that if an Eskimo takes whalemeat from the unlocked igloo of another Eskimo, then one of them is a knave and the other a fool. It is not that we disapprove of stealing and that the Eskimos do not, but that their circumstances differ so much from ours as to call for new consideration and a different judgment, which may be that in their situation stealing is innocent, or that in their situation there is no private property and therefore no possibility of *stealing* at all.

(4) Some tribes leave their elderly and useless members to die in the forest. Others, including our own, provide old age pensions and geriatric hospitals. But we should have to reconsider our arrangements if we found that the care of the aged involved for us the consequences that it might involve for a nomadic and pastoral people: general starvation because the old could not keep pace with the necessary movement to new pastures, children and domestic animals a prey to wild beasts, a life burdensome to all and destined to end with the extinction of the tribe.

"When I say that something is good or bad or right or wrong I commit myself, and reveal something of my attitudes and feelings."

This is quite true, but it is equally and analogously true that when I say that something is true or false, or even that something is red or round, I also commit myself and reveal something of my *beliefs*. Some emotivist and imperativist philosophers have sometimes failed to draw a clear enough distinction between what is said or meant by a particular form of expression and what is implied or suggested by it, and even those who have distinguished clearly and correctly between meaning and implication in the case of moral propositions have often failed to see that exactly the same distinction can be drawn in the case of non-moral propositions. If I say "this is good" and then add "but

I do not approve of it," I certainly behave oddly enough to owe you an explanation, but I behave equally oddly and owe you a comparable explanation if I say "that is true, but I don't believe it." If it is held that I contradict myself in the first case, it must be allowed that I contradict myself in the second case. If it is claimed that I do not contradict myself in the second case, then it must be allowed that I do not contradict myself in the first case. If this point can be used as an argument against the objectivity of morals, then it can also be used as an argument against the objectivity of science, logic, and of every other branch of enquiry.

The parallel between *approve* and *believe* and between *good* and *true* is so close that it provides a useful test of the paradoxes of subjectivism and emotivism. The emotivist puts the cart before the horse in trying to explain goodness in terms of approval, just as he would if he tried to explain truth in terms of belief. Belief cannot be explained without introducing the notion of truth, and approval cannot be explained without introducing the notion of goodness. To believe is (roughly) to hold to be true, and to approve is (equally roughly) to hold to be good.   Hence it is as unsatisfactory to try to reduce goodness to approval, or to approval plus some other component, as it would be to try to reduce truth to belief, or to belief plus some other component.

If we are to give a correct account of the logical character of morality we must preserve the distinction between appearance and reality, between seeming and really being, that we clearly and admittedly have to preserve if we are to give a correct account of truth and belief. Just as we do and must hope that what we believe (what seems to us to be true) is and will be in fact true, so we must hope that what we approve (what seems to us to be good) is and will be in fact good.

I can say of another "He thinks it is raining, but it is not," and of myself, "I thought it was raining but it was not." I can also say of another "He thinks it is good, but it is not," and of myself "I thought it was good, but it was not."

"*After every circumstance, every relation is known, the understanding has no further room to operate, nor any object on which it could employ itself.*"

This sentence from the first Appendix to Hume's *Enquiry Concerning the Principles of Morals* is the moral sceptic's favourite quotation, and he uses it for several purposes, including some that are alien to Hume's intentions. Sometimes it is no more than a flourish added to the argument from disagreement. Sometimes it is used in support of the claim that there comes a point in every moral dispute when further reasoning is not so much ineffective as impossible in principle. In either case the answer is once again a firm *tu quoque*. In any sense in which it is true that there may or must come to a point in moral enquiry beyond which no further reasoning is possible, it is in that same sense equally true that there may or must be a point in any enquiry at which the reasoning has to stop. Nothing can be proved to a man who will accept nothing that has not been proved. Moore recognized that his proof of an external world uses premises which have not themselves been proved. Not even in pure mathematics, that paradigm of strict security of reasoning, can we *force* a man to accept our premises or our modes of inference; and therefore we cannot force him to accept our conclusions. Once again the moral sceptic counts as a reason for doubting the objectivity of morals a feature of moral enquiry which is exactly paralleled in other departments of enquiry where he does *not* count it as a reason for scepticism. If he is to be consistent, he must either withdraw his argument against the objectivity of morals or subscribe also to an analogous argument against the objectivity of mathematics, physics, history, and every other branch of enquiry.

But of course such an argument gives no support to a sceptical conclusion about any of these enquiries. However conclusive a mode of reasoning may be, and however accurately we may use it, it always remains possible that we shall fail to convince a man who disagrees with us. There may come a point in a moral dispute when it is wiser to agree to differ than to persist with fruitless efforts to convince an opponent. But this by itself is no more a reason for doubting the truth of our premises and the validity of our arguments than the teacher's failure to convince a pupil of the validity of a proof of Pythagoras' theorum is a reason for doubting the validity of the proof and the truth of the theorum. It is notorious that even an expert physicist may fail to convince a member of the Flat Earth Society that the earth is not flat, but we nevertheless *know* that the earth is not flat. Lewis Carroll's tortoise ingeniously resisted the best efforts of Achilles to convince him of the validity of a simple deductive argument, but of course the argument *is* valid.

"A dispute which is purely moral is inconclusive in principle. The specifically moral element in moral disputes is one which cannot be resolved by investigation and reflection."

This objection brings into the open an assumption that is made at least implicitly by most of those who use Hume's remark as a subjective weapon: the assumption that whatever is a logical or factual dispute, or a mixture of logical and factual disputes, is necessarily *not* a moral dispute; that nothing is a moral dispute unless it is *purely* moral in the sense that it is a dispute between parties who agree on *all* the relevant factual and logical questions. But the *purely moral* dispute envisaged by this assumption is a pure fiction. The search for the "specifically moral elements" in moral disputes is a wild goose chase, and is the result of the initial confusion of supposing that no feature of moral reasoning is *really* a feature of moral reasoning, or is *characteristic* or moral reasoning, unless it is peculiar to moral reasoning. It is as if one insisted that a ginger cake could be fully characterized, and could only be characterized, by saying that there is ginger in it. It is true that ginger is the peculiar ingredient of a ginger cake as contrasted with other cakes, but no cake can be made entirely of ginger, and the ingredients that are combined with ginger to make ginger cakes are the same as those that are combined with chocolate, lemon, orange or vanilla to make other kinds of cakes; and ginger itself, when combined with other ingredients and treated in other ways, goes into the making of ginger puddings, ginger biscuits and ginger beer.

To the question "What is the place of reason in ethics?" why should we not answer: "The place of reason in ethics is exactly what it is in other enquiries, to enable us to find out the relevant facts and to make our judgments mutually consistent, to expose factual errors and detect logical inconsistencies"? This might seem to imply that there are some moral judgments which will serve as starting points for any moral enquiry, and will not themselves be proved, as others may be proved by being derived from them or disproved by being shown to be incompatible with them, and also to imply that we cannot engage in moral argument with a man with whom we agree on *no* moral question. In so far as these implications are correct they apply to all enquiry and not only to moral enquiry, and they do not, when correctly construed, constitute any objection to the rationality and objectivity of morality or of any other mode of enquiry. They seem to make difficulties for moral objectivity only when they are associated with a picture of rationality which, though it has always been powerful in the minds of philosophers, can be shown to be an unacceptable caricature.

I have criticised this picture elsewhere, and I shall be returning later in this article to some of its ill-effects. Here it is necessary only to underline once again that the moral sceptic is partial and selective in his use of an argument of indefinitely wide scope: if it were true that a man must accept unprovable moral premises before I could prove to him that there is such a thing as moral knowledge it would equally be true that a man must accept an unprovable material object proposition before Moore could prove to him that there is an external world. Similarly, if a moral conclusion can be proved only to a man who accepts unprovable moral premises then a physical conclusion can be proved only to a man who accepts unprovable physical premises.

"*There are recognized methods for settling factual and logical disputes, but there are no recognized methods for settling moral disputes.*"

This is either false, or true but irrelevant, according to how it is understood. Too often those who make this complaint are arguing in a circle, since they will count nothing as a recognized method of argument unless it is a recognized method of logical or scientific argument. If we adopt this interpretation, then it is true that there are no recognized methods of moral argument, but the lack of such methods does not affect the claim that morality is objective. One department of enquiry has not been shown to be no true department of enquiry when all that has been shown is that it cannot be carried on by exactly the methods that are appropriate to some other department of enquiry. We know without the help of the sceptic that morality is not identical with logic or science.

But in its most straightforward sense the claim is simply false. There *are* recognized methods of moral argument. Whenever we say "How would you like it if somebody did this to you?" or "How would it be if we all acted like this?" we are arguing according to recognized and established methods, and are in fact appealing to the consistency-requirement to which I have already referred. It is true that such appeals are often ineffective, but it is also true that well-founded logical or scientific arguments often fail to convince those to whom they are addressed. If the present objection is pursued beyond this point it turns into the argument from radical disagreement.

Now the moral sceptic is even more inclined to exaggerate the amount of disagreement that there is about methods of moral argument than he is inclined to exaggerate the amount of disagreement of moral belief as such. One reason for this is that he concentrates his attention on the admittedly striking and important fact that there is an enormous amount of immoral *conduct*. But most of those who *behave* immorally appeal to the very same methods of moral argument as those who condemn their immoral conduct. Hitler broke many promises, but he did not explicitly hold that promisebreaking as such and in general was justified. When others broke their promises to him he complained with the same force and in the same terms as those with whom he himself had failed to keep faith. And whenever he broke a promise he tried to *justify* his breach by claiming that other obligations overrode the duty to keep the promise. He did not simply deny that it was his duty to keep promises. He thus entered into the very process of argument by which it is possible to condemn so many of his own actions. He was *inconsistent* in requiring of other nations and their leaders standards of conduct to which he himself did not conform, and in failing to produce *convincing reasons* for his own departures from the agreed standards.

Here we may remember Bishop Butler's remark that the true system of morality can be found by noticing "what all men pretend," however true it may be that not all men live up to their pretensions.

The same point can be illustrated in national politics. When the Opposition complain against an alleged misdemeanour on the part of the Government, they are often reminded that they themselves, when they were in office, behaved in precisely the same way in closely analogous circumstances. They are then able to reply by pointing out that the *then* Opposition complained violently in the House of Commons. In such cases both sides are proceeding by recognized methods of argument, and each side is convicted of inconsistency by appeal to those methods.

"*Objectivism leads to authoritarianism: who are we to be so downright sure about what is good and bad, right and wrong?*"

A good illustration of this complaint is found in Professor P. H. Nowell-Smith's remark that "It is no accident that religious persecutions are the monopoly of objective theorists." This type of argument is radically misconceived; it consists in combination of several separate but equally serious confusions. In the first place we must notice that Nowell-Smith is here using a *moral* argument against objectivism. His objection depends on the moral proposition that religious persecution is morally wrong. I fully accept this moral proposition, but I claim that it gives no support to Nowell-Smith's attack on objectivism. For this moral proposition, and indeed every other moral proposition, is logically independent of the objectivist account of the nature of moral enquiry, in the sense that it would not be self-contradictory to deny objectivism and approve of religious persecution, or to condemn religious persecution and accept objectivism. In general, every philosophical proposition about the logical character of a class of propositions is logically independent of the truth or falsehood of any proposition of that class. This can be most decisively shown by pointing out that a philosophical proposition about the logical character of any particular proposition is also about the logical character of the *negation* of that proposition, since every proposition has the same logical character as its negation. (The negation of a moral proposition is a moral proposition, the negation of an empirical proposition is an empirical proposition, and so on.) It follows that if, as a matter of historical fact, "religious persecutions are the monopoly of objective theorists" this is not because the objective theory gives any logical ground for religious persecution, but because some objective theorists have made the very mistake of which I am now accusing Nowell-Smith, namely the mi take of supposing that it *does* give some logical ground for religious persecution.

This is in fact my second main objection to the argument from authoritarianism, that it not only depends on a moral proposition which is logically independent of objectivism, but also depends on a causal proposition which, like all other casual propositions, is logically independent of objectivism. It may be true that those who accept the objective theory are liable to argue mistakenly from it to the conclusion that religious persecution is justified. If this is so, while it is indeed not "an accident", but a causal phenomenon which can be scientifically or historically investigated and understood, it gives no ground of objection to the objective theory.

The fear of authoritarianism which prompts Nowell-Smith's complaint is also present in the minds of many of those who make the other objections that I have discussed. I shall return to this later, and show its importance for an understanding of the motives that lead to the rejection of the common sense account of moral knowledge. But the objection involves a logical point of great importance, and I must say something about it here if I am to make quite clear why I reject Nowell-Smith's complaint.

When a philosopher defends the certainty and objectivity of a particular branch of knowledge, he naturally provides examples of propositions of the kind with which he is concerned, and says of them that he knows them to be true. This is what Moore was doing when he said that he had two hands, or that the earth had existed for many years past. Now it is also very natural that a rival philosopher who is able to show that a proposition which is used as such an example is *not* true, or is at least very doubtful, should feel that he has damaged the philosophical position of the philosopher who used the example. And yet this feeling is wholly unjustified. For the example can be doubted or refuted only by making use of that very mode of reasoning which the philosopher who used the example was defending. An example will make the point clearer. If I am defending our knowledge of the external world against a sceptic, I may pick up an object from the table and say, in Moore's fashion, "I *know* that I have a pen in my hand." The sceptic may be able to point out to me that the object in my hand is not a pen, but a propelling pencil. But if he takes this opportunity, then, far from weakening my philosophical position, he grants me my case, because although it is true that I have made a mistake in saying that I *knew* that I had a pen in my hand, the sceptic's proof that I made that mistake is in itself sufficient to show that I was not mistaken in my claim that there can be knowledge of the external world. All that he succeeds in doing is to give me a better example than the one I had chosen for myself.

Similarly, if I am defending the objectivity of morals, and I give an example of a moral proposition which I claim that I know to be true, and the moral sceptic is able to convince me that it is *not* true, or that it is doubtful, he can only do this by making use of the very mode of reasoning whose possibility he seemed to be denying. As we have seen, this is how Nowell-Smith proceeds in his attack on objectivism: he makes use of a moral proposition. It is a recurrent feature of sceptical arguments that they rely on the very types of knowledge that they are meant to be attacking. When he reminds us of all the occasions when we were mistaken the sceptic fails to notice that he can identify the occasions when we were mistaken only because we now know *better*; that in fact the notion of *being mistaken* is necessarily connected with that of *not* being mistaken, and stands or falls with it.

So far I have been defending a particular type of account of moral enquiry against a number of objections. I maintain that the account I have defended is the common sense account, and that it can be defended against philosophical attacks in very much the same manner as that in which Moore's common sense account of our knowledge of the external world can be defended against philosophical attacks. At this point a new question arises. If I am right in claiming that my account is in accordance with common sense and common language, why has it been so vigorously attacked, and why in particular has it been attacked by philosophers who pride themselves on their fidelity to common sense and common language? I think we can find the key to the solution of this problem if we look further at Moore's treatment of our knowledge of the external world and at the sceptical objections against which he defended it. This will lead us to a brief consideration of the general form of philosophical scepticism of which moral scepticism and scepticism about the external world are particular instances.

After attending to Moore's defence of common sense and his proof of an external world we may ask, "Why in that case do so many philosophers maintain that common sense is mistaken, and that we do not in fact know anything about the external world?" The situation appears more puzzling still when we notice that Moore does not claim to be telling the sceptics anything that they do not already know. He propounds what has been called "Moore's paradox," that sceptical philosophers themselves know as well as Moore does that their conclusions are untrue.

When this puzzlement becomes more articulate it may take a rather different form. We may say, "Surely Moore must be *missing the point* of the sceptical philosophers. If they know as well as he does that we *do* have knowledge of the external world, then they cannot seriously mean to deny that we have knowledge of the external world. When they seem to deny what they and all of us very well know, they must really be doing something else, and we must not rest content with showing that what they *say* is false. Perhaps what they *say* is not what they *mean*." And this is what some philosophers have said about scepticism and Moore's answer to it. Professor John Wisdom has described Moore's procedure as "legalistic." While Moore is quite right in his arguments and in his conclusions, many of his readers remain dissatisfied, because they feel that his convincing disproof of the sceptical conclusion needs to be supplemented by a fuller account of the sources and motives and effects of scepticism.

This is just what Professor Wisdom, following a lead given by Wittgenstein, has undertaken to supply. The first hint was given in

Wittgenstein's *Tractatus* ("What the solipsist *means* is of course correct") and it was extended and elaborated in the researches that have now been published as *The Blue and Brown Books* and *Philosophical Investigations*. The story is taken further still in Wisdom's *Other Minds* and *Philosophy and Psychoanalysis*. In this paper it is neither necessary nor possible to give a full account of what has emerged from all these works. It will be sufficient if I can indicate in general terms how these enquiries bear on Moore's treatment of our knowledge of the external world, and how they can help us with our original question about common sense and morality.

We must ask, "What is the point that Moore is missing? If the sceptic, under the guise of doubting our claim to have knowledge of the external world, is really doing something else, what else is he really doing?" He is portraying the character of our knowledge of the external world by implicitly contrasting our knowledge of the external world with our knowledge of mathematics and our knowledge of our own minds. When he explicitly claims that we have no knowledge of the external world he is implicitly claiming that our knowledge of the external world is different in kind from these other forms of knowledge. He *says* that no proposition about the external world is certainly true: he *means* that no proposition about the external world has the same *kind* of certainty as some propositions about minds or some propositions of mathematics.

In general: a metaphysical paradox is a portrait of the character of a kind of enquiry, executed by the technique of implicit comparison of one kind of enquiry with another. The sceptical philosopher notices that what ultimately confirms a proposition of a given type is a set of propositions of another type, that is to say a set of propositions from which the original proposition does not follow deductively. He expresses this insight by saying that we have *no* ultimate reasons for asserting the propositions, since the only available evidence does not and cannot logically guarantee the conclusion. He thus comes into conflict with the common sense conviction that we do have knowledge of the kind in question, and also with other philosophers who defend this common sense conviction. They also make use of the paradox technique. Some of them agree with the sceptic that only deductive certainty will do, and are therefore led to claim that our ultimate evidence *is* deductively related to the conclusion, that the conclusion is *equivalent* to the evidence from which it is ultimately derived. The slogan of this party is that "The meaning of a statement is the method of its verification."

Others agree with the sceptic that the conclusion does not deductively follow from the premises, but deny that a deductive validation is required. Their slogan is that "Every sort of statement has its own sort of logic."

Other metaphysicians avoid the risks and surrender the rewards of paradox, and follow the safer, slower road of *direct* comparison and contrast, of detailed, literal description of the similarities and differences between kinds of knowledge. And sometimes the landscape painters and the nature poets bandy words with those who prefer theodolites and photogrammetry.

There is one peculiar feature of the sceptic's procedure which underlines this account of the nature of metaphysical conflicts. When he is purporting to cast doubt on any one kind of knowledge, the sceptic must make use of other kinds of knowledge as his standards of comparison, and these other kinds of knowledge, while they are being used in this way, are of course exempt from criticism. But each of them in turn may be doubted by the same procedure, and may even be implicitly and unfavourably contrasted with kinds of knowledge against which it was itself employed as a sceptical weapon. This is well illustrated in metaphysical arguments about time.

(1) The ultimate evidence for statements about the future is evidence about the present and the past. But from statements about the present and the past no statement about the future follows deductively. Therefore we have no knowledge of the future.

(2) The ultimate evidence for statements about the past is evidence about the present and the future. But from statements about the present and the future no statement about the past follows deductively. Therefore we have no knowledge of the past.

(3) The ultimate evidence for statements about the present is evidence about the past and the future. But from statements about the past and the future no statement about the present deductively follows. Therefore we have no knowledge of the present.

These three sceptical arguments together form an outline sketch of the nature of our knowledge of the past, the present and the future. Each of them taken separately proceeds by assuming that two of the three types of knowledge are sound, and using them to cast doubt on the third. Each in turn is questioned, and each in turn is taken to be sound and used as a sceptical weapon against the other two. If we take all this at its face value the account is therefore self-contradictory.

Even if a philosopher confines himself to attacking one of the types of knowledge by assuming the other two types to be sound, he cannot escape the charge of inconsistency, since it is clearly possible, even if he does not do it himself, to use his own method of argument against the types of knowledge that he chooses to exempt from it.

There is a general form of sceptical argument which can be applied in turn to every type of knowledge, even, as Lewis Carroll's tortoise shows, to deductive knowledge. A philosopher who uses this form of argument against any one type of knowledge must claim exemption for at least one other type of knowledge. But if he *seriously* means to doubt the type of knowledge against which he uses the argument, this is just what he cannot consistently do, since the type of knowledge that he chooses to exempt has no more and no less right to its exemption than the type of knowledge that he chooses to condemn. But of course, as Moore is aware and as Wisdom shows and insists, no sceptic does seriously mean to cast doubt on any type of knowledge, however much he may protest that this is what he is trying to do.

If we now return to the moral sceptic we can see that what he was doing was to draw implicit comparisons and contrasts between moral knowledge and other kinds of knowledge. When I defended the common sense view that we *do* have moral knowledge, I was being "legalistic" as Moore was being legalistic when he defended the common sense view that we have knowledge of the external world. In any sense in which he was missing the point of the sceptic of the senses, I was in the same sense missing the point of the moral sceptic. And just as the sceptic of the senses is not finally disposed of by showing that what he says is literally false, so the moral sceptic is not finally disposed of by showing that what he says is literally false. Each of them makes by his paradox a point which is quite compatible with the platitude which his paradox literally denies. But just as Moore rightly felt it worth while to demonstrate to the sceptic of the senses that his paradox *was* a literal denial of a platitude, because he suspected that the sceptic was not fully aware of the nature of his own procedure, so I have felt it worth while to demonstrate to the moral sceptic that his paradox is a literal denial of a platitude, because I suspect that many moral sceptics, even if they are fully aware that scepticism of the senses is a denial of a platitude, are not fully aware that moral scepticism is a denial of a platitude.

In moral philosophy, as in the philosophy of perception, to demonstrate the falsehood of scepticism and the unsoundness of sceptical arguments is an important beginning, but it is only a beginning. It needs to be followed by a positive exposition and description of the character of the knowledge that the sceptic declares not to deserve the name of knowledge, and an explanation of how its character prompts the sceptic to propound his paradoxes, and hence of how his paradoxes contribute to our understanding of its character. To do this for moral scepticism would be to write the book on moral knowledge for which this article cannot be more than a provisional first chapter.

Introduction to Jonathan Bennett

There are those who argue that certain kinds of things should never be done, no matter what the consequences of not doing them; while other sorts of things may sometimes be done. They defend the principle "It would always be wrong to . . . , whatever the consequences of not doing so" when the blank is filled, with for example, "kill an innocent human", but not when it is filled, for example, with "sing a song." Thus they say that some general rules of the form "It would always be wrong to . . . etc." are true; other rules of that form are false; and one can tell on rational grounds how to distinguish the true ones from the false ones. Those who hold such a position are referred to by Jonathan Bennett in the article below as "conservatives."

Bennett argues that conservatives are wrong. There are no good reasons for accepting *any* principle of the form "It would always be wrong to . . . etc." To show this he chooses the example of feticide to save the mother's life: if an operation to kill the fetus is performed, the mother will live; without an operation, the mother will die and the fetus will live. He then tries to show in detail that there are no good reasons to accept the principle "It would always be wrong to kill an innocent human (the fetus), whatever the consequences of not doing so." An innocent human will die whether the operation is or is not performed, and Bennett is concerned to show that the moral difference between killing (operating) and letting die (not operating) is not sufficient to bear the weight of an unequivocal preference for letting die over killing no matter what the consequences.

Bennett explicitly or implicitly offers answers to a number of important questions. How can we draw the line between *what* someone did and the *consequences* of what he did? Is there any role in moral argument for the use of admittedly fantastic examples? Are there good grounds for dividing acts into those which are "good in themselves" or "good by nature," those which are "bad in themselves" or "bad by nature," and those which are indifferent? May we ever do evil in order that good may come of it? Does one have more responsibility for what one does than for what one refrains from doing, for acts than for omissions? Is there a clear-cut rule that we can use in this mother vs. child case, and in others like it? If not, will not decisions be *ad hoc* and arbitrary?

'Whatever the consequences'*
by Jonathan Bennett

The following kind of thing can occur.[1] A woman in labour will certainly die unless an operation is performed in which the head of her unborn child is crushed or dissected; while if it is not performed the child can be delivered, alive, by post-mortem Caesarian section. This presents a straight choice between the woman's life and the child's.

In a particular instance of this kind, some people would argue for securing the woman's survival on the basis of the special facts of the case: the woman's terror, or her place in an established network of affections and dependencies, or the child's physical defects, and so on. For them, the argument could go the other way in another instance, even if only in a very special one—*e.g.* where the child is well formed and the woman has cancer which will kill her within a month anyway.

Others would favour the woman's survival in any instance of the kind presented in my opening paragraph, on the grounds that women are human while unborn children are not. This dubious argument does not need to be attacked here, and I shall ignore it.

Others again would say, just on the facts as stated in my first paragraph, that the *child* must be allowed to survive. Their objection to any operation in which an unborn child's head is crushed, whatever the special features of the case, goes like this:

To do the operation would be to kill the child, while to refrain from doing it would not be to kill the woman but merely to conduct oneself in such a

---

* Reprinted with permission from *Analysis*, XXVI, January 1966, pp. 83–102.
[1] J. K. Feeney and A. P. Barry "Hydrocephaly as a Cause of Maternal Mortality," *Journal of Obstetrics and Gynaecology of the British Empire*, LXI, pp. 652–56. R. L. Cecil and H. F. Conn (eds.), *The Specialties in General Practice*. (Philadelphia, Pa.: Saunders, 1957), p. 410.

127

way that—as a foreseen but unwanted consequence—the woman died. The question we should ask is not: 'The woman's life or the child's?', but rather: 'To kill, or not to kill, an innocent human?' The answer to *that* is that it is always absolutely wrong to kill an innocent human, even in such dismal circumstances as these.

This line of thought needs to be attacked. Some able people find it acceptable; it is presupposed by the Principle of Double Effect[2] which permeates Roman Catholic writing on morals; and I cannot find any published statement of the extremely strong philosophical case for its rejection.

I shall state that case as best I can. My presentation of it owes much to certain allies and opponents who have commented on earlier drafts. I gratefully acknowledge my debt to Miss G. E. M. Anscombe, A. G. N. Flew, A. Kenny, and T. J. Smiley; and to a number of Cambridge research students, especially D. F. Wallace.

THE PLAN OF ATTACK

There is no way of disproving the principle: "It would always be wrong to kill an innocent human, whatever the consequences of not doing so." The principle is consistent and reasonably clear; it can be fed into moral syllogisms to yield practical conclusions; and although its application to borderline cases may raise disturbing problems, this is true of any moral principle. Someone who thinks that the principle is laid down by a moral authority whose deliverances are to be accepted without question, without *any* testing against the dictates of the individual conscience, is vulnerable only to arguments about the credentials of his alleged authority; and these are not my present concern. So I have no reply to make to anyone who is prepared to say: "I shall obey God's command never to kill an innocent human. I shall make no independent moral assessment of this command—whether to test the reasonableness of obeying it, or to test my belief that it *is* God's command, or for any other purpose." My concern is solely with those who accept the principle: "It would always be wrong to kill an innocent human, whatever the consequences of not doing so", not just because it occurs in some received list of moral principles

---

[2] See G. Kelly, *Medico-Moral Problems* (Dublin: Clonmore, 1955), p. 20; C. J. McFadden, *Medical Ethics* (London: Burns and Oates, 1962), pp. 27–33; T. J. O'Donnell, *Morals in Medicine* (Westminster, Md.: Newman, 1959), pp. 39–44; N. St. John-Stevas, *The Right to Life* (London: Hodder and Stoughton, 1963), p. 71.

but also because they think that it can in some degree be recommended to the normal conscience. Against this, I shall argue that a normal person who accepts the principle must either have failed to see what it involves or be passively and unquestioningly obedient to an authority.

I do not equate "the normal conscience" with "the 'liberal' conscience". Of course, the principle *is* rejected by the "liberal" majority; but I shall argue for the stronger and less obvious thesis that the principle is in the last resort on a par with "It would always be wrong to shout, whatever the consequences of not doing so", or "It would always be wrong to leave a bucket in a hall-way, whatever *etc.*" It is sometimes said that we "should not understand" someone who claimed to accept such wild eccentricities as these as fundamental moral truths —that he would be making a logical mistake, perhaps about what it is for something to be a "moral" principle. I need not claim so much. It is enough to say that such a person, if he was sincere and in his right mind, could safely be assumed to have delivered himself over to a moral authority and to have opted out of moral thinking altogether. The same could be said of anyone who accepted *and really understood* the principle: "It would always be wrong to kill an innocent human, whatever the consequences of not doing so." This principle is accepted by reasonable people who, though many of them give weight to some moral authority, have not abdicated from independent moral thinking. Clearly, they regard the principle as one which others might be led to accept, or at least to take seriously, on grounds other than subservience to an authority. From this fact, together with the thesis for which I shall argue, it follows that those who accept the principle (like others who at least treat it with respect) have not thought it through, have not seen what it comes to in concrete cases where it yields a different practical conclusion from that yielded by "It is wrong to kill an innocent human unless there are very powerful reasons for doing so". I aim to show what the principle comes to in these cases, and so to expose it for what it is.

My arguments will tell equally against any principle of the form "It would always be wrong to . . . , whatever the consequences of not doing so"; but I shall concentrate on the one principle about killing, and indeed on its application to the kind of obstetrical situation described in my opening paragraph.

I need a label for someone who accepts principles of the form: "It would always be wrong to . . . , whatever the consequences of not doing so." "Roman Catholic" is at once too wide and too narrow; "intrinsicalist" is nasty; "absolutist" is misleading; "deontologist" means too many other things as well. Reluctantly, I settle for "conservative." This use has precedents, but I offer it as a stipulative definition—an expository convenience and not a claim about "conservatism" in any ordinary sense.

Well then: When the conservative condemns the operation described in my opening paragraph, he does so *partly* because the operation involves the death of an innocent human. So does its non-performance; but for the conservative the dilemma is asymmetrical because the two alternatives involve human deaths in different ways: in one case the death is part of a killing, in the other there is no killing and a death occurs only as a consequence of what is done. From the premiss that operating would be killing an innocent human, together with the principle: "It would always be wrong to kill an innocent human, whatever *etc.*", it does follow that it would be wrong to operate. But the usual conservative—the one I plan to attack—thinks that his principle has *some* measure of acceptability on grounds other than unquestioning obedience to an authority. He must therefore think that the premiss: "In this case, operating would be killing an innocent human while not-operating would involve the death of an innocent human only as a consequence" gives *some* reason for the conclusion: "In this case, operating would be wrong". I shall argue that it gives no reason at all: once the muddles have been cleared away, it is just not humanly possible to see the premiss as supporting the conclusion, however weakly, except by accepting the principle "It would always be wrong *etc.*" as an unquestionable *donnée*.

THE ACTION/CONSEQUENCE DISTINCTION

When James killed Henry, what happened was this: James contracted his fingers round the handle of a knife, and moved his hand in such a way that the knife penetrated Henry's body and severed an artery; blood escaped from the wound, the rate of oxygen-transfer to Henry's body-cells fell drastically, and Henry died. In general, someone's performing a physical action includes his moving some part or parts of his body. (The difference between "He moved his hand" and "His hand moved" is not in question here: I am referring to movements which he *makes*.) He does this in a physical environment, and other things happen in consequence. A description of what he *did* will ordinarily entail something not only about his movements but also, *inter alia*, about some of their upshots. Other upshots will not ordinarily be covered by any description of "what he did", but will be counted amongst "the consequences of what he did." There are various criteria for drawing the line between what someone did and the consequences of what he did; and there can be several proper ways of drawing it in a given case.

This last point notwithstanding, there are wrong ways of dividing a set of happenings into action and consequences. Even where it is not positively wrong to give a very parsimonious account of "what he did", it may be preferable to be more inclusive. If in my chosen example the obstetrician does the operation, it is true that he crushes the child's head with the consequence that the child dies, but a better account, perhaps, would say that he *kills* the child by crushing its head. There can certainly be outright wrongness at the other end of the scale: we cannot be as inclusive as we like in our account of "what he did". If at the last time when the operation could save the woman's life the obstetrician is resignedly writing up his notes, it is just not true that, as he sits at his desk, he is killing the woman; nor, indeed, is he killing her at any other time.

The use of the action/consequence distinction in the conservative premiss is, therefore, perfectly correct. Operating *is* killing; not-operating is not. What are we saying when we say this? By what criteria is the action/consequence distinction drawn in the present case? I shall try, by answering this, to show that in this case one cannot attach moral significance to the fact that the line drawn by the distinction falls where it does. Briefly, the criteria for the action/consequence distinction fall into two groups: those which could support a moral conclusion but which do not apply to every instance of the obstetrical example; and those which do apply to the example but which it would be wildly eccentric to think relevant to the moral assessment of courses of action. There is no overlap between the two groups.

ASPECTS OF THE DISTINCTION: FIRST GROUP

Some differences which tend to go with the action/consequence distinction, and are perhaps to be counted amongst the criteria for it, clearly do have moral significance. None of them, however, is generally present in the obstetrical example.

Given a question about whether some particular upshot of a movement I made is to be covered by the description of what I *did:*

(a) The answer may depend in part upon whether in making the movement I was entirely confident that that upshot would ensure; and this could reasonably be thought relevant to the moral assessment of my conduct. This aspect of the action/consequence distinction, however, is absent from most instances of the obstetrical example. The classification of not-operating as something other than killing does not imply that the obstetrician rates the woman's chance of survival (if the operation is not performed) higher than the child's chance of survival (if it is performed). If it did imply this then, by contraposition, not-operating would in many such cases have to be classified as killing after all.

(b) The answer may depend in part upon how certain or inevitable it was that that upshot would ensue from my movement, or upon how confidently I ought to have expected it to ensue; and that too may have a strong bearing on the moral assessment of my conduct. But it gets no grip on the obstetrical example, for in many cases of that kind there is moral certainty on both sides of the dilemma. If the conservative says that the action/consequence distinction, when correctly drawn, is always associated with morally significant differences in the inevitability of upshots of movements, then he is vulnerable to an argument by contraposition like the one in (a). He is vulnerable in other ways as well, which I shall discuss in my next section.

(c) The answer may depend in part upon whether I made the movement partly or wholly for the sake of achieving that upshot; and this is a morally significant matter. But the obstetrical example is symmetrical in that respect also: if the obstetrician crushes the child's head he does so not because this will lead to the child's death or because it constitutes killing the child, but because that is his only way of removing the child's body from the woman's.

To summarize: moral conclusions may be supported by facts (a) about what is expected, but in the example each upshot is confidently expected; (b) about what is inevitable, but in the example each upshot is inevitable; or (c) about what is ultimately aimed at, but in the example neither upshot is aimed at.

AN ASIDE: DEGREES OF INEVITABILITY

I have suggested that a conservative might say: "The action-consequence distinction is always associated with a morally significant difference in the degree to which upshots are certain or inevitable."

This is false; but let us grant it in order to see whether it can help the conservative on the obstetrical example. I concede, for purposes of argument, that if the operation is not performed the woman will pretty certainly die, while if it is performed the child will even more certainly die.

What use can the conservative make of this concession? Will he say that the practical decision is to be based on a weighing of the comparative desirability of upshots against the comparative certainty of their achievement? If so, then he must allow that there *could* be a case in which it was right to kill the child—perhaps a case where a healthy young widow with four children is bearing a hydrocephalic child, and where her chance of survival if the operation is not performed is *nearly* as bad as the child's chance of survival if it is performed. If a professed "conservative" allows that there could, however improbably, be such a case, then he is not a conservative but a consequentialist; he does after all base his final judgment on the special features of the case; and he has misrepresented his position by using the language of action and consequence to express his implausible views about the comparative inevitability of upshots. On the other hand, if the conservative still absolutely rules out the killing of the child, whatever the details of the particular case, then what could be his point in claiming that there is a difference in degree of inevitability? The moral significance of this supposed difference would, at best, have to be conceded to be an obscure one which threw no light on why anyone should adopt the conservative view.

A certain conservative tactic is at issue here. Miss G. E. M. Anscombe has said:

If someone really thinks, *in advance*, that it is open to question whether such an action as procuring the judicial execution of the innocent should be quite excluded from consideration—I do not want to argue with him; he shows a corrupt mind.[3]

The phrase "quite excluded from consideration" clearly places Miss Anscombe as what I am calling a "conservative." (The phrase "a corrupt mind," incidentally, tends to confirm my view that conservatives think their position can stand the light of day, *i.e.* that they

---

[3] G. E. M. Anscombe, "Modern Moral Philosophy," *Philosophy*, XXXIII (1958) p. 17.

do not see it as tenable only by those who passively obey some moral authority.) Now, in the course of a footnote to this passage Miss Anscombe remarks:

In discussion when this paper was read, as was perhaps to be expected, this case was produced: a government is required to have an innocent man tried, sentenced and executed under threat of a "hydrogen bomb war". It would seem strange to me to have much hope of averting a war threatened by such men as made this demand. But the most important thing about the way in which cases like this are invented in discussions, is the assumption that only two courses are open: here, compliance and open defiance. No one can say in advance of such a situation what the possibilities are going to be—e.g. that there is none of stalling by a feigned willingness to comply, accompanied by a skilfully arranged 'escape' of the victim.

This makes two points about the case as described: there might be nothing we could do which would have a good chance of averting a war; and if there were one such thing we could do there might be several. The consequentialist might meet this by trying yet again to describe a case in which judicially executing an innocent man *is* the only thing we could do which would have a good chance of averting a war. When he has added the details which block off the other alternatives, his invented case may well be far removed from present political likelihood; it may even be quite fantastic. Still, what does the conservative say about it?

Here is Miss Anscombe, at her most gamesome, on the subject of "fantastic" examples:

A point of method I would recommend to the corrupter of the youth would be this: concentrate on examples which are either banal: you have promised to return a book, but . . . and so on, or fantastic: what you ought to do if you had to move forward, and stepping with your right foot meant killing twenty-five young men, while stepping with your left foot would kill fifty drooling old ones. (Obviously the right thing to do would be to jump and polish off the lot.)[4]

The cards are now well stacked; but this is a game in which a conservative should not be taking a hand at all. Someone may say (i): "In

---

[4] G. E. M. Anscombe, "Does Oxford Moral Philosophy Corrupt the Youth?", *The Listener*, February 14, 1957, p. 267. See also the correspondence in ensuing numbers, and Michael Tanner, "Examples in Moral Philosophy," *Proceedings of the Aristotelian Society*, LXV (1964–65), pp. 61–76.

no situation could it be right to procure the judicial execution of the innocent: political probability aside, the judicial execution of the innocent is absolutely impermissible in any possible circumstances." Or someone may say (ii): "It is never right to procure the judicial execution of the innocent: a situation in which this would be right has never arisen, isn't going to arise, and cannot even be described without entering into the realm of political fantasy.' These are different. The former is conservatism, according to which "the judicial execution of the innocent should be quite excluded from consideration". The latter is not conservatism: according to it, the judicial execution of the innocent is taken into consideration, assessed in the light of the political probabilities of the world we live in, and excluded on that basis. The former is Miss Anscombe's large type; the latter, apparently, is her footnote. The difference between (i) "In no situation could it be right . . ." and (ii) "No situation is even remotely likely to occur in which it would be right . . ." can be masked by dismissing what is relevant but unlikely as "fantastic" and therefore negligible. But the difference between the two positions is crucial, even if in the first instance it can be brought out only by considering "fantastic" possibilities. The two may yield the same real-life practical conclusions, but (ii) can be understood and argued with in a way in which (i) cannot. If someone accepts (ii), and is not afraid to discuss a "fantastic" but possible situation in which he would approve the judicial execution of an innocent man, he can be challenged to square this with his contrary judgment in regard to some less fantastic situation. Whether he could meet the challenge would depend on the details of his moral position and of the situations in question. The point is that we should know where we stood with him: for example, we should know that it was *relevant* to adduce evidence about how good the chances would be of averting war in this way in this situation, or in that way in that. It is just this sort of thing which the unwavering conservative must regard as irrelevant; and that is what is wrong with his position. Miss Anscombe says: "No one can say in advance of such a situation what the possibilities are going to be"; but the central objection to conservatism is, precisely, that it says in advance that for the judging of the proposed course of action *it does not matter* what the possibilities are going to be. Why, then, go on about them—if not to disguise conservatism as something else when the going gets tough?

I have based this paper on the obstetrical example in the hope that, without being jeered at for having "invented" an example which is "fantastic," I could present a kind of case in which a conservative principle would yield a practical conclusion different from any likely to be arrived at by consequentialist arguments. The claim that in these cases there would always be a morally significant difference between the woman's chance of survival and the child's could only be another attempt to get the spotlight off conservatism altogether—to get the consequentialist to accept the conservative's conclusion and forget about his principle. In the obstetrical example, the attempt is pretty desperate (though, with the aid of judiciously selected statistics, it is made often enough); with other kinds of example, used to examine this or other conservative principles, it might be easier for the conservative to make a show of insisting on the addition of details which render the examples "fantastic". But this does not mean that the case against conservatism is stronger here than elsewhere. It means only that the obstetrical example gives less scope than most for the "there-might-be-another-way-out" move, or protective-coloration gambit, which some conservatives sometimes use when they shelter their position by giving the impression that it does not really exist.

A conservative might invoke inevitability, without comparing degrees of it in the consequentialist manner, by saying that if the operation is not performed the woman still has *some* chance of survival while if it is performed the child has *none*. Barring miracles, this is wrong about the woman; not barring miracles, it is wrong about the child. It could seem plausible only to someone who did not bar miracles but took a peculiar view of how they operate. Some people do attach importance in this regard to the fact that if the operation is not performed the woman may take some time to die: they seem to think— perhaps encouraged by an eccentric view of God as powerful but *slow*— that the longer an upshot is delayed the more room there is for a miraculous intervention. This belief, whatever the assumptions which underlie it, gives no help to the conservative position. For suppose the obstetrician decides to try, after operating and delivering the child, to repair its head by microsurgery. The woman's supposed "some chance" of survival if the child's head is not crushed is of the same kind as the obstetrician's "some chance" of saving the child after crushing its head: in each case there is what the well-informed plain man would call "no chance", but in each case it will take a little time for the matter to be finally settled by the events themselves—for the woman to die or the obstetrician to admit failure. Would the conservative say that the obstetrician's intention to try to save the child in this way, though hopeless, completely alters the sharp of the problem and perhaps makes it all right for the obstetrician to crush the child's head? If so, then what we have here is a morality of gestures and poses.

ASPECTS OF THE DISTINCTION: SECOND GROUP

I return to the main thread of my argument. Of the remaining three aspects of the action/consequence distinction, it was not quite true to say that all are present in (every instance of) the obstetrical example; for the first of them has not even that merit. The main point, however, is that even if it were always present it would not help the conservative— though it might help us to diagnose his trouble.

(d) Someone's decision whether an upshot of a movement of mine is to be covered by his description of what I *did* may depend partly on his moral assessment of my role in the total situation. Your condemnation of me, or perhaps your approval, may be reflected in your putting on the "action" side of the line an upshot which an indifferent onlooker would count as merely a "consequence". This aspect of the action/ consequence distinction—if indeed it is one independently of those already discussed—cannot help the conservative who believes that a premiss using the distinction tends to *support* a moral conclusion. That belief demands a relevance relation which slopes the other way.

There seems to be just two remaining aspects to the action/consequences distinction. Certainly, there are only two which do appear in all instances of the obstetrical example. These two must be the sole justification for saying that operating would be killing while not-operating would not be killing; and so they must bear the whole weight of any conservative but non-authoritarian case against killing the child.

(e) Operating is killing-the-child because if the obstetrician operates there is a high degree of *immediacy* between what he does with his hands and the child's dying. This immediacy consists in the brevity or absence of time-lag, spatial nearness, simplicity of causal connexions, and paucity of intervening physical objects. The relations amongst these are complex; but they are severally relevant to the action/consequence distinction, and in the obstetrical example they all pull together, creating an overwhelming case for calling the performance of the operation the *killing* of the child

(f) Not-operating is not killing-the-woman because it is not *doing* anything at all but is merely *refraining* from doing something.

Since (e) and (f) are so central to the action/consequence distinction generally, it is appropriate that they should sometimes bear its whole weight, as they do in the conservative's (correct) application of the distinction to the obstetrical example. But if (e) and (f) are all there is to the premiss: "In this case, operating would be killing an innocent human while not-operating would involve the death of an innocent human only as a consequence", then this premiss offers no support at all to the conclusion: "In this case, operating would be wrong."

The matters which I group under "immediacy" in (e) may borrow moral significance from their loose association with facts about whether and in what degree upshots are (a) expected, (b) inevitable or (c) aimed at. In none of these respects, however, is there a relevant asymmetry in the obstetrical example. The question is: why should a difference in degree of immediacy, unaccompanied by other relevant differences, be taken to support a moral discrimination? I cannot think of a remotely plausible answer which does not consist solely in an appeal to an authority.[5]

Suggestions come to mind about "not getting one's hands dirty"; and the notion of what I call "immediacy" does help to show how the literal and the metaphorical are mingled in some uses of that phrase. In so doing, however, it exposes the desire to "keep one's hands clean," in cases like the obstetrical example, as a symptom of muddle or primness or, worst of all, a moral egoism like Pilate's. (To be fair: I do not think that many conservatives would answer in this way. If they used similar words it would probably not be to express the nasty sentiment I have mentioned but rather to say something like: "I must obey God's law; and the rest is up to God." Because this suggests a purely authoritarian basis, and because it certainly has nothing to do with immediacy, it lies beyond my present scope.)

Similarly with the acting/refraining distinction in (f). I shall argue in my next section that our criteria for this distinction do not invest it with any moral significance whatever—except when the distinction is drawn on the basis of independently formed moral judgments, and then

[5] Conservatives use words like 'direct' to cover a jumble of factors of which immediacy is the most prominent. Pius XII has said that a pain-killing, life-shortening drug may be used "if there exists no direct causal link, either through the will of interested parties or by the nature of things, between the induced consciousness [*sic* and the shortening of life . . ." (Quoted in St. John-Stevas, *op. cit.*, p. 61.)

it cannot help the conservative case for the reason given in (d). And if neither (e) immediacy nor (f) acting/refraining separately has moral significance, then clearly they cannot acquire any by being taken together.

ACTING AND REFRAINING

Suppose the obstetrician does not operate, and the woman dies. He does not kill her, but he *lets her die*. The reproach suggested by these words is just an unavoidable nuisance, and I shall not argue from it. When I say "he lets her die", I mean only that he knowingly refrains from preventing her death which he alone could prevent, and he cannot say that her survival is in a general way "none of my business" or "not [even *prima facie*] my concern". If my arguments so far are correct, then this one fact—the fact that the non-operating obstetrician *lets the woman die* but does not *kill her*—is the only remaining feature of the situation which the conservative can hope to adduce as supporting his judgment about what ought to be done in every instance of the obstetrical example.[6] Let us examine the difference between "X killed Y" and "X let Y die."

Some cases of letting-die are also cases of killing. If on a dark night X knows that Y's next step will take him over the edge of a high cliff, and he refrains from uttering a simple word of warning because he doesn't care or because he wants Y dead, then it is natural to say not only that X lets Y die but also that he kills him—even if it was not X who suggested the route, removed the fence from the cliff-top, *etc.* Cases like this, where a failure-to-prevent is described as a doing partly *because* it is judged to be wicked or indefensible, are beside my present point; for I want to see what difference there is between killing and letting-die which might be a *basis for* a moral judgment. Anyway, the letting-die which is also killing must involve malice or wanton indifference, and there is nothing like that in the obstetrical example. In short, to court these cases as relevant to the obstetrical example would be to suggest that not-operating would after all be killing the woman—a plainly false suggestion which I have disavowed. I wish to criticise the conservative's argument, not to deny his premiss. So from now on I

---

[6] In a case where the child cannot survive anyway: "It is a question of the *direct taking* of one innocent life or merely *permitting* two deaths. In other words, there is question of one *murder* against two deaths . . ." Kelly, *op. cit.*, p. 181.

shall ignore cases of letting-die which are also cases of killing; and it will make for brevity to pretend that they do not exist. For example, I shall say that killing involves moving one's body—which is false of some of these cases, but true of all others.

One more preliminary point: the purposes of the present enquiry do not demand that a full analysis be given either of "X killed Y" or of "X let Y die". We can ignore any implications either may have about what X (a) expected, (b) should have expected, or (c) was aiming at; for the obstetrical example is symmetrical in all those respects. We can also ignore the fact that "X killed Y" loosely implies something about (e) immediacy which is not implied by "X let Y die", for immediacy in itself has no moral significance.

Consider the statement that *Joe killed the calf*. A certain aspect of the analysis of this will help us to see how it relates to *Joe let the calf die*. To say that Joe killed the calf is to say that

(1) Joe moved his body

and

(2) the calf died;

but it is also to say something about how Joe's moving was connected with the calf's dying—something to the effect that

(3) If Joe had not moved as he did, the calf would not have died.

How is (3) to be interpreted? We might take it, rather strictly, as saying

(3'): If Joe had moved in *any* other way, the calf would not have died. This, however, is too strong to be a necessary condition of Joe's having killed the calf. Joe may have killed the calf even if he could have moved in other ways which would equally have involved the calf's dying. Suppose that Joe cut the calf's throat, but could have shot it instead: in that case he clearly killed it; but (3') denies that he killed it, because the calf might still have died even if Joe had not moved in just the way he did.

We might adopt a weaker reading of (3), namely as saying

(3''): Joe could have moved in *some* other way without the calf's dying.

But where (3') was too strong to be necessary, (3'') is too weak to express a sufficient connexion between Joe's moving and the calf's dying. It counts Joe as having killed the calf not only in cases where we should ordinarily say that he killed it but also in cases where the most we should say is that he let it die.

The truth lies somewhere between (3'), which is appropriate to "Joe killed the calf in the only way open to him", and (3''), which is appropriate to "Joe killed the calf or let it die." Specifically, the connexion between Joe's moving and the calf's dying which is appropriate to "Joe killed the calf" but not to "Joe let the calf die" is expressed by

(3'''): Of all the other ways in which Joe might have moved, *relatively few* satisfy the condition: if Joe had moved like that, the calf would have died.

And the connexion which is appropriate to "Joe let the calf die" but not to "Joe killed the calf" is expressed by

(4): Of all the other ways in which Joe might have moved, *almost all* satisfy the condition: if Joe had moved like that, the calf would have died.

This brings me to the main thesis of the present section: apart from the factors I have excluded as already dealt with, the difference between "X killed Y" and "X let Y die" *is* the difference between (3''') and (4). When the killing/letting-die distinction is stripped of its implications regarding immediacy, intention *etc.*—which lack moral significance or don't apply to the example—all that remains is a distinction having to do with where a set of movements lies on the scale which has "the only set of movements which would have produced that upshot" at one end and "movements other than the only set which would have produced that upshot" at the other.

This, then, is the conservative's residual basis for a moral discrimination between operating and not-operating. Operating would be killing: if the obstetrician makes movements which constitute operating, then the child will die; and there are very few other movements he could make which would also involve the child's dying. Not-operating would only be letting-die: if throughout the time when he could be operating the obstetrician makes movements which constitute not-operating, then the woman will die; but the vast majority of alternative movements he could make during that time would equally involve the woman's dying. I do not see how anyone doing his own moral thinking about the matter could find the least shred of moral significance in *this* difference between operating and not-operating.

Suppose you are told that X killed Y in the only way possible in the circumstances; and this, perhaps together with certain other details of the case, leads you to judge X's conduct adversely. Then you are told: "You have been misled: there is another way in which X could have killed Y." Then a third informant says :"That is wrong too: there are two other ways . . . *etc.*" Then a fourth: "No: there are three other ways . . . *etc.*" Clearly, these successive corrections put no pressure at all on your original judgment: you will not think it relevant to your judgment on X's killing of Y that it could have been carried out in any one of *n* different ways. But the move from "X killed Y in the only possible way" to "X killed Y in one of the only five possible ways" is of the same *kind* as the move from "X killed Y" to "X let Y die" (except for the latter's implications about immediacy); and the moral insignificance of the former move is evidence for the moral insignificance of the latter move also.

The difference between "X killed Y" and "X let Y die" is the sum-total of a vast number of differences such as that between "X killed Y in one of the only *n* possible ways" and "X killed Y in one of the only *n*+1 possible ways". If the difference between ". . . *n* . . ." and ". . . *n*+1 . . ." were morally insignificant only because it was *too small* for any moral discrimination to be based upon it, then the sum-total of millions of such differences might still have moral significance. But in fact the differences in question, whatever their size, are of the *wrong kind* for any moral discrimination to be based upon them. Suppose you have judged X adversely, on the basis of the misinformation: "X killed Y in the only way possible in the circumstances"; and this is then replaced, in one swoop, by the true report: "X did not kill Y at all, though he did knowingly let Y die". Other things being equal, would this give you the slightest reason to retract your adverse judgment? Not a bit of it! It would be perfectly reasonable for you to reply: "The fact remains that X chose to conduct himself in a way which he knew would involve Y's death. At first I thought his choice could encompass Y's death only by being the choice of some rather specific course of conduct; whereas the revised report shows me that X's choice could have encompassed Y's death while committing X to very little. At first I thought it had to be a choice to act; I now realize that it could have been a choice to refrain. What of it?"

There are several things a conservative is likely to say at this point —all equivalent. "When we know that the crucial choice could have been a choice to refrain from something, we can begin to allow for the possibility that it may have been a choice to refrain from doing something wrong, such as killing an innocent human." Or: "You say 'other things being equal,' but in the obstetrical example they aren't equal. By representing letting-die as a kind of wide-optioned killing you suppress the fact that the alternative to letting the woman die is killing the child."

Replies like these are available to the conservative only if he does not need them and can break through at some other point; for they assume the very point which is at issue, namely that in every instance of the obstetrical example it would be wrong to kill the child. I think that in some cases it would indeed be wrong––(I do not press for a blanket judgment on all instances of the example—quite the contrary); and in such a case the obstetrician, if he rightly let the woman die, could defend his doing so on the basis of the details of the particular case. Furthermore, he might wish to begin his defence by explaining: "I let the woman die, but I did not kill her"; for letting-die is in general likely to be more defensible than killing. My analysis incidentally shows one reason why: the alternatives to killing are always very numerous, and the odds are that at least one of them provides an acceptable way out of the impasse; whereas the alternative to letting-die is always some fairly specific course of conduct, and if there are conclusive objections to *that* then there's an end of the matter. All this, though, is a matter of likelihoods. It is no help in the rare cases where the alternatives to killing, numerous as they are, arguably do *not* include an acceptable way out of the impasse because they all involve something of the same order of gravity as a killing, namely a letting-die. The conservative may say: "Where innocent humans are in question, letting-die is not of the same order of gravity as killing: for one of them is not, and the other is, absolutely wrong in all possible circumstances." But this, like the rejoinders out of which this paragraph grew, assumes the very point which is at issue. All these conservative moves come down to just one thing: "At this point your argument fails; for the wrongness of killing the child, in any instance of the obstetrical example, *can* be defended on the basis of your own analysis of the acting/refraining distinction— plus the extra premiss that it would always be wrong to kill the child."

THE STRESS ON THE SPECIFIC

My argument is finished; but its strategy might be thought to be open to a certain criticism which I want to discuss.

The obsterical example is a *kind* of situation, on every instance of which the conservative makes a certain judgment. I have argued that this judgment, as applied to many instances of the example, cannot be defended except by the unquestioning invocation of authority. This would have been damaging to the conservative position even if I had appealed only to "fantastic" kinds of instance such as seldom or never occur; but in fact my claims have been true of many real-life instances of the obstetrical example. Still, a conservative might resist my drive towards the relatively specific, my insistence upon asking: "What is there about *this* kind of instance which justifies your judgment upon it?" He might claim that even my opening paragraph presents so special a kind of situation that he cannot fairly be asked to find in *it* something which supports his judgment other than by a blanket appeal to his general principle that it would always be wrong to kill an innocent human. There are two ways in which he might defend this stand: they look alike, but their fatal defects are very different.

The first is by the use of a sub-Wittgensteinian argument from the nature of language. Although I have never encountered it, it is a possible and plausible objection to my strategy of argument. The conservative might say: "Granted that facts about (a) expectation, (b) inevitability and (c) intention are irrelevant to the way the action/consequence distinction applies to the obstetrical example; it does not follow that when we apply the distinction to the example *all* we are doing— apart from (d) reflecting our already-formed moral judgments—is to report facts about (e) immediacy and (f) acting/refraining. Language and thought don't work like this. When we say: 'Operating would be killing; not-operating would not be killing though it would have death as a consequence', we are not *just* talking about immediacy and specificity of options. We are using words which, *qua* works in the language, are laden with associations having to do with (a)–(d); and these associations of the words cannot simply be ignored or forgotten in a particular case. Language is not atomic in that way, and it would be at best a clumsy instrument if it were."

I agree that we often do, and perhaps must sometimes, decide our conduct in one situation partly through verbal carry-overs from others in which similar conduct could be justified more directly. But I think that everyone will agree that the more serious a practical problem is, the greater is our obligation to resist such verbal carry-overs and scrutinize the particular problem in order to see what there is about *it* which would justify this or that solution to it. A practical problem in which human lives are at stake is a deeply serious one, and it would be an abdication from all moral seriousness to settle it by verbal carry-overs. I am not saying: "Take pity on the poor woman, and never mind what the correct description of the situation is." I am opposing someone who says: "This is the correct description of the situation—never mind what its force is in this particular case."

The second objection to my stress on the particular case, or the specific kind of case, is one which conservatives do sometimes use; and it connects with a muddle which is not special to conservatives. It goes like this: "We must have rules. If every practical problem had to be solved on the spot, on the basis of the fine details of the particular case, the results would be disastrous. Take a situation which falls under some rule which I know to be justified in most situations. There may not be time or means for me to learn much more about the present situation than just that it does fall under the rule; the details of the case, even if I can discover them, may be too complex for me to handle; my handling of them, even if intellectually efficient, may without my knowing it be self-interested or corrupt; by deciding, however uncorruptly, not to follow the rule on this occasion, I may weaken its hold on me in other situations where it clearly ought to be followed; and even if I could be sure that I was in no such danger, I might help others into it by publicly breaking the rule."[7]

This is all true, but it does not help the conservative. Notice first that it tells against undue attention to individual cases rather than against undue attention to limited kinds of case: its target is not the specific but the particular. Still, it could be developed into an attack on over-stressing very specifically detailed kinds of case: its opening words would then have to be replaced by: "We must have rather general rules." This is true too, but it is still no help to the conservative.

This argument for our bringing practical problems under rather general rules is based on the consequences of our not doing so: it points to the dangers attendant on suspending a general rule and considering whether one's practical problem might be better resolved by applying a less general one. But sometimes these dangers will be far too slight to justify doing what a given general rule enjoins in a particular situation. If the thesis under discussion is to have any practical upshot which is not ludicrous ("Never break any general rule which would enjoin the right action in more cases than not"), or vague to the point of vacuity

---

[7] For a gesture in this direction, see St. John-Stevas, *op. cit.*, pp. 14–16. See also McFadden, *op. cit.*, p. 133.

("Always apply some fairly general rule"), or merely question-begging ("Never break a rule forbidding an action which really is absolutely impermissible"), then it must allow us to raise questions of the form: "Need we be deterred by the dangers attendant on suspending *this* rule in favour of *this* more specific rule in *this* kind of situation?" The answer will depend upon what the challenged general rule is, what the proposed substitute for it is, the intelligence and character of the agent, and the likelihood that his breaking the rule (if it comes to that) would become generally known and, if known, demoralizing to others. These matters need not be so complex as to defeat finite intelligence, or so primrose-strewn that fallen man dare not venture among them. Furthermore, they can themselves be embodied in rules carefully formulated in advance—meta-rules about the kinds of situation in which this or that ground-level general rule may be suspended in favour of this or that more specific one.

Here is a possible case. A certain obstetrician accepts the rule, "Do not kill innocent humans," as applicable in every kind of situation he has thought of except the kind described in my opening paragraph. He wants a rule for this kind too, as a shield against the confusions, temptations and pressures of the concrete situation; and after reflection he adopts the following: "If the child is not hydrocephalic it is not to be killed. If it is hydrocephalic it is to be killed unless either (a) the woman is bound to die within a month anyway, or (b) the woman has no other children under eighteen and she is known to be a chronic acute depressive. If (a) or (b) or both are true, the child is not to be killed."

By preferring this rule to the more general one for instance of the obstetrical example, the obstetrician is not rendering it likely that in some situations he will flounder around not knowing what rule about killing to apply. For he has a clear enough meta-rule: "If the only way to save a woman's life is to kill the child she is bearing, apply this rule: . . . ; otherwise apply the rule: Do not kill innocent humans."

The obstetrician is not satisfied with his ground-level rule for instances of the obstetrical example, and he hopes to be able to improve it. Still, he is resigned to his rule's ignoring various matters which, though they are relevant to what the ideally right action would be, would involve him in the dangers of over-specificity mentioned above. "Is the woman a potential murderess or the child a mongol?"—the answers are probably unobtainable. "In what ways would the woman's death represent a real loss to others?"—the answer, even if discoverable, could be so complex as to elude any manageable rule. "Would either course of action bring the medical profession into undeserved but seriously damaging disrepute?"—it would be too easy for that to be unconsciously conflated with the question of which course would best further the obstetrician's own career. "Would the child, if delivered alive, be especially helpful to students of hydrocephalus?"—asking that could be the first step on a downward path: by allowing one woman to die partly because her child will be medically interesting if alive, even an uncorrupt man may ease the way towards allowing some other woman to die partly because *she* will be medically interesting when dead.

Although he pays heed—neurotically pays far too much heed—to the conservative's warnings against over-specificity, this obstetrician arrives at a conclusion quite different from the conservative's. That is the crux. The conservative who warns against the dangers of over-specifying is trying to find a consequentialist basis for his whole position. Unlike the "protective-coloration gambit" discussed earlier, this is legitimate enough in itself; but it simply does not yield the conservative position on the matter under discussion. For it to do so, the conservative would have to show that our obstetrician's more specific rule is *too* dangerous in the ways mentioned above; and he would have to do this without applying danger-inflating standards which would commit him also to condemning as too dangerous the suspension of the general rule: "Never leave a bucket in a hall-way." He may object: "Buckets in hall-ways are not important enough to provide a fair analogy. Where something as grave as killing is in question, we should be especially sensitive to the dangers of suspending a general rule." But then when something as grave as letting someone die is involved in applying the rule, we should be especially reluctant to accept, without good empirical evidence, popular clichés about the dangers of suspending general rules. The two points cancel out.

Of course, there are these dangers, and we should guard against them. To assess them at all precisely, though, would require more than we know of sociology, psychology and the philosophy of mind; and so our guarding against them can consist only in our keeping the urge towards specificity under some restraint, our remembering that in this matter it is not always true that the sky is the limit. The conservative who hopes to secure his position by pointing out these dangers must claim that he *can* assess them, and can discover in them a simple, sweeping pattern which picks out a certain list of general rules as the ones which ought never to be suspended by anyone in any circumstances. No one would explicitly make so preposterous a claim.

"So you do at any rate retreat from act- to rule-utilitarianism?" No. Rule-utilitarianism can be presented (1) as a quasi-mystical doctrine about the importance of rule-following "*per se*," or (2) as a doctrine about the importance of rule-following because of what rule-following empirically *is*, because of what happens when people follow rules and what happens when they don't. In version (1), rule-utilitarianism is a distinct doctrine which has nothing to recommend it. In version (2), it is just part of a thorough act-utilitarianism. (In most actual presentatations, there is a cloudy attempt to combine (2)'s reasonableness with (1)'s rejection of act-utilitarianism.) In this section I have been discussing what the consequences might be, for myself or others, of my suspending or breaking a given general rule. These are among, not additional to, the consequential factors whose relevance I have been urging all through the paper. There has been no retreat.

CONCLUSION

Principles of the form: "It would always be wrong to . . . , whatever the consequences of not doing so" seem defensible because the action/consequence distinction does often have a certain kind of moral significance. But in proportion as a situation gives real work to the rider ". . . whatever the consequences of not doing so", in proportion as it puts pressure on this rider, in proportion as the "consequences of not doing so" give some moral reason for "doing so"—to that extent the action/consequence distinction lacks moral significance in that situation. The obstetrical example is just an extreme case: there the rider serves to dismiss the entire moral case against applying the principle; and, proportionately, the action/consequence distinction carries no moral weight at all.

The phenomenon of conservatism, then, can be explained as follows. The conservative naturally thinks that the action/consequence distinction has great moral significance because of its frequent connexion with differences concerning (a) expectation, (b) inevitability, (c) intention and (d) independently formed moral judgments. He then encounters cases like the obstetrical example, where (a)–(d) are irrelevant but where the distinction can still be applied because of facts about (e) immediacy and (f) acting/refraining. Failing to see that in these cases the distinction has lost absolutely all its moral bite, and perhaps encouraged by a mistake about "rule-following *per se*", he still applies his principle in the usual way. Those who do not follow him in this he finds lax or opportunist or corrupt; and many of them half agree, by conceding to his position a certain hard and unfeeling uprightness. Both are wrong. Conservatism, when it is not mere obedience, is mere muddle.*

* For a response to this article, see P. J. Fitzgerald, "Acting and Refraining," *Analysis*, XXVII (1967), pp. 133–39. Bennett's rejoinder "Acting and Refraining," is found in *Analysis*, XXVIII (1967), pp. 30–31. And cf. James Cargile, "On Consequentialism", *Analysis*, XXIX (1969), pp. 78–88; and R. W. Beardsmore, "Consequences and Moral Worth," *Analysis*, (1969), pp. 177–186.

Introduction to A. C. Ewing

The question to which A. C. Ewing addresses himself is this: to what extent is Christian ethics compatible with utilitarianism? There is, however, relatively little discussion of the nature or content of characteristically Christian ethics, and his article is mainly an answer to this question: to what extent does utilitarianism prove to be a satisfactory ethical theory, a theory capable of providing for moral problems answers which are in accord with our moral sensibilities? Ewing's general answer is that utilitarianism, suitably understood and interpreted, can answer most, if not quite all, of the objections that can be raised against it; and that in any case, utilitarian considerations must play a very large part in any sound moral theory.

Among the objections raised against utilitarianism are these. Few people believe it right or a duty to break a promise if only a little more good can be done by breaking it than by keeping it; but utilitarianism commands this. Few think it right to steal from the rich to give to the poor even if human welfare would be thereby promoted; but utilitarianism commands this. Few would punish an innocent man even if this would improve his character or otherwise promote his welfare; but utilitarianism commands this. And so on. Ewing shows that these objections do not have all the force they might at first be thought to have. Most would as a matter of fact be willing to break a promise or punish an innocent person if the consequences of keeping the promise or of not punishing the innocent person were sufficiently bad. And still other moves are available to the utilitarian; he can draw conclusions compatible both with utilitarianism and with moral common sense if he stresses indirect consequences, or broadens the notion of consequences, or emphasizes the avoidance of evil over the promotion of good, or the like. Ewing however sees the utilitarians as unable easily to account for the preference people have for actions based on good

150

motives or intentions rather than on bad motives or intentions even if the consequences happen to be the same; or to account for the preference people have for the altruistic over the egoistic action when the consequences for human welfare are equivalent. The utilitarian could argue that both consequences and action-in-itself have a certain value, and that if the goal is the production of good, both the goodness of the act and the goodness of the consequences must be evaluated and a tradeoff ratio established between them. This move however virtually eliminates the differences between the utilitarian and his opponent, for each can now speak both about the intrinsic nature of the act and about the consequences of the act.

Finally, the utilitarian can pretty well account for the obligation one has to seek human welfare, but finds it rather more difficult to account for the moral fact that one must have the right frame of mind when he seeks this welfare.

Christian Ethics and Utilitarianism
by A. C. Ewing

If one believes in ethics it is only reasonable to aim at a rational justification of one's ethical beliefs. Now the most plausible mode of justification and the one that has most commonly been used by philosophers in the past is by reference to the consequences of our actions. That is the doctrine of utilitarianism. One distinction must however at once be made. Utilitarianism has been used in a narrower sense to stand for hedonism and in a wider sense by G. E. Moore and others to stand for the view that our only duty is to do what will produce, or it might be said, will tend most to produce the greatest good, "good" being understood as including but not limited to happiness. I do not wish to embark on the old discussion as to whether happiness is the only good, so I shall consider utilitarianism in the wider sense of the term. Now up to a point Christianity certainly goes with utilitarianism. "Loving one's neighbour as oneself" does indeed involve seeking his welfare in the highest sense of the word. Yet on the other hand it is clear that a morality which merely considered consequences would meet with the severe disapproval of most Christians. It is plainly a very important question for discussion, not without practical bearings, whether and how far this disapproval is justified.

Now it has struck many philosophers as self-evident that we ought just to seek the greatest good, not indeed selfishly just the greatest good for ourselves, but the greatest good we can produce for people in general, and this seems, taken in the abstract, a very plausible proposition indeed. Seeking good of course includes the attempt to produce or lessen evils. What else could there be to aim at, it may be asked, what other ground could there be for doing something except that it will produce or is at least reasonably likely to produce some good or remove some evil? This seems true and from it one is inclined to infer that we ought always to aim simply at producing as much good as we can, including again under the "production of good" the reduction of evil. But that this is not so clear we shall see soon.

One thing I had better mention first. The question I am asking calls for answers whatever view we take of the definition of good. Some thinkers hold that to say a thing is good is just to say that it is conducive to human satisfaction in some way, ultimately a psychological judgement. In that case the question is whether to act rightly is just to try sincerely and reasonably to produce the greatest satisfaction. Others think that the meaning of good cannot be *reduced* to this, but still may confine the things which are ultimately good to those which satisfy conscious beings and so on this earth to those mainly which satisfy human beings. They have still to consider then whether what makes something a duty is solely the tendency to produce these satisfactions and diminish the dissatisfactions. The question may indeed be thought to have been settled by a definition if we define good as what we ought to bring about, but it will still be a question on which differences will arise whether we ought to perform some actions for their own sake or only always for their results in producing consequences of some kind.

Even those who deny objective validity to ethical judgements, if they stop short of complete ethical scepticism, will admit that it is in some sense rational or right to base our ethical judgements on these satisfying experiences, and the question may still be asked whether it is *only* because of such consequences that we feel ready to approve, commend or advocate actions.

In speaking of satisfying experiences I had better add that I am not suggesting the view, held by the older utilitarians including Bentham and even Sidgwick but not Mill, that the quality of the satisfying experience does not matter and that quantity of satisfaction (or pleasure) produced is the sole criterion for determining what we ought to do. One might hold that the only things ultimately good were satisfying experiences and still agree with Mill in maintaining that a small amount of satisfaction got from the "higher" pleasures may be of much greater value than a much larger amount got from the "lower" pleasures, although one may well criticize Mill for his inconsistency in still maintaining pleasure to be the only good. If pleasure is really the only good, it can only be the quantity of the pleasure which counts.

We should distinguish between counting satisfactory experiences and counting satisfaction as the only good.

In any case utilitarian considerations must play a very great part in moral argument. Certainly, at the present day at least, in ordinary moral discussions the most usual although not the only, type of moral argument is utilitarian, i.e. it proceeds by reference to consequences. And Christianity must at least go a long way with it, for at the very least the chief Christian duty in relation to other men is to aim at their good. But can all duties be reduced to a matter of good consequences? To this most Christians would say No. Certainly there are seemingly strong objections to utilitarianism or at least to the view that it can be reconciled with our ordinary ethical beliefs even without presupposing any specifically Christian doctrine. Few people in any or almost any civilization would regard it as right, still less their duty, to break a promise whenever it seemed that a little more good could be done by breaking it than by keeping it, although they might agree if a very great deal more could. Few would think it right to steal money from a rich man in order to give it to the Freedom from Hunger campaign, although a great many lives would be saved thereby. Few would hold it right to punish an innocent man even if it were possible to show that you would improve his character thereby and deter potential criminals as effectively as would punishment of the guilty. Most people feel themselves under a much greater obligation to produce good for members of their own family than to produce an equal good for strangers. Further, utilitarianism would seem to entitle and even require us to do evil that good may come provided the amount of evil in the means does not outweigh the amount of good in the end to be attained. Christians in particular have felt the strongest objection to this doing of evil that good may come.

Utilitarians have commonly replied by stressing indirect effects. Even where it would do a little more good to break a promise than to keep it, it is said that this is outweighed by the effect on general confidence in promises. If the poor cheat the rich even for a good cause, general security will be in peril. If it is known that innocent people may be punished on utilitarian grounds, nobody will feel safe. If some people adopt evil means, e.g. theft and cheating where the general good is furthered by them, others will follow their example and adopt such means either in misguided fanaticism or out of selfish or mixed motives where great harm is done on the whole and not good. But as has been pointed out often, the force of these replies depends on the actions in question being *known* to have occurred. Should not the moral for the utilitarian be, it may be urged,—Do these things but do them in secret? If the deeds in question are not discovered they will not provide a bad example or diminish security. Now crooks would generally agree that their deeds should be kept secret, but this does not make their morality a very creditable one.

If it is then suggested that the deeds are wrong because they have a bad effect on the agent's character, it is replied that this argument is circular. Unless it is independently known that it is wrong to do them, why should the deeds have a bad effect on one's character?

Some utilitarians or would-be utilitarians have tried to meet such difficulties by a distinction between what they call act-utilitarianism and rule-utilitarianism. "Act-utilitarianism" is the doctrine that for any individual act to be right it must produce at least as much good as any possible alternative action, or at any rate be an act such that it is more rational or not less rational to choose it than any other in view of the data at the disposal of the agent, taking account only of the relative value and probability of the effects that he could rationally anticipate of the particular action. The second, qualified statement is introduced in order to allow for human fallibility and ignorance. We do not ordinarily say that a person ought not to have done what he did just because his act had some bad effects which he could not possibly be expected to foresee, although some philosophers have used "ought" in such a sense. However this distinction is not of importance for the present point; I only mention it for the sake of clarity and completeness. The difference between act-utilitarianism and rule-utilitarianism is that while the former in determining what is right or what we ought to do considers only the effects, actual or possible, of the particular act under consideration, the latter considers instead in many cases the usual effects of the observation of a general rule that acts of a certain kind should be performed or avoided. According to rule-utilitarianism for an act to be right or even obligatory it is not necessary that it should be useful; all that is needed is that it should belong to one of certain classes of acts which are in general useful. For instance there is no doubt that the practice of keeping promises is generally useful, and this, it is maintained, puts me under an obligation to stick to the general rule and keep my promises even in some particular cases where it is not useful.

But it seems to me that a rule-utilitarian has really abandoned utilitarianism. If it is my duty to perform some acts which it would not be right for me to choose to do if I considered only how much good they were likely to do in comparison with alternative possible acts, production of good is not the only ground of obligation. Further unless some additional explanation is given, the view has failed to provide a reasonable ground for the obligation to make an exception to utilitarianism in these cases. Why ever should it be my duty to do what I have good ground to think will not give the best results in a particular case, because it usually does so? What should we think of a doctor who insisted on prescribing penicillin for a patient who he had good reason to think was allergic to it on the ground that penicillin was good for most patients with his disease? Why should we think any better of a man who keeps a promise which it is harmful to keep just because it is usually beneficial to keep promises?

Part of the answer to the problem is that it really is sometimes better to break a promise or make an exception to other general moral rules if the consequences of keeping them are sufficiently bad. Hardly any philosophers I have met and very few thinking people would now defend Kant's view that one ought not to tell a lie even to save a man's life from a murderer. It has been suggested that it is absolutely never right to punish the innocent, but would it be wrong to fine an innocent man ten pounds or imprison him for a month in order to mollify a mad dictator and prevent him from unleashing a war? Even to the rule against murder I should make with many others an exception in the most unusual case of Hitler, and at least if murder is not defined in such a way as to debar the application of the term to cases of consent or "presumed" consent, in many cases of mercy killing. There are not many crimes that it would not be right to commit if they were really necessary to prevent a third world war. Certainly no one except a thoroughgoing pacifist can consistently object in all cases to doing or bringing about evil that good may come or at least that greater evil be prevented, for certainly any war involves this in an appalling fashion.

But when we have said all this, we must admit that it cannot possibly be the whole answer for a man whose ethical principles accord with Christianity or for that matter with the standards of any or almost any community known to us. I fancy about the nearest approach to a purely utilitarian ethics is that preached in communist states (though I certainly do not wish to say that in its application communist ethics is really more useful than ours but the reverse). Even there however this utilitarian ethics is applied not so much to individual relations as to actions done on behalf of the state. A moral man will feel that he ought not to break a promise just because some slight extra good is done by breaking it to a person other than the promisee, or murder a politician if he is convinced that the continuance of the latter's life will do more harm than good. It is certainly not a mark of high morality always to look round with great care before you fulfil a promise in order to make sure that you could not do anything more useful with your time and energy. If that were the accepted practice, I am afraid few promises would be fulfilled. Even if there are exceptions to these general laws regarding moral action, a moral man will find them rare, much rarer than he would if he were a consistent utilitarian.

Bishop Butler seems to have a suggestion which I have heard used in some form by modern theologians, whether they took it from him or not. God, according to a plausible interpretation of Butler, is himself a pure utilitarian or at least may well be, but men must not be so on any account whatever. Men must always obey the recognized general moral laws even if it seems to do more harm than good in a particular instance, but if we do so God will arrange that in the long run, including the life to come, the evil consequences of obeying the law are outweighed by the good. So what we do if we do our duty will in fact always produce the greatest good, but what it is our duty to do does not depend only on the consequences of our action in the way of producing good, at least as we see them, but often on general laws known independently of consequences.

To deal with this argument we need not discuss the question of the existence of God. Whether God exists or not I think there is a defect in the argument. It might perhaps be consistently used if the moral laws other than any capable of complete utilitarian justification were held to be revealed by God in the Bible or through some inspired person or persons and accepted simply on that account. In that case ethics would be dependent on theology. This is not Butler's view nor is it mine, and this is not the occasion to discuss questions of revealed theology. Butler did indeed believe that the moral laws were revealed by God, but he insisted that we can also see their truth by the use of our reason independently of revelation. Now the defect in the argument is shown when we ask how we can know or have good reason to think that God will act like that. What reason can there be for thinking that

He will bring it about that our acts have better consequences if we obey the laws in question than if we are simply utilitarian and go according to our own estimate of consequences? Is it because the right act must be the act which does the greatest good? But that is utilitarianism. Is it because to obey the laws is right apart from its consequences and so deserves reward on its own account and to disobey them on account of the consequences is wrong and so deserves punishment? Then we must either know or have good reason to believe that the acts are right or wrong independently of the question whether God will reward or punish them. But if our judgment of the acts is based independently of this, the introduction of God is of no help in the argument.

The argument attributed to Butler has another defect which may be brought out by comparing it to an argument of Sidgwick, Professor of Moral Philosophy at Cambridge in the late nineteenth century. Sidgwick said he could not resist either the conviction that it was rational to seek one's own greatest good to the exclusion of all else or the conviction that it was the rational course to seek the greatest good of all sentient beings, and he tried to reconcile the conflict between these two beliefs by postulating that God had arranged the after-life in such a way that you only got your own greatest good if you sought the greatest good of others. It has rightly been objected to Sidgwick that this would not remove the inconsistency between these two beliefs, as the conflicting propositions that the rational course is to seek only your own good and that the rational course is to seek the good of everyone are not reconciled, even if the consequences of the two lines of action are the same. The two propositions give rival views as to what we ought to seek as an end in itself and it is irrelevant to this question if the two courses of action do produce the same result as means. It would no doubt be practically very useful in controlling their external actions if people inclined to be selfish could be convinced that to seek the good of others would ultimately be to their own advantage, but if they sought it only for that reason they would still undeniably be embracing an ethical principle irreconcilable with that of the unselfish man, and it is morally very important not to do the right thing for the wrong reason. Similarly Butler cannot reconcile the proposition that we ought always to seek the greatest good with the proposition that any particular kind of action, e.g. lying, ought always to be avoided as wrong in itself, by maintaining that the two courses lead to the same results. The question is about the ultimate ground for not lying. The view that lying is necessarily always wrong can be refuted simply by pointing out that it obviously would be right to tell a lie if that were the only way of averting the total destruction of the human race. Even if it be the case that such a situation will never arise, that is sufficient because if it were involved in the nature of lies that they ought never to be told, this would imply that not only no actual but no possible consequences could ever justify them. Butler seems indeed to be guilty of two inconsistencies. He seems to be assuming both a non-utilitarian ethics so as to be able to say that we can see lies, for example, to be wrong apart from their consequences and a utilitarian ethics so as to be able to say that the right act will produce the greatest good after all. And he seems also to be maintaining that if the right action in fact leads to the greatest good, this will reconcile the necessarily inconsistent propositions that we ought to perform some actions a ends in themselves irrespective of whether they produce the greatest good and that we ought only to seek the greatest good.

We are thus confronted with a situation in which we seem to have to admit that, if we are to have an ethics that a good man would tolerate in practice, we must not judge the rightness of actions simply in terms of the consequences we can calculate. But there is still a way out for the utilitarian which will at least mitigate the case against him. I have referred to the consequences we can calculate, but we must allow for the limitations of human capacity for this calculation. On such grounds Moore although a utilitarian defends a view in *Principia Ethica* which comes near Butler in its practical conclusions without his introduction of God. Moore says that, since we are very liable to make mistakes in calculating consequences and in estimating the good or evil in them relatively to that in the consequences of alternative actions, it is safer to keep to general laws in cases where the law is one that is usually observed and one the observation of which we generally think has good consequences. He reinforces this argument by saying that the cases where we might be inclined to break such general laws are mostly cases where we think it to our interest or to the interest of friends to do so and in such cases we should be specially liable to go wrong in our estimate of effects through being prejudiced in favour of breaking the law if we allowed it as an ethical possibility at all. I should not go as far as Moore went and say on this account that we ought never to break the laws, and I remember him admitting to me in conversation

40 or 50 years after he had written the book that he had gone too far here. It seems to me that, for example, no elaborate calculation of consequences would be ordinarily needed to decide that I should tell a lie in order to prevent a murder. It is true that more good might always have *conceivably* been done by my not preventing it. For anything I know the man I saved might die next week in a much more painful way or go mad and do the most terrible things and the murderer might, if enabled to commit the murder, have been so shocked by what he had done that he repented and led an exemplary life ever afterwards, while had he been prevented, he might have gone on to live wickedly and sometime commit two murders, but this is unlikely and we can only go on probable consequences. But action is not wrong because it has bad effects which the agent could not possibly have foreseen. Moore's point is however of much importance for less extreme cases, and it can be used by utilitarians to bring their moral practice more into conformity with that of most good people. To take an example, there are not many things more repugnant than the deliberate punishment on utilitarian grounds of innocent people. But even a utilitarian might justify the general condemnation of this by saying that, although there no doubt are some cases where you would do more good than harm by punishing an innocent man, no human being and, I should be inclined to add, especially no government organization, could be trusted to decide which these are and it would be a source of endless trouble and abuses if utilitarian calculations were allowed here. A further point arises which deserves much emphasis: there are good empirical grounds for thinking that beyond any definite harm we can foresee resulting from the use of evil means there is likely to be a considerable extra amount of evil produced the nature of which we cannot in detail foresee. This then should be taken into account before deciding to adopt plainly evil means. And in general it is very hard to be sure that the evil means which sometimes seem to be needed to attain a good end, or, more plausibly, to prevent a still greater evil, will really serve the end for which they are adopted or not also produce evil which outweighs the good, or again that with more thought one might not find means that would not involve the evil and yet produce the good. It is human fallibility and lack of knowledge which makes the case different from that which I cited earlier of a doctor who should prescribe penicillin for a patient who was allergic to it because it was good for most patients. I was assuming that he knew or had very good reason

for thinking that the patient was allergic. In the great majority of cases people who use evil means for good ends cannot have adequate grounds for thinking that these means are necessary for the attainment of the ends and that, if they are used, the evil resulting will not outweigh the good. The case is rather analogous to one where the doctor has not at his disposal means of determining whether the patient is or is not allergic to penicillin before using the drug and therefore has no option but to go on general laws derived from a consideration of the great majority of patients. In most cases we are not entitled to have the same confidence that a doctor may well be entitled to have about a patient being allergic when we consider whether we can attain a particular good end by evil means without incurring dangers of further evil which more than neutralize its advantages. I am not arguing that these general moral rules to which I have been referring should never be broken but only that the considerations I have mentioned have the effect of making it after all very hard to show that the practical conduct which a rational utilitarianism would dictate is inconsistent on many points with what an enlightened Christian ethics would dictate. In most cases when we are confronted with plain general moral rules, utilitarian grounds themselves make it undesirable even to attempt a calculation of good produced because of the risk of developing a habit of mind in which we are liable to be led astray by the prospect of a definite good which, because it is definitely foreseeable as at least a not unlikely fruit of action, may well wrongly come to outweigh in many minds the intangible risks I have mentioned. Where an act seems quite likely to produce some clearly envisaged good but is still more likely because of its shady character to do some greater harm which however we cannot clearly envisage, there is a great danger of being tempted to plump for the good we clearly foresee at the expense of the evil we ought to anticipate but cannot definitely envisage.

There is however a residuum of cases where this is not so and rules ought to be broken in the interests of the greatest good because the harm done by keeping them would be too serious. That we cannot lay down watertight rules as to where this residuum begins and ends is an inability common to all ethical theories that I know. We cannot cut the knot by laying down a set of universal rules to which there are no exceptions if only because two such laws may clash in a particular case. But this admission may well be made by a non-utilitarian. It is for this reason that Sir David Ross introduced the concept of *prima facie* duties, as obligations which hold in most cases but not in all because they may clash with other *prima facie* duties, as well as with utilitarian considerations, to which he also allowed a limited validity. It seems to me that the only way in which a non-utilitarian ethics can be made plausible is by introducing this concept of *prima facie* duties: and further I think that Ross's account corresponds much better with the way in which we actually do think on moral questions than does utilitarianism. But it leaves the various *prima facie* duties unexplained just taken as given in intuition and not connected in any system, and I think that something more than this is needed to complete Ross's work.

It is then not so easy as might be expected to show that utilitarianism is incompatible with the principles accepted in Christian ethics as understood in a way that is at all enlightened. It would be easier to show that it was incompatible with the teaching of a person who in the name of Christian ethics should forbid the use of contraceptives however menacing the population explosion, or advocate intolerance in religious matters. But I at least should insist that the utilitarians would be in the right here, as would by now, I think, most Christians Utilitarianism, it may be argued, is then after all able to justify on its principles the ordinary moral laws as generally obligatory and this is the most that any reasonable ethical theory can do. But there is a snag. I have only been talking about rules regarding outward behaviour and this is not the whole of Christian ethics; when we go deeper a clash does arise, indeed not only between utilitarianism and Christian ethics but between utilitarianism and the ethical beliefs of probably any community. The point I wish to make is this. We all feel that we have not just a general obligation to produce good for all and sundry. Although we certainly have an obligation not to harm strangers and also to help them in case of need, we also feel that we have special obligations to some men that we do not have to others. We feel ourselves under special obligations to our creditors and in general to those to whom we have made promises, to members of our family, to those who have rendered us special services and also to those whom we have injured to make them any reparation in our power. We feel obliged to do for all these in various ways what we should not feel obliged to do for strangers with whom we had had no previous relations. Christian ethics in particular further lays great stress on a man's motives and finds in them a good or evil which is quite apart from that of the action's effects. Again most moral teachers and certainly most Christians emphasize altruism as being a duty in a way in which the production of an equal amount of good for oneself is not. All this disagrees with the utilitarian doctrine that the one thing that matters is to produce as much good as possible irrespective for whose benefit the good is produced. Now the utilitarian has various devices by means of which he can plausibly reconcile his doctrine with the principles I have mentioned, in the sense of showing that he can from his own point of view justify the kind of outward action which these principles require, but whereas the obligations are felt by us as direct these are all indirect justifications. He can say that, if we break our promises or punish the innocent, harm will probably be done in certain indirect ways even where the immediate effects seem more good than bad and that the risk of this is too great for it to be right to act in such ways, but this would not give us a direct obligation to avoid breaking promises or punishing the innocent because these things are wrong in themselves. But does not the very notion of a promise entail some obligation to keep it and the very notion of punishment already and without going into consequences entail an obligation to avoid punishing the innocent? The utilitarian can say for instance that the great goods involved in family life would not be realized if different members of the same family did not give special consideration to each other's interests in a way in which it is not practicable to expect them to do with strangers, but a consistent utilitarian will still have to admit that a man has no more obligation to his wife or children as such in themselves than he has to a stranger. His obligations to his family thus become only derivative from his indiscriminate obligation to everybody to promote their good, though it just happens that usually he can produce more good by attending to their needs than by attending to those of a perfect stranger. It would seem very ungracious for a man to say to good parents or any benefactors by whom he has been greatly helped at great cost to themselves "I am under no special obligation to you more than to anybody else; but it is just that my obligation to people in general requires me to make special efforts on your behalf." The utilitarian will ordinarily justify the special attention given to motives by simply saying that if a man does something externally right from wrong motives we have no ground to expect him to act rightly on other occasions, while if he does it from right motives we have. Christian ethics on the other hand seems committed to the view that there is something inherently good about acting on right motives rather than wrong even if the consequences were the same, and I should agree with this view. Again as regards the Christian emphasis on altruism the utilitarian may say that, since men are liable to be more averse to or more quick to realize the danger of harm for themselves than for others, they do not need to dwell on their obligation not to harm themselves unnecessarily so much as on their obligation not to harm others. But this is not adequate to account for the extreme difference we see between the action of a man who deliberately hurts another in order to secure a lesser advantage for himself and that of a man who sacrifices a much greater good of his own for the sake of a lesser good for somebody else. The former is just morally deplorable, the latter is in some respects praiseworthy although perhaps foolish. It is no doubt true that altruism can be carried too far. It may be more blessed to give than to receive, but at any rate for the greater blessing to be obtained there must always be somebody to enjoy the less. But when we have made all necessary reservations, the distinction I have mentioned between sacrificing somebody else's good to one's own and one's own good to somebody else's still holds and is quite incompatible with unqualified utilitarianism.

Some utilitarians would try to meet these points by maintaining that certain actions are preferable to others, the consequences of which would have been better, because the action in itself has a certain value or because the alternative action which would have led to better consequences would have been intrinsically bad. Thus where a man sacrifices good A in order to provide good B for another man, even if good A is of slightly more value than good B, the total state of affairs may still be better for the sacrifice because to assess its total value one will have to include not only the consequences of his unselfish act but the intrinsic value of the act itself. Similarly it might be my duty to keep promises and refrain from cheating not only because of consequences but also because breaking promises and cheating are evil in themselves, and this evil might in some cases be the decisive factor by outweighing the extra good gained by, for instance, breaking a promise. This view would no longer be utilitarian in the sense of making the rightness of an action dependent on its consequences, but it would still be utilitarian in the sense of maintaining that the right act is always the act of those possible in the given situation which is most conducive to the production of good. This type of utilitarianism could also justify the emphasis on the importance of having good motives by reference to the intrinsic value of action from good motives.

and to the intrinsic evil in acting from bad, as well as by an appeal to consequences, which still must be part of the reason in any case. And it might explain the special obligation to parents, wife or children by saying that towards these a man is usually able to act with a special love which gives an intrinsic value to the action that can enable it to outweigh in the scale of value even an act somewhat more beneficial in respect of its consequences directed to a person not linked to him by special ties of affection.

But if the utilitarian adopts this line, it will be difficult to decide between him and his opponent, at least at the level at which the discussion has usually been conducted. He has now come too near to his opponent for them to be easily distinguished. How are we going to tell whether among the reasons against telling lies we are to include the fact that lying is intrinsically evil or the fact that we are under a special ultimate obligation not to tell lies? But while it is difficult to decide this, it may be doubted whether it matters very much which we say. At least this is now a question of little interest to anybody but professional philosophers. Actually there is a plausible definition of good (bad) according to which to say in the context of this argument that something was intrinsically good (bad) would be to say that it ought to be pursued (avoided) for its own sake or, if it is an action, done (avoided) for its own sake, and in that case the doctrines of the two sides would become identical.

But even if there need be no important difference between this much modified form of utilitarianism and Christian ethics, the utilitarians have usually not made enough modifications or realized how far their modifications might carry them. In the controversy as usually conducted there have been two issues involved of great, even of great practical importance, in one of which I think the utilitarians were more in the right, in the other their opponents. To take the second point first, most utilitarians have thrown the whole emphasis on consequences and have in answering the question how the rightness or wrongness of actions is to be determined neglected their aspect as expressing certain attitudes of mind, while the ethics inspired by Christianity has much emphasized the latter. This obviously can be carried too far; if a person is sufficiently lacking in intelligence, actions that express a sincerely good state of mind may be disastrously wrong, but we have seen the dangers of relying too much on the calculation of consequences foreseeable by us where it is a question of making exceptions to general principles of moral action on utilitarian grounds. This is to a large extent due to human fallibility, which when the principle of action is in general a good one and two such principles do not conflict, makes it usually even from the point of view of consequences desirable to rely on the principle rather than to go in for the calculation. But the state of mind in which the action is performed is also relevant and, I think, not only because a good state of mind in the agent increases the likelihood of good consequences. The utilitarian indeed may allow for this without giving up his view that the right act is the act most conducive to the production of good, since the good produced by an action must include not only the good in its consequences but also any good residing in the act itself. Unless he is going to say that the only good is pleasure, in the wide sense of this term in which it has been used by philosophers to cover the feeling-side of any satisfying activity from eating one's dinner to apprehending the highest philosophical truths and even communing with God, a view which has often been predominant among moral philosophers in the past but which they would usually reject today, he must consider other candidates for the title of intrinsic goodness as opposed to goodness merely as a means. But there is, it seems, nothing which has a stronger claim to be ranked as an intrinsic good than moral goodness, although I am not suggesting that it is the only intrinsic good or that pleasure is not a good also. Now apart from its expression in voluntary actions and states of mind moral goodness is only an unrealized disposition, and a mere unrealized disposition is in itself nothing actual at all, nothing more than a set of purely hypothetical propositions. Therefore if moral goodness is good in itself, morally good states of minds and actions must also be good in themselves, and if so the question about the amount of good they produce is not merely a question about good or bad consequences. But although utilitarianism might be developed in such a way as to make allowance fully for what I have said, this has rarely, if ever, been done by utilitarians. Further if it were done I think we should find it impossible to treat good in so purely quantitative a way as utilitarianism implies. But I have no time to go into this last point on the present occasion. However I must insist that a utilitarianism which does not allow for the points I have mentioned is a practical and not only a theoretical danger. It will leading to the recommending of some actions which even from the point of view of consequences are undesirable.

In the second place, however, we must not carry our criticism of utilitarianism so far as to maintain that we can know by intuition or *a priori* argument that certain acts, e.g. keeping promises, are obligatory (or for that matter wrong) irrespective of their relation to the conscious states of anyone. The moral judgement as to what ought to be done, I think, must always be justifiable by reference to conscious states which the act is thought to produce or, if not produce, express. Conscious states are the only things in the world we know of value as ends in themselves. This has not always been allowed for adequately by opponents of utilitarianism and those Christians who stuck too much to the letter of the law, but I think it is implied in the Christian doctrine that our sole duty aside from religious duty to God is to love our neighbors as ourselves, which must involve both seeking their good and having the right spirit in seeking it.

Introduction to B. J. Diggs

The naïve view of morality is that living morally is pretty nearly wholly a matter of following prevailing moral rules. The "new moralities" of every age cause concern because they question the rightness of the prevailing rules, and the most extreme of them take an antinomian position and go so far as to question the rightness or usefulness of any moral rules at all. Most situationists are very much attracted to antinomianism but usually stop short of it and affirm a position according to which moral rules are much like the act-utilitarian's "rules of thumb." But the care with which most situationists and their opponents use the term "rule" leaves much to be desired. The article which follows is offered as a model of philosophical analysis of a key moral term, a model which deserves emulation by those concerned with situationism.

A brief outline may be helpful.

I. The central question for Professor Diggs is this: what sort of rule is a moral rule?

He first discusses instrumental rules, those prescribing actions believed to contribute to the attainment of a goal. Some of these are practical maxims which one follows at his own pleasure, e.g. "Be sure that the surface to be painted is thoroughly dry." One follows such a rule if and only if one thereby gets the job done more satisfactorily. Another sort of instrumental rule is more complex, being legislated or handed down by some authority, and one who is subject to the authority is not free to choose at his own pleasure not to follow the rule, e.g. the employee is not free to disobey the painting contractor's rule: "Use a four inch brush when painting large walls."

There is a clear-cut distinction between the justification of authoritative instrumental rules (Is this a good rule?) and the justification of a particular action falling under a rule of this type in force (What ought I to do?). If an employee breaks a rule in force, he might not be entitled to his pay, even though he more effectively achieved the goal which the rule itself was intended to achieve.

II. Rule utilitarians regard moral rules as authoritative instrumental rules: the criterion of morally right *action* is conformity to a system of rules, and the criterion of the rightness of the *rule* is the production of as much general happiness as possible. The difficulty with this is that everyone knows that the rules in force in any society are non-ideal and will not maximize happiness, and so sometimes one must choose between following relatively poor existing rules and acting to maximize happiness, between *rules* and *utilitarianism*. If the criterion of right action is taken rather to be an ideal set of rules which, if adopted, would produce general happiness, the difficulty is that unadopted rules are not rules at all, and so cannot be authoritative rules.

III. Another model for moral rules is conceivable. Consider the constitutive rules of a game like baseball or chess, e.g. "A batter hit by a pitched ball goes immediately to first base." These are non-instrumental rules, they are not bridges to something else. Such games do not have "purposes" and so their rules cannot be criticized as failing to contribute maximally to purposes. *Winning* might be said to be the goal or "object" of the game, but one cannot by breaking a constitutive rule better achieve such a goal; if one allows six strikes instead of three for being called "out," one is simply not playing *baseball*.

The playing of games, however, also involves skills and tactics and strategies, and in this regard players may follow instrumental rules ("Players must take batting practice before each game") laid down by the manager or coach. Unlike the very rules of the game, these latter rules are evaluated instrumentally, as for example, failing to promote winning this game.

IV. The analysis of games reveals that although one may do many things as means to ends in the course of playing a game, this does not show that the game itself is a means. Similarly the fact that one has a purpose when he speaks, or makes a promise, or deals in property, does not show that speech or promising or property are, as the utilitarian alleges, instruments for the promotion of goals logically independent of these institutions and practices. It seems rather that institutions and practices create or establish most goals which men pursue, in the sense that these goals would be logically impossible without such institutions and practices.

One may avoid cheating in a game not because cheating somehow prevents one from reaching his goal, but because the game is less fun when cheating goes on, because one misses the values of good sportsmanship, etc. One avoids cheating or breaking the rules not for narrowly "moral" reasons, but out of love of the game. Similarly one may avoid lying or stealing or adultery not because somehow one thereby reaches his goal, is happier, or the like, but because such an act would detract from the values social communication could have, because one would miss the satisfaction of honest assumption of responsibility, etc.

In sum, the utilitarian says of moral rules: Play the game of life by the rules— and you will win the prize! He thereby misses the very point of morality, for the right thing to say is: Play the game of life by the rules—it is more fun that way!

Rules and Utilitarianism*
By B. J. Diggs

Although moral rules have had a prominent place in recent moral philosophy, their character is not clear. One reason for this is the vagueness and ambiguity which infect the use of the term "rule": Philosophers tend to conceive of moral rules on some particular model, sometimes in a confused way, often innocently and without a clear view of the alternatives. J. Rawls called attention to one important instance of this: He pointed out that the tendency to regard rules as convenient guides, or as summaries of earlier experiences, seems to have blinded some philosophers ". . . to the significance of the distinction between justifying a practice and justifying a particular action falling under it. . . ."[1]

Partly as a consequence, utilitarianism has been interpreted in a special way, as asserting that the rightness and wrongness of particular acts is decidable on general utilitarian grounds. This form of utilitarianism, so-called "act utilitarianism," is open to serious and well-known objections.[2]

The appeal of the recently more popular "rule utilitarianism" is that it is able to meet some of these objections, and still retain the tie between morality and "the general welfare," which is one of the most attractive characteristics of utilitarianism. I shall argue in this paper, however, that rule utilitarians (and some of their critics, and many others who view moral rules in the same general way) have also tended

* Reprinted from *The American Philosophical Quarterly*, *I* (1964), pp. 32–44.
[1] John Rawls, "Two Concepts of Rules," *Philosophical Review*, LXIV (1955), pp. 29–30.
[2] Cf. e.g., R. B. Brandt, *Ethical Theory* (Englewood Cliffs, N. J.: Prentice-Hall, 1959), chap. XV.

unwittingly to adopt a particular kind of rule as the model of a moral rule. When this kind of rule has been delineated, and alternatives noted, I think rule utilitarianism loses much of its initial appeal.

My object in this paper, however, is not so much to refute rule utilitarianism as to contribute to the clarification of moral rules. By distinguishing two kinds of rules I shall try to illuminate one of the fundamental options (as well as one of the fundamental confusions) open to moral theory. (1) The first kind of rule is exemplified by the rules which workers follow as part of their jobs; these rules may be used to describe a job. (2) The other kind of rule characterizes such common games as baseball, chess, and the like. Both kinds of rule define "practices," but the practices are very different. I think the easy tendency to confuse them may have blinded moral philosophers to significant distinctions between justifying a system of rules designed to contribute to some goal or product, justifying a system of rules which defines a "form of life," and justifying moral rules. Marking these distinctions should help clarify certain steps taken in recent moral philosophy: One should be able to appreciate more fully the point of Baier's assertion that although moral rules are "for the good of everyone alike," they are not designed to promote the greatest good of everyone.[3] One should also be able to see more clearly why Rawls maintains that the decision on the rules of justice is not properly conceived on the utilitarian model, as an administrative decision on how to promote the greatest happiness.[4] The analysis of rules is illuminating, moreover, not only because it helps mark major differences of this kind, but also because it shows what is behind some of the twists and turns of moral theory.

I

1.0 The first kind of rule which I shall describe belongs to a large class of rules which I call "instrumental." All rules in this large class are adopted or followed as a means to an end, in order to "accomplish a purpose" or "get a job done." The simplest of these rules is the "practical maxim" which one ordinarily follows at his own pleasure,

---

[3] K. Baier, *The Moral Point of View: A Rational Basis of Ethics* (Ithaca, N. Y.: Cornell, 1958), pp. 200–204.

[4] John Rawls, "Justice as Fairness," *Philosophical Review*, LXVII (1958), pp. 164–94. It will be clear that Rawl's analysis in "Two Concepts of Rules" does not support a utilitarian theory.

such as "Be sure the surface to be painted is thoroughly dry" or "Do not plant tomatoes until after the last frost."[5]

The instrumental rule to which I call attention is more complex. On many occasions when one wants a job done, either he is not in a position or not able or not willing to do the job himself. If he is in a position of power or authority, or if he has money, he may simply order or hire others to "do the job" and leave it to them. In numerous cases, however, he himself lays down rules of procedure, and establishes "jobs" or "roles" in the institutional sense. A "job" in the latter sense is not a job to be "done," but a job to be "offered to" or "given" to a person. If a person "takes" or is "assigned" "the job" then we often think of him as under an obligation to "do his job," and partly consists in his following rules. Instrumental rules of this kind, unlike practical maxims, have a social dimension: It *makes sense* to ask whether a job-holder (or role-taker) is *obligated* to follow a particular rule, or whether this is one of his *duties*, and the penalty attaching to a breach of the rules does not consist simply in his not "getting the job done."

Rules of this kind are found in very different institutions. Some are rules of a "job" in the ordinary sense. Others apply to anyone who voluntarily assumes a "role," such as "automobile driver." Others characterize a position which one is obliged to take by law, for example, that of private in the army. The goals which the rules are designed to serve may be ordinary products of labor, such as houses, steel beams, etc.; or fairly specific social goals such as "getting vehicles to their destinations safely and expeditiously"; or goals as general as "the national defense." In some cases the rules, differing from job to job, mark a division of labor, as the rules which say what factory workers, or the members of a platoon, are to do. In other cases, the same rules apply more or less equally to all, as in the case of (at least some) rules regulating traffic.

Notwithstanding their variety, these rules can be classified together because they share two fundamental characteristics: (1) The rules prescribe action which is thought to contribute to the attainment of a goal. This is the "design" of such rules, at least in the sense that if the prescribed action does not effectively contribute to the attainment of the goal, for the most part, then the rule itself is subject to criticism.

[5] Cf. Max Black, "Notes on the Meaning of 'Rule'," *Theoria*, XXIV (1958), pp. 121–122; reprinted in his *Models and Metaphors* (Ithaca, N. Y.: Cornell, 1962), pp. 95–139.

(2) The rules are "laid down" or "legislated" or "made the rule" by a party which has power or authority of some kind; one cannot learn "what the rules are" simply by determining what general procedures most effectively promote the goal. This latter characteristic sharply differentiates these rules from what I have called practical maxims, although both share the first characteristic and are "instrumental."[6]

I shall now consider each of these two characteristics in turn.

1.1 Since rules of this kind are designed to serve a goal, the "best" set of rules is that set, *other things equal*, which is most effective in promoting the goal. The qualification is important: One ordinarily asks the question, "Is this a good rule?" in order to determine whether or not the action to be prescribed by the rule, together with other acts, will most efficiently produce the goal, without violating certain other rules, and in a way that harmonizes best with other aims, assuming persons can be persuaded to follow the rule.[7]

Consider a factory planner designing an assembly line, or an army officer considering platoon reorganization, or a traffic planning commission trying to decide whether a street should be made a throughway. In each case rules are proposed, but there is no contradiction in saying that action on the rules will not contribute to the goal. Within its context the question "Is this a good rule?" is one of practical fact and

---

[6] Practical maxims should not be dismissed, however, as "mere rules of thumb" on the one hand, or as "simply stating relations between means and ends" on the other. When one follows a maxim the rule *directs* action and is a *criterion* of certain kinds of rightness and wrongness in acting.

In passing note that Rawls's "summary conception," as a whole, does not properly apply to practical maxims, although several features of this conception do apply. Rawls's analysis, admirable as it is, is very apt to mislead. For the "summary view," as he calls it, is a blend of two quite distinct conceptions: In part it is a confused conception or a misconception of a rule, as a summary or report. In other respects it is an accurate conception of what I have called a practical maxim. This may account for an ambivalence in Rawls's article: Cf. ". . . it is doubtful that anything to which the summary conception did apply would be called a *rule*." [(p. 23) "Two Concepts . . ."] with "Some rules will fit one conception, some rules the other; and so there are rules of practices (rules in the strict sense), and maxims and 'rules of thumb'." (p. 29). The point is that maxims are rules in a *different* sense from other kinds of rules, whereas no rule, *qua rule*, is a summary or report.

The importance of this point is that there are two possible confusions here, not one: A person may conceive moral rules as summaries or reports, or he may conceive moral rules on the model of maxims. The texts of Austin and Mill, which Rawls cites, together with Rawls's discussion, suggest that the latter, more than the former, was their mistake. *V.*, however, note 13 below.

[7] Cf. my "Technical Ought," *Mind*, LXIX (1960), pp. 301–17.

experience. This indicates one sense in saying that the goal is "over and beyond" the action and the rules.

There is another sense in saying this: In practice a goal is often described in terms of rules or procedures which are thought to produce it (when, for example, a beam is to be built according to procedural specifications). Moreover, at the time of action one may not be able to say just what he wants in other terms. Nevertheless, there is no contradiction, explicit or implied, in saying that this person got the goal (in the sense that he can truthfully say "This has all the desirable features of what I wanted") without anyone's having laid down or followed rules. Although the beam was not constructed according to specifications, tests may now show that it is as strong as one could have wished for. In this sense it is *logically* possible for one to attain the goal which a set of instrumental rules is designed to serve without these rules having been followed. I shall refer to this characteristic by saying that the goal of any set of instrumental rules is "logically independent" of these rules.

Although an instrumental action is *properly* described in many ways, depending on the context, it can always be *truthfully* described in terms of a goal, as a "trying to get or produce G." For a goal is essential to such action, and to the rules which guide it. Nevertheless, it is clear that it is logically possible to act and follow instrumental rules without attaining the goal, and to attain the goal without following rules.

Moreover, although obviously one cannot act *on* a rule of any kind if there is no rule, one can act *in the way* specified by a set of instrumental rules (as well as attain a desired result) without *these* rules having been adopted. A group of workers, for example, may hit upon certain procedures which are so effective that they are made "the rule"; in such a case we may say, somewhat misleadingly, that one discovered a good rule by observing the actual results of a line of action. In complex cases it is very unlikely that men will act in the way rules would prescribe if the rules have not in fact been enacted. Nevertheless, there is no contradiction in saying that men acted in this way but there were no rules prescribing this course of action.[8]

Thus in the case of instrumental rules the action as well as the goal may be said to be logically independent of the rules.

[8] Cf. Rawls, ibid., p. 22.

1.2 Now consider the second major characteristic of rules of this kind, namely, that they are "laid down," "legislated," "made," or "adopted."

It is clear enough that an employer, for example, who "informs" his employee of the rules, is not simply "giving information." Moreover, this act or performance is very different from one's "adopting" a practical maxim or making a rule "a rule for himself." Note that in the case of a maxim the adoption of the rule is "incomplete" so long as one simply resolves to follow it. Rules of the present kind, however, are normally made for others to follow: To make their adoption complete, one must get at least some of these others "to agree," in some sense, to follow the rules.

This is so in spite of our sometimes speaking, in the sense indicated earlier, of one's "discovering a good rule" of this kind. We also speak of an administrator's "thinking of a good rule," "deciding on a rule," and "informing an employee of the rules decided on." It is quite clear, however, that "thinking of a rule" and "deciding on it" are steps taken *in the direction of* adopting a rule; the latter corresponds roughly to the stage of "resolution" in the case of a maxim. They are only steps; the rule will not become effective, and strictly speaking, will not *be* a rule, until it is "put in force" or "made a rule."

Legislation is one way of putting such a rule in force. In this case parents and guardians "teach" their children what the laws are; they do not ask for consent. In other cases the members of a group, working co-operatively, "decide on the rules," or an employer or a sergeant "tells one the rules." By such an act those subject to the rules are "directed to follow them," and the rules are then "in force." The rules serve on the one hand as guides to action—they tell one what to do—and on the other as criteria of correctness of action—acts in accord with them are said to be *right* and breaches of them are said to be *wrong*. The rules thus tell one both *what* to do, and *that* he should do it. They are useful just on this account: One may lay down rules of this kind to make use of unskilled labor, or to gain the benefits of a division of labor, or simply to co-ordinate activity as in the case of an efficient traffic system.

The analysis of what the various cases of adopting a rule have in common, and what it is to be subject to rules, takes one to the difficult problem of what constitutes an authority. For our purpose the following will suffice: A party seems to be constituted as a *de facto* authority when one accepts the fact, that this party prescribes an act, as a *reason* for following the prescription (a rule of the present kind being one form of prescription). This indicates the somewhat technical sense of saying that the rule follower "agrees to" follow the rules.[9] In the case of rules of the present kind authority is ordinarily constituted, and agreement to follow the rules obtained, by contract, law, convention, or the like. Some such arrangement is necessary to induce a person to follow rules of this kind, since persons other than the rule-follower "are interested in" the goal, and normally he himself does not get (more than a share of) the product of his labor. The contract, law, or convention both promises some reward to the rule-follower, and at the same time converts others' "being interested in" the goal to their "having an interest in it"—in a legal or quasi-legal sense. This, of course, is why one who follows rules of this kind, unlike one who adopts a maxim as his guide, is not free to alter or follow the rules "at his pleasure."

The point which needs particular emphasis here, however, is that the contract, law, or convention is essential to the rule's being a rule; it is not "external" to the rule, since without it one's "laying down the rules" would be only so much rhetoric. When a contract is simply "to do a job," notice that the criterion of correctness is simply "getting the job done." If I hire a person to paint a house, he has done what he is supposed to do when the house is painted. On the other hand, to the extent to which a contract lays down rules specifying how the job is to be done, the rules are the criterion. If a painter contracts to follow certain procedures, and then fails to follow them, he has not done what he is supposed to do. This should make it quite clear that it is the contract, law, or convention which determines in a given case that rules will be the criterion of correctness. The "agreement" secured by contract, law, or convention thus makes a rule a rule, and without something like it there could be no rules of this kind.

1.3 The discussion of the two major characteristics of these rules reveals two criteria of correctness. On the one hand, there is the criterion of a "good" rule. On the other, there are rules *in force*

[9] Cf. Black, pp. 120–121. Black's analysis of the "laying down of the rules" in terms of "promulgator activities" and "subject activities" (pp. 139–146) is illuminating, as is H. L. A. Harts's recent analysis of the complex idea of "acceptance" in the case of the law. V. *The Concept of Law* (New York: Oxford Univ. Press, 1961), chaps. IV–VI, esp. pp. 107–114.

constituting a criterion in certain respects of the *right thing to do*. In the case of these rules there is thus a clear distinction between the justification of a rule or practice and the justification of a particular action falling under it. Perhaps on this very account some have been led to view moral rules as rules of this kind.

1.3.1 Before going on to moral rules let us notice that this distinction is not important simply because acts are judged by rules which are judged in turn in another manner, in this case by reference to a goal. The significance of the distinction derives more from the fact that the two criteria are "independent" in the following way: One may do the thing which most contributes to the goal, yet violate the rules in force; and one may act according to the rule in force when the rule is a poor one.

Moreover, the rules *in force*, not the rules which are *best*, constitute (at least under certain conditions) the criterion of right and wrong acts. This is evident in practice: A worker who does his job is *entitled* to his pay, whether or not the rules he follows in doing his job are *good* rules. This question, whether or not the rules in force are "good," ordinarily does not have to be settled for them to serve as a criterion of right action. Normally it does not even arise.

Of course, one might criticize the rules *in force* as "illegitimate" or as laid down by one who lacks rightful or proper authority, and *on this account* argue that they are not the "true" criterion of right action. However, the question of the "legitimacy" of the rules is not settled by determining which rules are best. To try to have it this way would be to invite disagreement concerning which rules *are* best, and to have no effective rule at all.[10] It would be wholly impractical to accept as authoritative or binding, and as the criterion of right action, only "the rules which are best". Who, for example, would lay down, or contract to follow under penalty, rules characterized only in this way?

Thus, even though rules of the present kind are explicitly designed to promote a goal, the rule follower is not generally at liberty to use the goal as his criterion of the right thing to do. The distinction between the two criteria so far remains firm.

---

[10] Cf. Hume's remarks on the need of a "determinate rule of conduct," or "general rules," in his discussion of justice, both in the *Treatise of Human Nature* (Cleveland: World Publishing Co., 1962) and *Inquiry Concerning Human Understanding* (Chicago: Regnery, 1956). Hume, however, does not make precisely the same point.

1.3.2 Nevertheless, the independence of these two criteria can be overemphasized. For one thing, the criterion of good rule, in virtue of its being used by those who adopt rules, is an indirect criterion of right action. The rules which are the criterion of right and wrong action do not prescribe action which just *as a matter of fact* contributes or fails to contribute to the goal; the rules are *criticizable* if they are not good rules. Thus it does not "just so happen" that the right act *tends* to contribute to the goal. If it did not generally do this it would not be called "right," for there would be no such rules.

Second, no statement of a rule includes reference to all conditions pertinent to its application; one would not wish so to encumber it, even if every contingency could be foreseen. This implies that every rule follower is expected to know "what he is doing" in a sense larger than "following the rules"; and if the rules are instrumental he is often expected to know the goal to which his rule-directed action supposedly contributes—to know "what he is doing" in this sense. Not always, to be sure, but often he could not make a sound judgment of when and how to apply the rule without this knowledge.

For both of these reasons it is a mistake to say, in a pedestrian and casuistical way, that "the criterion of right acts is the rules." It is a mistake to think of *every* exception and *every* case as somehow included in the rule. The motive for doing so, presumably to preserve the authority of rules, is mistaken: There is an important difference between interpreting a rule, or violating it *in special circumstances*, and deciding each individual case just as if there were no rules. A person subject to rules who follows the latter course merits a special kind of criticism. Although it is difficult to specify conditions in which the violation of an instrumental rule is proper, surely the bare fact, "that by doing so one can better promote the goal," is not sufficient. The rule follower is not the sole or final authority on the propriety of breaking a rule, even when it is for the benefit of the other party.

This brings us back to the independence of the two criteria. However, it should now be clear that these criteria are interrelated and operate together. Moreover, since there are two criteria in the case of rules of the present kind, it always *makes sense* to ask if an action right by the rules is also right in the respect that it is good that a rule prescribes it. It not only *makes sense* to speak of its being proper to violate a rule, "successful violations" tend to be commended.

II

2.0 As soon as rules of the foregoing kind have been described it is rather obvious that many moral theorists, intentionally or not, have cut moral rules to their pattern. Anyone who regards the standard of morally right action as itself a means to an end will have this tendency, and this is typically true of rule utilitarians: The distinctive characteristic of their theory is that a system of rules is the criterion of morally right action and these rules in turn are to be judged good or bad according to the consequences which action on the rules either generally produces as a matter of fact, or would produce if people could be persuaded to follow them.[11] The consequence which has been thought to be critical in assessing the soundness of a system of rules has been variously identified, as "the happiness of all," "public utility," "security," "the general welfare," etc. Nevertheless, in spite of the difference in name and even in conception, this has been taken to be a consequence, real or possible, and as an end or goal which a good system of rules would first promote and then ensure. The question of which system of rules will be most successful in this respect generally has been thought to be, at least broadly speaking, empirical: Fact and practical experience will decide which system is best. The theory thus implies that the goal, and goal promoting action, both, in senses indicated earlier, are *logically* independent of any system of rules. This fundamentally instrumental

---

[11] See, for example, J. O. Urmson's "The Interpretation of the Moral Philosophy of J. S. Mill," *Philosophical Quarterly*, III (1953), pp. 33–39. By and large I agree with this interpretation of Mill, although Mill showed other tendencies, not only toward a more radical utilitarianism but, in the opposite direction, toward the ethics of Bradley. John Austin is sometimes said to be a good representative of this point of view, but his conception of moral rules as commands, learned in the way we learn practical maxims, is a hodgepodge (see *The Province of Jurisprudence Determined* (New York: Noonday Press, 1954), Lectures I–III. In some respects Hume's discussion of the artificial virtues, especially justice, is a much better (and perhaps the best) classical example of this type of theory.

Among contemporaries (and apart from useful textbook presentations: see Brandt, *loc. cit.*, and J. Hospers, *Human Conduct* (New York: Harcourt, 1962)). S. Toulmin in *An Examination of The Place of Reason in Ethics* (Cambridge: University Press, 1950) and P. H. Nowell-Smith in *Ethics* (Baltimore, Md.: Penguin, 1954) have come closest to an explicit statement of the theory.

An examination of actual cases of this kind of theory, with all the proper qualifications, especially if the theory is extended beyond utilitarianism, would require considerable space. I do not undertake the historical investigation here. In my judgment, the theory has a popularity which exceeds its merit, and some tendencies which are pernicious (see Section IV below). By isolating the germ, the disease may be better understood—its valuable antibodies notwithstanding.

and telic character of the system of rules, and indirectly of rule-directed action as well, is a distinctive feature of utilitarianism.[12] Moreover, as I pointed out above, it is an essential feature of rules of the foregoing kind that persons other than the rule follower are "interested" in the product; this "interest" is expressed in some kind of contract, convention, or law which gives the rules authority. In utilitarian theory the "party-in-authority" tends to be "the people"; directly or indirectly they enter conventions, "adopt" rules, then enforce them, so that all may share the fruits of the rule-directed action. The product is shared, the goal is the good of all.

2.1 Moral rules on the rule utilitarian view thus have the basic characteristics of the rules which I discussed in (I). When the two are compared, and the analysis in (I) is brought to bear, it quickly reveals that rule utilitarianism is faced with a fundamental problem. If the position is to have the advantage over act utilitarianism that is claimed for it, then the criterion of right action must be a system of rules and not general utility. Rules are a criterion of right action, however, only on condition that they are "rules-in-force" and in some sense "agreed to." But obviously the rules which are "in force" or "agreed to" may or may not be the rules which maximize utility; and to the extent that they are not, then the "best rules" by the utilitarian standard, not having been "adopted," are not the criterion of right action. The best rules may not even be known. The "rules" and the "utilitarianism" in "rule utilitarianism" thus constitute two independent criteria, and they may not be in much accord.

2.1.1 The analysis in (I) not only clearly shows the nature of this difficulty, but also helps one to understand some of the directions in which utilitarianism has moved in an effort to avoid it. Some good utilitarians, mindful of evil in ordinary conventions, tend to say that just as men *ought* to adopt a rule only if it maximizes utility, so one is *obligated* to follow a rule only if it maximizes utility. This doctrine implies that one may freely disregard a rule if ever he discovers that action on the rule is not maximally felicific, and in this respect makes moral rules like "practical maxims." It deprives social and moral rules

---

[12] It would be a mistake to say that utilitarians maintained this deliberately, after considering alternatives, or even that they did so consistently. John Stuart Mill, in Chapter IV of *Utilitarianism*, seems to have been unaware of the issue when he discussed happiness as "a concrete whole" and virtue as one of its "parts." Cf. below 4.5.

of their authority and naturally is in sharp conflict with practice. On this alternative rule utilitarianism collapses into act utilitarianism.[13]

2.1.2 Other rule utilitarians, equally concerned to avoid an ethical conventionalism, either close their eyes to the difficulty or else overlook it. They either just declare an ideal set of rules to be the criterion, or else say that the criterion of right action is the system of rules which, *if* adopted, *would* maximize utility, or something of the sort. Such a formulation clearly does not acknowledge that rules must be adopted if they are to be rules: The "if adopted" is only a way of describing the ideal and actually obscures the necessity of a rule's being adopted.

The fact that it is commonly the case that some moral principles and rules to which a person subscribes are not "in force" in his society raises important issues for *any* moral philosophy of rules. I cannot even try to do them justice here. Nevertheless, surely it is a mistake to maintain that a set of rules, thought to be ideally utilitarian or felicific, is the criterion of right action. If the rules are simply described in this way, and are not enumerated, we so far do not have any rules and are not likely to get any.[14] On the other hand, if we are presented with a list, but these are not rules in practice, the most one could reasonably do is to try to get them adopted. A manager in the quiet of his office may dream of a system of rules which will maximize production, and a utilitarian may build a theory around the set of rules which will maximize utility. Surely the latter would be as foolish as the former if he said that these ideal rules are the criterion of right and wrong acts. As previous analysis has shown, acts are not judged by proposed rules, ideal rules, and rules-in-theory: for these do not fully qualify as rules.[15]

[13] For a clear recent statement of this position, see J. J. C. Smart, "Extreme and Restricted Utilitarianism," *Philosophical Quarterly*, VI (1956), pp. 344–54. Notice that Smart argues explicity that moral rules are "rules of thumb."

[14] Cf. above, 1, 3.1.

[15] See 1.2 and 1.3.1 above. Since utilitarianism is rather often associated with reform, it tends to be formulated in ideal terms. See, for example, J. S. Mill's most explicit statement of his position in Ch. II, paragraph 10 of *Utilitarianism* ". . . the standard of morality, which may accordingly be defined 'the rules and precepts for human conduct', by the observance of which an existence such as has been described might be, to the greatest extent possible, secured to all mankind . . ." In this passage, how is "possible" to be taken? Does it mean "possible, within the framework of existing institutions?" For one attempt to avoid in this way the difficulties inherent in an ideal formulation, see R. B. Brandt, *op. cit.*, pp. 396–400. This attempt goes only part of the way in meeting the difficulty. On the difficulty itself cf. H. J. McCloskey, "An Examination of Restricted Utilitarianism," *Philosophical Review*, LXVI (1957), esp. pp. 475–81; and J. Austin, *op. cit.*, Lecture III.

2.1.3 Other rule utilitarians show a finer appreciation of the logic of their position: They interpret moral rules on analogy with the rules in (I), even if it forces them to admit that the criterion of right action is not the set of rules which maximizes utility. This alternative seems to be popular with those whose primary allegiance is to a "morality of rules," and who are utilitarian only because they suppose that "welfare" *must* have something to do with morality. (After all, what else *can* serve as a criterion of rules?)

On this alternative it always makes sense to ask whether or not a "moral or social convention" subscribed to in practice is best, and this gives sense to the question, sometimes asked, whether a people who follow their conventions act in the best way they could. At the same time the question, whether an individual ought to do something in particular—for example, repay money borrowed—is quite a different question, to be answered by referring, at least in part, to the practices and conventions of that society. Such a view does not make the blunder of taking an ideal system of rules as the criterion of which particular acts are right, and yet it does not endorse conventions which are obviously questionable. One may seek earnestly to reform the moral conventions of a people, and yet insist that these conventions, some of which are in need of reform, are the general criterion by which a man must decide what in particular he ought to do, and by which his acts are to be judged. At the same time, such a view need not dichotomize the two criteria. As we found above, rules of this kind have an open texture which permits the criterion of the rules to enter into their proper interpretation. I think we may presume, moreover, that there are instances in which one should violate the letter of a moral rule when following it would clearly be to the detriment of the general welfare, or the welfare of all parties concerned. Rule utilitarians could no doubt take instances of this sort to support their theory. As we also found above, one may admit this without depriving rules of their authority.[16]

---

[16] I think this is the most favorable interpretation which can be given to the utilitarianism of the nineteenth century reformers: They framed a theory which would make sense of reform, but at the same time had too much practical (if not always philosophical) sense to advocate the use of the criterion of rules as the criterion of acts. It is as if they perceived the importance of moral rules and practices but were unable fully to accommodate these to their theory. I think that the presence of the two criteria, which the analysis of the rules in (I) clearly reveals, explains for example the "tension" between chapter two of Mill's *Utilitarianism* on the one hand, and chapters three and five on the other.

III

3.0 A careful development and criticism of rule utilitarianism, as just outlined, would be worth while, but it is outside the range of this paper. Even without this development, however, it can be shown that rule utilitarians, by using the kind of rule in (I) as a model, have exercised a definite option, and I want to indicate the general character of this option. To do this, I shall first consider briefly the rules of certain kinds of games.[17]

3.1 Rules of common competitive games, such as baseball, chess, and the like, say how a game is to be played. They state the "object of the game," "the moves," "how the counting should go," etc. Often they are stated in "rule books," and sometimes they are enforced by referees appointed by an acknowledged authority. These formalities, however, are not at all necessary. The rules must be "laid down" or "adopted" in some sense, but all that is required (in the case of those games being discussed) is that a group of players "agree" on a set of rules. This agreement may consist simply in their following and enforcing rules which they all have learned: Think, for example, of a group of small boys playing baseball, and think of the difference between one's knowing the rules and playing the game. In such cases there is no formally agreed-upon authority; each player—in principle— is both rule-follower and rule-enforcer. No player has the authority to modify the rules at will, but the players together can change them in any way they see fit. As one should expect, there are many variations.

In the latter respects game rules of this kind are quite like the rules in (I). These game rules, however, noticeably lack the first major characteristic of those rules: They are not designed to yield a product. More precisely, they are not adopted to promote the attainment of a goal which, in the senses indicated earlier, is "over and beyond" the

---

[17] I can be brief because rules of this kind have been discussed by others. I shall mostly confine myself to points not previously mentioned, or at least not emphasized. I am perhaps most indebted to Rawls's acute analysis of what he calls the "practice conception," and on the whole agree with it. The name is misleading since very many "practices," as we ordinarily think of them, are defined by rules (e.g., by job rules) which are quite unlike those to which his "practice conception of rules" properly applies. Although unimportant in itself, it is just this kind of thing, I suspect, which has led moral philosophers into serious error. One can sympathize since it is almost impossible to find a conventional expression which is not misleading in some important respect.

rules.[18] They do not serve a goal which is "logically independent" of the game which they define.

3.1.1 Of course people who play games do so with various motives, and some of the goals which motivate them are logically independent of the game; for example, exercise, recreation, the opportunity to talk to friends or make a conquest. Undoubtedly games are popular because they serve so many ends. Nevertheless, motives and goals of this kind are not essential. Many players participate (so far as can be determined without psychoanalyzing them) "just because they want to" or simply "from love of the game." Actually this kind of motive, even if it is not typical, is that which is most distinctive of players: One who "loves a game" commonly regards another, who lacks the motive, as poorly appreciating "the quality of the game." This is apt to be missed just because games have been turned into instruments, for exercise, diversion, etc., to such a great degree. The point is, they *need* not be.

Moreover, games *qua* games do not seem to have a design or goal *different* from the motives of the rule-followers, in the way rules of jobs commonly do. What is this goal? One who most appreciates a game speaks about it rather as if it were an aesthetic object, worth playing on its own account and apart from any product or result; and if he is asked to justify his claim that it is good, he seems to have a problem analogous to that of justifying an aesthetic judgment.[19] Sometimes, to be sure, the rules of games are changed, and in particular instances violated, in order to change the consequences. Many official rules, for example, have been changed in order to lessen player injuries; and particular persons may find a game played by the official rules too strenuous, or pursuit of the ball after a bad drive too troublesome. These facts, however, do not imply that the rules are designed to produce consequences, such as the right amount of exercise or exertion, or the good health of the players. Changes of the kind mentioned simply indicate that the rules of a game, like the rules of a job, are

[18] Some games have become instruments to such a considerable degree, and some instrumental activities have become so much like games, that no description will prevent the intrusion of dubious and borderline cases.

[19] This reminds one of the ancient distinctions between "doing" and "making," and between (what the medievals called) "immanent" and "transitive" activity. I do not mean to deny that some jobs are worth doing "on their own account," but even when "one enjoys a job," there is a discernible purpose which it is designed to promote.

adopted in a context by persons who have many desires and many obligations other than "to play the game" and "follow its rules." Games are often altered to make them harmonize better with such contextual features. It is true, of course, that persons who have turned games into instruments change or violate the rules more readily. As we say, these people do not take the game as seriously.

Some philosophers are inclined to say that even when one plays a game "just because he wants to" or "for love of the game," the game is still an instrument—to "his enjoyment" or "pleasure." This stand depends for its cogency on our being able to describe this pleasure or enjoyment without referring to the game, which should be possible if the pleasure or enjoyment really were something separate from playing he game. However, although it is clearly possible to play a game and not enjoy it, the converse does not appear plausible. To be sure, one sometimes says that he gets about the same enjoyment from one game as another, especially when the two are similar. But this is apt to mean that he has no strong preference for one game over another, that he likes one as well as the other, not that there is a kind of pleasurable feeling which in fact results from both, more or less equally, and which *conceivably* could be had from very different activities or even from being acted *on* in some way. (Similarly, when one says that he "likes to talk to one person about as much as another," this clearly does not mean that talking to the two persons produces the same kind of pleasure in him.) Moreover, when we speak of getting about the same enjoyment from two games, sometimes the "enjoyment" does not appear to be, strictly speaking, the enjoyment "of playing the game," but rather the enjoyment of exercising, talking to friends, etc. I do not deny, however, that games can become instruments. I want to argue that they need not be, often are not, and that in calling them games we do not imply that they are instruments.

The kind of goal the pursuit of which to some degree *is* essential to the playing of the game is the "object of the game," as defined by the rules, and the various sub-goals which promote this object according to the rules. Such goals as these, for example, "to score the most runs," "to get the batter out at second base," obviously are not logically independent of the rules of the game—if there were no rules it would be logically impossible to try to do these things. It is just nonsense to speak of changing the rules so that one can better attain the object of the game.

3.1.2 Since the action within a game is designed to attain goals defined by the rules, the action as well as the goal logically depends on the rules: In important respects a move in the game has the consequences it has because the rules say it has; *in these respects* the rules define the consequences and determine the character of the action.[20] Since the character of instrumental action is fixed at least partly by the goal which the action is designed to serve, the action can be described in this essential respect, as a "trying to get the goal," without referring to or presupposing rules. In the case of play in a game, unless the game has become an instrument, this is not possible; if one describes the action in a game apart from the rules, as a "trying to catch a ball," he leaves out the design. On account of this difference one may feel inclined to say that whereas rules of the kind described in (1) *may* be used to describe an action, game rules by defining new kinds of action just constitute "forms of life."[21]

3.2 However, this is but one side of the story, and if it were the only one it is not likely that the two kinds of rules would be confused. To see the other side, which is equally important, one should attend to the fact that the play in a game is not wholly defined by the rules of the game. "The kind of game he plays" ordinarily does not refer to the game as defined by the rules; "to play a game" ordinarily means more than following the rules. The point is that although the object of the game is defined by the rules, since the action in a game normally consists in "trying to attain that object," and since the game rules do not determine success in this respect, the action in *this* respect is instrumental. Players often develop tactics and strategies and skills in playing. Sometimes they follow what I have called practical maxims, and at other times they follow team rules agreed on among themselves or laid down by the "manager." The latter are, of course, examples of the rules described in (I). Obviously they should not be confused with rules of games, as I have described them. For one can be said to play a game without his following any particular set of instrumental rules.

The point of greatest importance here is that although game rules are not themselves instruments, they support, as it were, a considerable mount of instrumental activity, much of which logically could not be

---

[20] This is the point which Rawls emphasized.
[21] Cf. A. I. Melden, "Action," *Philosophical Review*, LXV (1956), pp. 523–541.

carried on without them. To play a game is typically to follow the rules of the game *and* engage in this instrumental activity; a "good player" does more than just follow the rules. Even one who "loves the game for its own sake" derives his satisfaction from the kind of *instrumental* activity which the rules of the game make possible. Games make new goals, new pursuits, and new skills available to men.

In this situation it is not surprising that some should regard games themselves as instruments. To regard them in this way, however, would be to confuse their function.

IV

4.0 The rules of games just considered differ most significantly from the rules described in (I) because they are, by our criterion, "non-instrumental." This point of difference between the two kinds of rules is one of the most important to be found. I have been concerned to mark it here to focus attention on the thesis, maintained by many utilitarians, that moral rules and social institutions are instruments designed to promote a goal logically independent of the rules and institutions. The thesis is only rarely discussed, and I think that failure to discuss it helps account for the recurrent popularity of utilitarianism. However, morality is obviously not a game, and if the thesis is to be fully assessed, moral rules must be carefully analyzed and alternatives considered. This is out of the question here. In the remainder of this paper I shall note a complexity which is too often overlooked, and just indicate the critical force of certain recently developed lines of argument. However, the fundamental issue here is not at all new.[22]

[22] Historically one perhaps first senses the issue in his reading of Plato and Aristotle. Is man's end somehow "writ in his nature" in such a way that it can be determined apart from a determination of virtue? If so, it might be reasonable to regard virtue as a *means* to the end, and instruction in virtue as a matter of learning from practical experience the best means. On the other hand, if man's end cannot be determined without the determination of virtue—if man's end is properly defined in terms of virtue, as activity in accordance with it, and man's nature is defined as potentialities for this end—then virtue is not a means and its discovery in practical experience must be understood differently. Although the second interpretation is the sounder, there were tendencies in medieval thought to favor the first—undoubtedly deriving from the fact that God, who is certainly different from man, was said to be man's end. Moreover, the desire of God was said to be implanted in man's nature. This inclination was said to be a natural participation of the eternal law, and natural virtue was said to be an insufficient means to God. I think myself, however, that the second interpretation gives a sounder account of the ethics not only of Augustine but also of Aquinas. Yet it is not surprising that out of this tradition there should

4.1 Consider the rule "Do not cheat." Often it is taught in the context of a game, and it acquires a rather specific sense in this context. The rule in this use can be paraphrased as "Do not violate the rules of the game in order to gain an advantage for yourself." In this use the rule logically presupposes games as social institutions; if there were no games, the rule could not have this use and this meaning.

The same general point applies to many other moral rules, such as "Keep your promises," "Do not steal," and "Do not lie." Each of these logically presupposes institutions and practices, such as "promising," "a system of property," "a language." Since these moral rules presuppose such practices, they cannot be understood apart from them; the practice, constituted by its own rules, makes the moral rule meaningful. Philosophical analyses which have attempted to clarify moral rules apart from institutionalized practices have surrounded them with theoretical perplexities and turned them into "mere forms" of morality.[23]

However, the fact that these moral rules presuppose institutions or practices does not *in itself* decide the question whether or not they are instrumental and utilitarian. In some respects the rules "Do not cheat," "Do not lie," etc., are like the rules "Do not violate traffic lights," "Do not drive on the wrong side," etc. These rules obviously presuppose practices, and the rules and practices appear to be primarily instrumental and utilitarian. We can easily conceive of the practices being changed in order to provide a more effective system of traffic control.

have come the contrary (Lockian) doctrine that natural law applies to man in a "state of nature," and that men by compact make societies as a remedy for natural evils and as a means to natural goals. This doctrine in turn, by way of reaction, stimulated theories according to which the distinction of right and wrong is not founded in nature, but in contract, convention, or rules. In the nineteenth century the opposition between the two general points of view assumed more of its original form when idealists worked out their own interpretation of the social contract, and opposed utilitarianism. (See, for example, Bradley's "Pleasure for Pleasure's Sake" in *Ethical Studies* (New York: G. E. Stechert, 1911) and Bernard Bosanquet's *Philosophical Theory of the State* (New York: St. Martin's, 1923).) Very recent philosophy in some respects strongly resembles idealism, undoubtedly because it itself is a reaction to a kind of philosophy which arose in reaction to idealism. For one example, cf. Bosanquet, *op. cit.*, with A. I. Melden, *Rights and Right Conduct* (New York: Humanities Press, 1959).

This is, of course, only a fragmentary account of the historical origins of the issue.

[23] This misinterpretation accounts for some criticisms of a morality of rules. Cf. A. Macbeath, *Experiments in Living* (London: Macmillan, 1952), Lecture XIII.

On the utilitarian view moral rules and the institutions which they presuppose are rather like a system of this kind. The assumption is that men have various destinations which they want to reach and the social aim is to provide the system of institutions which will be most effective in helping them along. As men together devise such public instruments as roads and bridges, which no one alone could construct, and then regulate the use of these instruments for the "public good," so on this view men together have developed such institutions as "promising," "a system of property," etc. These institutions may not have arisen through deliberate design, although (there often seems to be the assumption that) if an institution or practice has arisen, then it *must* have been rewarding, and consequently *must* have served some purpose. The instrumental character of these institutions is evidenced more directly, however, by the fact that persons hold and dispose of property, make promises, and, quite generally, engage in the life of their institutions with goals in mind. If these reasons are decisive, moreover, one's language, too, should be viewed as a social tool.[24] Certainly men have purposes in speaking.

As in the case of a traffic system, however, on occasion it is to a person's advantage to break the rules of their institutions. Men must be taught not to; they must be made to realize that temporary advantage is far outweighed by the more permanent benefits to be gained if all can be depended on to follow the rules. Moral rules, such as "Keep your promises," "Do not steal," "Do not lie," like the rules "Always obey traffic signals," "Do not drive on the wrong side," seem to be conceived as deriving from the occasional but recurrent conflict between private advantage and public institutions. Utilitarians commonly make the point that if a person in his own interest is sometimes led to violate a rule, he will nevertheless insist, also in his own interest, that others follow the rule: The "security" which derives from a system of public institutions is given an important place in moral theory. Moral rules of this kind thus seem to be conceived as supports for and ancillary to the public institutions which they presuppose. If these rules could only be made to serve a system of truly *rational* (i.e., utilitarian) institutions, the aforementioned conflict would be minimized, as the happiness of all was promoted. The negative morality of rules would be lost in liberal affection for the general welfare.

[24] Cf. Hume's *Treatise of Human Nature*, ed. L. A. Selby-Bigge (New York: Oxford Univ. Press, 1941), III, II, II. Esp. p. 490.

4.2 Moral rules of this kind in a sense do *tend* to support the institutions and practices which they presuppose: They *tend* to receive their effective interpretation from the character of the institutions, and they are both taught and reaffirmed most vigorously when persons from self-interest show an inclination to violate the rules of the institutions. As a consequence (and for an additional reason which will soon be apparent[25]) these institutions and practices have, as it were, a "moral dimension" or a "moral part." Nevertheless, in assessing rule utilitarianism it is important to distinguish moral rules on the one hand from other rules which also define and characterize the underlying institutions and practices. For it is possible to learn the rules of a game, and to play the game, without being tempted to cheat, without grasping the concept of "cheating," and without learning the moral rule "Do not cheat." It is not uncommon for children to do this. Children ordinarily also learn to speak correctly, in the sense of learning many rules of the language, without learning the rule "Do not lie," thus without grasping the moral concept of a lie. It may not be so evident, but it is also the case that one can learn many rules governing property, can learn to make a promise, etc., without grasping the moral force of the rules "Do not steal," "Keep your promises," etc. There are surely legal experts on property and contract who have, as we say, very little moral understanding.[26]

In considering the soundness of rule utilitarianism, there are thus two interrelated questions. The first is whether or not the institutions of promising, property, language, etc., are instruments serving goals logically independent of these institutions. This bears on the question of the soundness of utilitarianism not only as a *moral* but as a *social* theory. Then there is the more restricted question whether rule utilitarianism offers a sound account of moral rules.

[25] See 4.5 below.

[26] Although an adequate description of property and promising in a sense implies that theft and promise-breaking are morally wrong, a person may fail to "see" the implication. When we teach a child what property and promising are, we commonly say that it is wrong for him to take what belongs to another and wrong for him not to do what he has promised to do. So far, however, the child is not guilty of theft or promise-breaking, and until he has witnessed them, or an inclination thereto. in himself or another (since he has not yet had occasion to *use* the rules "Do not steal" and "Keep your promises"), he will have little practical understanding of these rules. Before he reaches this point, however, he may have learned enough of the underlying rules to exchange property, make promises, etc. Growth in moral understanding is long and complex and participation in ordinary practices does not wait upon it.

4.3.1 Several lines of thought, some recently developed, bear on these questions. To take one example, primarily as it applies to the first of the questions: Utilitarians, as already indicated, have put considerable emphasis on "security," if not as *the* goal, nevertheless as an important "part" of the goal. A person cannot be "secure," however, without being able to *count on* others to act and refrain from acting in a variety of ways. His counting on others, moreover, is in a great many cases not "an expectation" based on an ordinary induction. For most often the expectation involved in one's counting on another is based on the fact that the action or restraint in question is governed by rules which define rights, obligations, duties, etc.: One can count on another because the other (presumably) is acting on such rules.[27] For this reason the expression "counting on another" in many occasions of its use makes no more sense apart from rules than "deciding to act" or "acting" makes apart from reasons for acting. There is also the related point that the action which one counts on another to do, itself, in many cases presupposes rules; for example, just as one could not count on a person to "play first base" if there were no game of baseball, so one could not count on another to "keep his promise" or "respect property" if there were no practice of promising or institution of property.[28] Although "security" is an ambiguous term, in the sense in which it refers to a significant social goal it could not mean what it does without rules which define institutions and practices.

For both these reasons "security" just does not appear to be a goal which is logically independent of the rules of institutions and practices like property, promising, language, etc. Moreover, it would seem very strange to think of the greatest number having the greatest happiness or pleasure or welfare without being fairly secure. The utilitarian position thus appears to be quite vulnerable, even apart from the fact that its proponents have notoriously failed to give "happiness," "pleasure," "welfare," and the like the clarity of meaning which they must have to function as goals.

4.3.2 Furthermore, as the earlier analysis of games revealed, the fact that one does many things as a means to an end when engaging in a practice gives no support to the claim that the practice itself is a means. The fact that one uses various devices to win a game does not

[27] Cf. Hart, *op. cit.*, pp. 54–7.
[28] Cf. Hume, *loc. cit.* Black and many others make the same point.

imply that the game is an instrument, and similarly, the fact that one uses words as tools, or makes a promise or deals in property for some purpose, does not support the view that institutions and practices such as language, promising, and property are instruments for the promotion of goals logically independent of these institutions and practices. Nor does this appear plausible: It seems rather to be the case that institutions and practices create or establish most of the goals which men pursue, in the sense that these goals, like the object of a game, would be logically impossible without the institutions and practices. It also appears that persons who engage in business, or make speeches, or follow intellectual pursuits ultimately because "they just enjoy doing these things" are rather like players who enjoy a game for its own sake—in the respect that they derive their enjoyment from instrumental activity which is also made possible by institutions and practices.

At this point, however, it becomes apparent that much requires to be worked out before one can replace the utilitarian view of social institutions with another which is more adequate.

4.4 When one turns to consider utilitarianism as a theory of moral rules, *to some extent* the same arguments apply. For some moral rules *are* in some respects ancillary to the practices and institutions which they presuppose, and in so far as this is the case, then generally speaking moral rules are just as utilitarian as, and no more utilitarian than, these practices and institutions. Notice that the most common uses of the moral rules "Do not lie," "Do not steal," and the like presuppose not only underlying institutions and practices, but also, as suggested above, a tendency or inclination of some persons at some times not to conform to the institutions and practices. This seems to explain why persons living in a law-abiding community use these moral rules so little. This in turn suggests that moral rules are "protective devices," rather like a police system, which also is little used in a law-abiding community and which also presupposes both institutions and an inclination on the part of some persons to violate them. The "police" view of moral rules is partial, but it is also partly true: It helps one see why moral rules are so often conceived as "external" to an individual, imposing restraints on him (and why some philosophers tend to pattern moral rules on rules in a prison!) At the same time it helps one understand why some people "internalize" moral rules in the way they do. For some insist on the importance of following moral rules only because they value a system of institutions and the "happiness and security" which the institutions afford. Seeing that valued institutions would cease to exist if people generally did not act in the way moral rules prescribe, they teach these rules—although morality for them is primarily a matter of promoting individual or public welfare, and it would be better if moral rules had little use. This interest in morality is epitomized in the person who regards moral rules as a protector of life, liberty, and property; breaking the rules breeds fear, ruins business, and disrupts the game. This is the internalization of moral rules as ancillary to institutions; it tends to characterize utilitarians past and present.

4.5 Moral rules, however, may be internalized in quite another way, and on this account utilitarianism as a *moral* theory is open to an additional criticism specific to itself.

For a person who values an institution constituted by rules may come to see that rules by nature apply to all members of a class. One who sees this may then be led to look upon the rules which characterize some particular institutions and practices not simply as "applying to all," but at the same time as constituting "a common standard of correctness." And in this way one may be led to the abstract but practical conception of "a community of men living under the idea of law," of which particular institutions afford so many possible examples. In so far as one thinks that others as well as himself act under this conception, he will no doubt value a particular game or language or any other such institution not only *qua* game, *qua* language, etc., but also as a particular instance and a particular form of such a communtiy.

When the idea of such a community is attained and made to govern practice (as it seems to have been, for example, by the Socrates of the *Crito*) then the moral rules "Do not lie," "Do not steal," etc., will appear in a new light. One who acts under such an idea will teach these rules neither as primarily negative and restraining, nor primarily as supports or protections for particular institutions. For although he may view the rules in these ways, he will regard them primarily as affirming in so many different ways the fundamental principle "Live under the idea of law." The principle may be stated negatively, in the form "Do not make an exception of oneself," but his primary aim in teaching the rules will be to raise one to the conception of a moral community. Since such a community potentially includes all men, part of the challenge may be to find particular institutions in which the conception can be realized.

Moral rules regarded in this way of course still presuppose particular institutions and practices. However, they are no longer, properly speaking, "ancillary to" the institutions and practices: They now "add something" to the institutions and practices which they presuppose; the institutions and practices now have a new dimension. Cheating comes to be deplored not primarily because it tends to disrupt a game but because it detracts from the quality which a game can have. If there is cheating, one may simply prefer not to play. In a similar way, lying may be deplored because it detracts from the quality of speech, theft because it detracts from the quality of exchange, etc. Put affirmatively, the idea of a moral community is realizable analogically— only in a variety of forms—in sportsmanship, morally mature speech, honest argument, etc. It should be evident that common institutions and practices are often not in fact logically independent of morality; one has to form a limited or abstract conception of them to make them so.

When moral rules are regarded in this way,[29] then obviously they do not serve a goal logically independent of themselves. In the language of Mill, virtue has now become a "part" of the end, a "part of happiness." Only it is clear that when Mill said this, with his usual willingness to sacrifice theory to good sense, he deserted utilitarianism. The instrumental and utilitarian pattern just will not fit.

V

Further discussion of moral rules is beyond the aim of this paper. My primary purpose has been to contribute to the clarification of moral rules by clarifying a fundamental option open to moral theory. To this end I have both analyzed the general utilitarian view of social rules and practices, along with some variations, and I have tried to lay bare the (largely implicit) utilitarian view of moral rules. I have analyzed moral rules, however, only to the point where the character and significance of the option, and the force of some of the arguments which apply, will be fairly clear. I do not want to suggest that all moral rules are like those which I have considered. The analysis of

[29] Cf. K. Baier, *op. cit.*, pp. 200–204, and W. D. Falk's comments on "natural obligation" and "mature moral thinking" in "Morality and Convention," *Journal of Philosophy*, LVII (1960), pp. 675–685.

games, in distinguishing the moral player from the good player, may remind one that there are two traditions in the history of ethics, one emphasizing an exoteric ethic and a moral law known to all, the other an esoteric ethic and a virtue reserved for the wise. I have been concerned, almost exlcusively, with the former, and not all of that.

In the course of the discussion attention has been called to the fact that moral rules can be (and thus tend to be) conceived as summaries, reports, practical maxims, rules designed to promote a goal, rules which define institutions, rules which protect institutions, and as particular forms of the fundamental principle of justice.[30] Marking the important differences between these alternatives should remove more than one confusion and at the same time provide *some* of the subtlety which will be needed if the discussion of moral rules is to make genuine advances in the future.

[30] The list is not meant to be exhaustive. Cf. e.g., D. S. Shwayder, "Moral Rules and Moral Maxims," *Ethics*, LXVII (1957), pp. 269–285.

Introduction to Eugene Fontinell

Professor Eugene Fontinell believes that before we can be clear about the role of situationist ethics in our world, we must first be clear about the sort of world we live in, and how it differs from past worlds or world views. Only after we get clear about our "metaphysical" presuppositions can we make sense of and evaluate the dependent variable in the equation, ethical theory.

Our world is the world of contemporary science, the world revolutionized by Copernicus and Darwin and Freud. In the sphere of ethics the traditional polarization between relativism and absolutism is no longer illuminating, for the classical world of substance and accident, subject and object, act and potency is gone forever. Gone too are the days when religion could be taken to supply satisfactory answers to the ultimate questions in ethics, for it is now sure that all ethical truth results from the reflective experience of the community.

We can make sense of the *radical novelty* of our world, of the sense in which a really new man lives in a really new world first by learning to see that ours is a world *in process*. The second significant aspect of our world is that it is no longer the traditional world of substances but is rather a world of relations, a world in which it is exactly true that "to be is to-be-with," as Marcel put it. Ours is a world, in short, of *processive relationalism.*

Man himself can no longer be viewed as an essentially independent being who then enters into relations with others. He is rather, like all else, a processive relational being and his ethics is thus an ethics of relationships. In the past, men tended to simplify moral decisions by isolating some values and protecting these by absolute general laws; all others were ignored. An ethics of relationships calls for the use of the pragmatic test, the test of consequences, to identify laws and values

197

which are relatively permanent, but these are nonetheless not beyond review or criticism.

An ethics of relationships does not furnish us with an easy-to-use key to moral problems, but does enable us to avoid some blind alleys. A crucial example of such a blind alley is that of the basic and allegedly irresolvable conflict between the rights of the individual and the rights of society. Traditional analyses could do no more than attempt to weigh and balance what appeared to be the very different claims of each, to avoid the destructive extremes of individualism and collectivism. The basic error here is that of cutting man off from society. In an ethics of relationships, by contrast, the human person is viewed as an essentially communal entity, as one who can, paradoxically, achieve greater individuality only by greater participation in the various sorts of communities, family, culture, church, etc., of which he is the expression. Decision-making is thus not a matter of applying rules to situations but of weighing and evaluating a diversity of relationships, claims, and values. This may *appear* to be no more than the sanctification of whim, but there is, in point of fact, no viable substitute for the view which takes account of man in the world science has given us, and this is the world of processive relationalism.

Towards an Ethics of Relationships*
by Eugene Fontinell

In an article "Context versus Principles: A Misplaced Debate in Christian Ethics,"[1] Professor James A. Gustafson has argued that the debate has ceased to be a fruitful one inasmuch as significantly different thinkers were classed together on both sides of the question. For the most part, this plea has gone unheeded; if anything, the controversy centering around situation ethics or "the new morality" has intensified. Gustafson's contention that the present form of the debate is not particularly enlightening is undoubtedly correct, but it should be added that one of the reasons why the opponents in this moral controversy often argue at cross purposes is their failure to clarify their assumptions or, if I may, their metaphysical presuppositions.

It is the intent of this paper to indicate what I believe to be the only conditions within which an adequate ethics can be developed. While it will briefly touch upon the decision making aspect of ethics, it will be primarily concerned with ethics as a metaphysics of morality, that is, with the effort to ground, explain, and defend the reasons or principles employed in the concrete act of making a moral decision.

In the history and development of any philosophical question a certain degree of polarization is almost inevitable. Certainly, no philosopher likes to admit that his philosophy is one-sided or overlooks relevant data. A philosophical idealist, for example, is convinced that he has incorporated into his system whatever is valid in philosophical realism, and vice versa. However, from the history of

* This paper was originally given as part of a lecture series sponsored by the Institute for Religious and Social Studies, Jewish Theological Seminary of America.
[1] James A. Gustafson, "Content Versus Principles: A Misplaced Debate in Christian Ethics," *Harvard Theological Review*, LVIII (1965), pp. 171–202.

philosophy it is evident that after a period of time the very terms and categories within which a philosophical question is phrased become obstacles to further development of that question. When that happens, nothing will suffice but a fundamental recasting of the entire question. Such is the situation I believe to obtain in the polarization of ethics in the form of moral relativism and moral absolutism.[2] The language and concepts employed are no longer useful, but the relativistic critique of static absolutism, though necessary, has not brought forth a viable and meaningful ethic.

Instead of using the terms "absolutism" or "relativism" it might be more helpful to change the terminology and acknowledge the need for both continuity and development. Without continuity, one is reduced to anarchic atomism; without development, one is stratified in an abstractionism that becomes increasingly impervious to new

[2] An example of this polarization is found in the debate on "the new morality" between Joseph Fletcher and Herbert McCabe in *Commonweal*, LXXXIII (Jan. 14, 1966), pp. 427–40. This, of course, is but a contemporary version of a dispute which begins with the Greeks and recurs in varying forms down through the ages. I have already stated that, in my opinion, "the present form of the debate is not particularly enlightening." It is always a bit unfair to dismiss other viewpoints in a few words or in a footnote. I do not totally dismiss either Fletcher or McCabe, but it might be helpful to indicate just where I diverge from them. Fletcher has presented his position in a full-length study, *Situation Ethics* (Philadelphia: The Westminster Press, 1966), and since my own approach can properly be called a form of "situation ethics," it is necessary to spell-out in a bit more detail my divergence from him.

First, and most important, I contend that the basic need is to develop a metaphysics adequate to the ethical situation. Fletcher seems to understand metaphysics exclusively in terms of "rationalistic metaphysics" and this he totally rejects. I would argue that everyone, including Fletcher, has at least an implicit metaphysics and that his is basically that which characterizes British Empiricism from Locke to Mill. The chief source of the metaphysics which I am employing is found in William James and John Dewey. Though Fletcher claims to be a follower of James and Dewey, he seems unaware of the fundamental difference between "experience" as employed by them and the "experience" of classical British empiricism. For a "brief statement of some of the chief contrasts between the orthodox description of experience and that congenial to present conditions," see John Dewey, "The Need for a Recovery of Philosophy," included in *On Experience, Nature and Freedom*, ed. and intro. by Richard J. Bernstein (New York: The Liberal Arts Press, 1960), p. 23. For almost a decade now, such thinkers as John E. Smith, Richard J. Bernstein, Ralph Sleeper and John J. McDermott have been stressing this "American metaphysics of experience." I have referred to it as "a metaphysics of relations and process" and have attempted to describe its central features in "Religious Truth in a Relational and Processive World," *Cross Currents*, XVII (1967), pp. 287–300.

My second disagreement with Fletcher has to do with his use of "love" as an absolute norm. I believe that this is much too easy and in the final analysis compromises his "situationism" in that love is held to be good regardless of the situation or

insights and experiences. Much, of course, depends on how one understands the terms "continuity" and "development." Does development of self-consciousness mean simply becoming more aware of what one has always been, or does it involve a more fundamental modification of what one is? Is man a being whose nature or essence is given by God, and whose task is simply to discover this and act accordingly? Or is man a being who is actually involved in the making of himself, who must struggle to form himself without any foreordained pattern against which he can definitively judge his actions?

The meaning which one attaches to the term "continuity" will depend on one's understanding of development. Continuity is more easily accounted for by doing as the Greeks first did, namely, positing certain unchanging principles which permeate all changing beings.

context. Hence, Fletcher is still an absolutist, even though he has only one absolute. My rejection of absolutes is total—there cannot be even one value or principle which can be used as a norm to evaluate or render good an ethical act without consideration of other factors and relations which enter into the constitution of that act.

Finally, Fletcher claims he is a pragmatist but I would contend that his "love absolutism" dilutes and possibly destroys his pragmatism. The kind of pragmatism to which I subscribe allows for no *a priori* judgments, even one which says, "love only is always good." There is evidence, I believe, that the consequences of love are *not* always good. Consider, for example, the love of parents for their children or the love of the patriot for his country. Would anyone suggest that every consequence which has stemmed from such loves has been good? If the objection is raised that the acts from which harmful consequences proceeded were not truly acts of love, then we destroy the utility of "love" as an antecedent norm or guide for decision-making. Nowhere is self-deception more likely than in the experience of love. Certainly the mother who consumes her child through possessiveness firmly believes that she is acting through love. In like fashion, the patriot claims to love when he says, "my country, right or wrong." Someone has referred to nationalism as a "love that hates." Hence, I would argue that love is itself situational or contextual, that love is but one of a variety of factors which must be considered in any concrete act of deciding.

As for the ethical views of Herbert McCabe, I have only the above-mentioned article on which to base my appraisal. Ironically, I think that he, rather than Fletcher, has a better grasp of the relational or contextual or situational structure of man. He is right on the mark when he states: "I exist, in fact, in many contexts and the problem of morality—the problem of really being myself—is not simply to do justice to one selected context but to get the priorities right" (*op. cit.*, p. 436). McCabe's "contextualism" is able to sustain absolutes, however, because it is ultimately static. His metaphysics, at least as presented in this article, does not give even a hint of that process which characterizes reality. He speaks of the "total human situation" which is the basis for his "absolute moral demands" as if it were an unchanging reality over against which human acts are to be judged. If one subscribes, as I do, to a processive view of reality in which the "total human situation" is itself in process, then it is not possible to sort out and safeguard any "absolutes" which would exist and have their reality independent of this process.

If one rejects such unchanging principles, as contemporary thought has overwhelmingly done, then continuity can only mean that the new man emerges out of the old by transformation rather than by either the actualization of an already existing potency or simple negation. In any event, there is a great difference between these two views of man.

Those who adhere to the classical or traditional view of man's nature as essentially unchanging inevitably argue that the contemporary, evolutionary view is destructive of man's moral life and leaves him as a rudderless ship at the mercy of the unpredictable sea of life. The appeal of the traditional position cannot be underestimated. It could not have attracted so many men in the past and continue to attract so many in the present unless it touched deeply certain human needs. Any ethic which fails to recognize those needs and take account of the traditional response is unquestionably shortsighted and superficial. A mystique of the new and of change is nothing more than the other side of the mystique of the old and of permanence.

Nevertheless, no moral philosophy will be adequate which is either inconsistent with or merely superficially consistent with the view of man and the world that has slowly emerged in the last several hundred years. This is not to suggest any simplistic scientism or identification of science and morality. It does, however, call into question any partitioning of territory in which man's moral life can remain fundamentally untouched by revolutions in man's knowledge of himself and the world.

From an historical point of view it was quite understandable that when the more specialized scientific methods could find no room for values, the needs of man's moral life were met by religions or philosophies which held themselves essentially independent of science. However necessary this dualism might have been to avoid a superficial scientism and rationalistic mechanism, it is now clear that a new morality must be forged. It must address itself to the aspects of man and the world which contemporary science has not only discovered but to some extent created.

This monumental task will not be accomplished by one man or even by one generation. But we cannot wait for the emergence of any definitive ethics, for no such ethics is forthcoming. Men are compelled to decide and act here and now, in the midst of complex, confusing, and often apparently contradictory data and principles. Of necessity, any ethics must be somewhat tentative and incomplete, for, as William

James put it, "there can be no final truth in ethics any more than in physics until the last man has had his experience and said his say."[3] For many, this concession would indicate the worthlessness of such an ethic. There are others, however, who are willing to acknowledge that such an approach may not be due simply to the inadequacy of its proponents, but may be rooted in the human situation. While it is commonplace that we live in an age permeated by insecurity, this is not merely an accidental feature of the twentieth century. It would be more accurate to say that we have become more acutely aware than were our ancestors of the human condition.

As much as any thinker, John Dewey has contributed to this awareness, but it does not lead him to despair. His view of the human situation as involving in uneasy tension both the precarious and the stable enabled him to indicate a path between the Scylla of nihilism and the Charybdis of absolutism.[4] Because no one can exist for any length of time in a situation of complete and total peril, the necessity for stability is evident. This is what the traditional view has always sought as a minimum, but it did so by reducing the precarious to the realm of the superficial. The world was divided into the eternal and the temporal, and values were to be found in the eternal world untouched by the contingency of the everyday world. Whatever nostalgia there may be for this world view, and however much indebted we are to it for having served man so long and so well, the harsh truth, as I see it, is that it is no longer a viable view.

The absolute certainty and unfailing security which were the marks of this world are no longer possible human options. In contrast, the contemporary world is characterized by uncertainty and insecurity. The initial recognition of this situation, whether individually or collectively, cannot help but be traumatic. The most dramatic way of expressing this experience at the present time is through the myth or the metaphor of the "Death of God." No reflective man can avoid asking with Dostoevski, "If there is no God, then are all things permitted?" The believer's version of this might be, "If God has given us no absolute values or commands, then are all things permitted?"

---

[3] *The Writings of William James*, ed., intro., annotated bibliography by John J. McDermott (New York: Random House, 1967), p. 611.
[4] This theme permeates most of Dewey's writings but see in particular, *The Quest for Certainty* (New York: Minton, Balch & Company, 1929), pp. 243 ff., and *Experience and Nature* (New York: Dover Publications, 1958), pp. 51 ff.

Ironically, many religiously committed persons are in agreement with the nihilists on the response to this question. Both groups agree that man cannot fully commit himself in the absence of a God who is the guarantor of absolute certitude in the realm of values. There are other religiously committed persons, however, who share the desire with many nontheistic humanists to build a moral life which will give some meaning to human existence in the absence of absolute certitude.

There would seem therefore to be a need for an ethic which is accessible to and helpful to a certain range of contemporary men. This ethic must allow for diversity, even diversity of fundamental beliefs, but must not lead to a destructive division of men into isolated, ghettoized, or antagonistic groups. This ethic must not be simply the lowest common denominator of those values on which most men agree. Rather, it must include the diversities in such a way that men from different cultures and traditions can interact so that the human situation will be continually enriched. Such an ethics would even be capable of involving a plurality of religious perspectives.

This would not be easy either to describe or to achieve. It is possible only on the assumption—and it is a very large assumption—that no ethical truth as such is given or revealed, since all truth, on my hypothesis, results from the reflective experience of the human community. While I do not rule out the possibility that this reflective experience takes place within the presence of another, whom one might call God, this other can never be used as a problem solver who would enable men to escape the continuing painful task of honing his values out of his experience.

Finally, this ethic must be both concrete and universal, as has been the ideal of every ethic. Clearly a concrete ethic which admits of no generalizations and transfer of insight and experience is worthless, for since every situation is radically different from every other one, it would provide no guidance, direction or aid. On the other hand, a universal ethic which divides the ethical situation up into principles which are given once and for all and which are not essentially affected by their incorporation into a concrete situation, inevitably falls into an abstractionism unfaithful to the experiential richness of the ethical situation.

It has been suggested from the outset that every ethic depends implicitly or explicitly upon the way in which man views himself and his world, upon some kind of metaphysical perspective or world view. An effort to achieve a greater consciousness of ourselves and the world is a first step in any ethic. This effort to describe a world view is never easy, for in contrasting the traditional or common sense world view on the one hand, and the contemporary world view on the other, one is not working with hard and fast categories. Nevertheless, though no one philosophy fully fits the view of the traditional or the contemporary, the distinction is not purely arbitrary and distinct worlds do emerge one from the other.[5] The contemporary world view to which I am referring has emerged out of the variety of revolutions—scientific, philosophical, political, artistic and religious—that have taken place over the past four hundred years.

The great difficulty in communicating what is involved in these revolutions is the lag in understanding between the frontier men who are effecting the revolutions and the men who ultimately are to be formed by the results of those revolutions. The fact that it was almost one hundred and fifty years after Copernicus first put forth his hypothesis that his world-view became widely accepted by the greater part of reflective men manifests how difficult it is at any particular moment to understand the new revolutions that are taking place.

This problem is rooted in the fact that the present revolution is so proximate that only a few are aware of what is taking place, and even they see only partially and somewhat confusedly. A book which manifests the resultant problem of communication is *Human Potentialities* by the psychologist, Gardner Murphy,[6] in which a frontier thinker attempts to explain a new revolution. It is akin to the work of Marshall McLuhan, whose questioners inevitably say, "We don't understand you," while he replies, "I know you don't understand me." This is doomed to go back and forth seemingly to no avail because there is as yet no adequate

---

[5] This point has been expressed exceptionally well by Thomas Berry, C.P., in "The Threshold of the Modern World," *Teilhard Conference Proceedings* (New York: Fordham University, 1964), p. 57: "We have acquired radically new ways of seeing the world. We experience a very different world in a thoroughly different manner. Earlier forms of intellectual and cultural life are breaking under the universal pressure resulting from our new ways of knowing. This new knowledge is not derived from the old but emerges from immediate experience of reality such as man has apparently never known before. This time no simple adjustment can be made between the old and the new. Certainly the new cannot be considered as merely an addendum to the old."

[6] Gardner Murphy, *Human Potentialities* (New York: Basic Books, 1958).

language for him to communicate what he sees, or at least thinks he sees[7].

Despite this difficulty of understanding and communication, an effort must be made. Almost thirty years ago, Alfred North Whitehead wrote the following: "When we survey the subsequent course of scientific thought throughout the seventeenth century up to the present day, two curious facts emerge. In the first place, the development of natural science has gradually discarded every single feature of the original common sense notion. . . . There is a second characteristic of subsequent thought which is equally prominent. This common sense notion still reigns supreme in the work-a-day life of mankind."[8]

The "common sense notion" that "still reigns" is the view of the world which serves us from day to day and for the most part, serves us fairly well. It is a world that is thought to be made up at the inorganic level of atomic bits and pieces; structured in itself and independently of man; containing substantial things with their own internal natures or essences; divided into subjects and objects; and, finally, formed by unchanging, universal principles and changing particulars. With numerous changes along the way, this world view was formulated and articulated first by the Greeks, continued through the Middle Ages, and maintained fundamentally into late modern times. Only now is it beginning to be recognized that this is no longer the formative world at work in the frontiers of science and art, and indeed in all spheres of experience.

CONTEMPORARY WORLD VIEW: Process and Relations

It is much more difficult to attempt to describe the contemporary world view inasmuch as this is still in formation. It appears in a variety of thinkers and experiences, but never in any fully explicated form. However, two features stand out: a world in process and a world in relation. Both of these go together and most people have some awareness of both, though neither is easy to grasp.

The first feature is a world in process, rather than merely a world involving process. No one from the earliest Greek to the present has

[7] In one such exchange, McLuhan stated "You're exploring my statements, not the situation. I'm not interested in my statements. I don't agree with them. I merely use them as probes. And if they don't help me get into the situation, I throw them away at once. They're expendable." Cited by Stanley Frank, "Who Said TV Has to Make Sense?" in *TV Guide*, May 13–19, 1967.

[8] Alfred North Whitehead, *Modes of Thought* (New York: Capricorn Books, 1958, f.p. 1938), p. 177.

ever denied that the world is in some sense processive, with some change, growth and development. As expressed by "a world in process" these factors are immensely more radical and pervasive, and would perhaps be best expressed by the word "novelty" or "the new." Man and his world are in the process of becoming a new man, a new world. This claim of the emergence of a new man is more than a rhetorical or metaphorical ploy. Gardner Murphy understands it so seriously that he is led to say, "It seems virtually certain that mankind, having created for itself a new environment and having undergone various transformations in the process, will not recognize itself in the mirror of a few thousand years hence."[9] In a similar vein, the Jesuit paleontologist Teilhard de Chardin has said: "Our modern world was created in less than 10,000 years, and in the past 200 years it has changed more than in all the preceding millennia. Have we ever thought what our planet may be like, psychologically, in a million years time?"[10]

Even more difficult to express in a few words is that second or "relational" feature of contemporary thought. In place of a world of substantial things, constituted essentially in themselves and independent of others, many contemporary thinkers offer a world of "fields" or "constellations of focused relations." There is a variety of expressions of relational theories in the realms of physics, psychology, and sociology in such thinkers as William James, John Dewey, George Herbert Meade, and Alfred North Whitehead, and in such contemporary philosophical movements as phenomenology, existentialism and personalism. Though they are all somewhat unique, they appear to possess a common thrust. Again Whitehead is most perceptive when he points out that the world which emerges from the new physics is one in which "the whole spatial universe is a field of force, or in other words, a field of incessant activity. . . . The notion of self-sufficient isolation is not exemplified in modern physics. . . . There are no essentially self-contained activities within limited regions. . . . Nature is a theatre for the inter-relations of activities."[11]

In the realm of psychology, of course, it was Kurt Lewin who developed a highly complex explanation of man which he described as

---

[9] *Op. cit.*, p. 326.
[10] Teilhard de Chardin, *The Future of Man* (New York: Harper & Row, 1964), p. 71.
[11] *Op. cit.*, pp. 186, 191.

"field theory."[12] Gardner Murphy points out that Lewin and "other creative thinkers in the land of 'field theory' have undertaken to show that the 'life space' of man is a function neither of man's inner existence nor of his environment nor of some bland formula regarding the interaction of the two but of *new creations of possible systems of relationship* between man and environment."[13] There is no simple way of communicating the full import of this development, but it is expressed in part by Murphy when he says, "Nothing springs from *me*, and nothing from my environment, but everything from the inter-action, the 'life space' in which I, as a person, navigate. . . . Both man and his environment need to be seen not as two realities but as two phases of one reality."[14]

Contemporary existentialists and personalists express relational views in a variety of forms. Gabriel Marcel, for example, expressed it most concisely when he said, "to be is to-be-with." The Dutch theologian, Luchesius Smits expresses this relational viewpoint most emphatically when he states: "St. Thomas doesn't approach the problem of man this way. He speaks of the person in himself, or *in se*. Then, afterwards, he speaks of the person's relations to other things. But for us who think existentially, you can't have a person standing alone. For us, the person *is* relation. We no longer say that man is a social being because he needs to be helped. We say he is social because *his essence is being together with* other persons in a world."[15]

It is my contention that this relational structure of man's being is a central presupposition for any ethics of relationships; a world of "Processive relationalism" is presupposed for any such ethics and has important bearing on questions both of values, especially "absolute values," and of conscience.

---

[12] Lewin's work is extremely difficult and technical from the point of view of a layman in psychology. Two collections of his papers give a good indication of what he is about: *A Dynamic Theory of Personality*, trans. by Donald K. Adams and Karl E. Zener (New York, McGraw-Hill, 1935), and *Field Theory in Social Science*, ed. by Dorwin Cartwright (New York: Harper Torchbooks, 1951). For a relatively short and reasonably readable introduction to Lewin's theory, see "Lewin's Field Theory," in Calvin S. Hall and Gardner Lindzey, *Theories of Personality* (New York: John Wiley & Sons, 1957), pp. 206–56.

[13] *Op. cit.*, p. 21.

[14] *Ibid.*, pp. 303, 307.

[15] Quoted in the *National Catholic Reporter*, April 13, 1966, p. 2.

PROCESSIVE RELATIONISM AND VALUES

Men are tempted to resolve ethical questions in the abstract or in terms of absolutes by the complexity of the concrete situation. Since it is not possible to consider all the factors involved in any situation, it is felt that the only way to avoid a destructive relativism and scepticism is to isolate some general laws or values which remain basically untouched by the context in which they enter. Is it possible to acknowledge both general laws and values, without either being affirmed as absolutes? An ethics of relationships such as that which I am suggesting implies that this is possible.

Values can be affirmed as relatively permanent on the basis of the quality of life which their pursuit brings forth. I would suggest that only some form of the pragmatic method is adequate for revealing those values which endure. Since only consequences can ultimately reveal the quality of life implicit in an action or a decision, such a method would have to be quite refined and involve acute attention to the cumulative experience not only of one's individual self but of mankind in general.[16]

This suggestion is hardly considered to resolve simply one of the most vexing questions that concern reflective men. Undoubtedly, many

---

[16] In "Religious Truth," *op. cit.*, pp. 305–306, I have indicated something of what a "pragmatic ethic" would involve. "The controlling principle, of course, is that there is no necessity for going beyond human experience in order to ground values. Though it is not usually expressed as such, I would maintain that there is a necessary phenomenological dimension to any pragmatic ethic. The primary or ultimate value of life, for example, is grasped immediately and irreducibly in that it is not justified in terms of some more basic or ultimate value. It must be stressed, however, that the 'life' which is the determining value for pragmatism is not some external or 'transcendent' norm; it is the existential life of the human community. *Within* this community it is possible to judge by comparison that one mode of life is better (more valuable) than another. Just as one line can be judged longer than another, though there exists no longest line, so one state can be judged better than another, though there exists no best state. 'Quality of life,' therefore, is not an abstract norm, gratuitously assumed; it is present at every moment of a community's existence. The quality of life which characterizes any community is the 'consequence' of a variety of factors. I will mention but three crucial ones and briefly indicate the basis for judging the 'quality of life' which ensues. First, an economic system which results in people being fed, housed and clothed is better than one which does not. Second, an educational system which results in people being able to understand science, appreciate art, literature and the like is better than one which closes people off from these goods. Finally, a religion which heightens man's sense of reverence for life and stimulates him to develop the resources of the world and to serve his fellow man is better than one which leads to exclusiveness and destruction."

values or principles present themselves with such force and clarity that they appear to be irreducible, sought for their own sake, or as they are usually described, absolute. Nevertheless, the present hypothesis suggests that values came into existence as the result of long community experience, and that their salutary consequences for the good of the individual and the community has burned them into the collective conscience. Though such a grand hypothesis is not easy to verify, it not only takes cognizance of the universality and permanence which undoubtedly are aspects of the ethical life, but is faithful to the processive and relational features of the human situation. By asserting this organic continuity of man and his moral life, this hypothesis is able to allow for the possibility of an emergence of values which signify an irreversible thrust to human life. Such values might become so embedded in the human community—not merely a stem of the community—that they will last as long as man.

John Dewey, himself a relativist of sorts, nevertheless stated that the "fundamental conceptions of morals are, therefore, neither arbitrary nor artificial. They are not imposed upon human nature from without but developed out of its own operations and needs. Particular aspects of morals are transient; they are often, in their actual manifestation, defective and perverted. But the framework of moral conceptions is as permanent as human life itself."[17]

While values can acquire a kind of permanence and universality, one cannot have absolute certainty about such values in the sense that they have a privileged position of being beyond review and criticism. No values are protected from critical scrutiny and reinterpretation on the basis of developing thought and experience. All values must continually be capable of being not merely asserted, but justified in the human community. If some values can now be called universal and permanent, it should be possible to show here and now why they are so.

It should be stressed, however, that it can still be maintained there are certain values after which man should fashion himself. Concerning these, one must have the courage of his beliefs and be willing to dedicate his life to the realization of such values even in the absence of any absolute certainty.[18]

---

[17] John Dewey, *Theory of The Moral Life* (New York: Holt, Rinehart and Winston, 1960, f.p. 1908), p. 176.

[18] Henry Margenau, *Ethics and Science* (New York: D. Van Nostrand Co., 1964), pp. 147–48, calls attention to an instructive irony when he states: "The reverential

PROCESSIVE RELATIONISM AND CONSCIENCE

Conscience is a reality that does not admit of strict definition. For present purposes, it can be understood as the human self directing its own activity in that dimension of life designated as moral. There is, of course, no conscience in a vacuum, no isolated individual conscience. The self, including the ethical self, is constituted by a variety of relationships. It is only within this constantly, often imperceptibly but at times radically shifting set of relationships that there gradually emerges what is called the individual person. Hence, freedom of conscience cannot be discussed apart from the culture and society in which the person exists.

The earliest and the most fundamental formation of conscience is nonreflective. It is a formation that comes about through cultural, familial, religious and numerous other individual and communal relationships. The distinguished philosopher of science, Henri Margenau, has said that conscience "is the instinctive residue in man's mind of the results of the ethical experimentation of the race through history."[19]

We must distinguish therefore that aspect of conscience which is inherited or received, and which is here called nonreflective, from that which results from conscious reflective activity. The first task in forming one's conscience is to be aware of the parental, cultural, religious, and other factors by which one has been fashioned. Secondly, one must attempt the lifelong process of evaluating these factors. The fact that one has originally accepted values or goals or articles of faith unreflectively is not in itself destructive, but to the extent that one achieves a certain level of reflection he must evaluate and eventually affirm, reject or modify these values.

Man is not a being constituted in himself who then enters into relationships; instead, he is a processive relational being in a processive relational world. This notion of a processive relationism has not been fully developed and it is confronted by formidable problems of which the most important is perhaps that of personal self-identity. Further, it is not being suggested that an ethics developed within the categories

moralist refuses to accept principles unless they are indubitable, sacrosanct, and eternal. . . . The effectiveness of ethics seems to depend upon the existence of absolute and universal truths. Consider against such attitudes the patent fact that science, odious as it may be to many, has flourished immensely under the regime of tentative postulates."

[19] *Ibid.*, p. 260.

of processive relationism will definitely resolve vexing ethical problems; in fact, a controlling presupposition here is that there are no absolutely definitive resolutions for live problems. It is suggested, however, that an ethics of relationships may enable one to deal more fruitfully with these questions, if only by leading to their recasting in such a way that certain dead-end resolutions are avoided.

Consider, for example, the classical controversy concerning the rights of the individual versus the rights of the community. As long as one continues to think in terms of individual men fully structured in themselves who then enter into relationships with other men in order to form a community, there will be a tendency to resolve this question either in the direction of a destructive individualism or a destructive collectivism. When, however, it is recognized that the human person is essentially communal, that in a sense the person is the individualized focus or expression of the community, that paradoxically one can achieve individuality only by greater participation in community, then it becomes apparent that any either/or resolution is unacceptable, and that the perspective of both the individual and the community is transformed. On the one hand, the individual person becomes obligated to determine whether or not his actions respect his varied relationships and are thereby in keeping with the deepest ideals of the community or communities by which he is continually being formed. On the other hand, the community must ever be on guard against betraying itself in the direction of a choking uniformity through a failure to recognize its most insightful and farseeing representatives.

The role of the prophet seems to illustrate this, for the prophet is not an egotistical rugged individualist who places himself in neurotic opposition to the community. Rather he is the one who at a particular moment in history is the best expression of the community inasmuch as he illuminates the community's self-betrayal and urges it to be faithful to those ideals which give to it its identity.

The premise that man is constituted by his relationships to the world, to his family, to his culture, to his fellow man, to his church, to his synagogue or to God has a crucial bearing on the human decision making process. It quite obviously suggests that in decision making one must be as faithful as possible to the totality of the person and must avoid centering on one aspect of the person in isolation from other aspects. Since not all the relationships which constitute the totality of the life of a person are equally important in determining the morality of a particular act, the crux of the decision making process which characterizes the human person is the weighing and evaluation of the diversity of relationships, their claims and values. This is not an easy process, either to describe or to perform, though it is easily caricatured as an excuse for following one's whims.

In conclusion, it must be emphasized that the complexity and multifactored characteristics of the moral situation do not excuse one from taking a stand; despite the fact that one can have no absolute certainty, one must reflect, decide, and act. In so doing, even the most exhaustive listing of relevant relationships and factors will not in itself result in an ethical decision. There is no substitute for that personal response which must always be permeated by a kind of faith and tinged with a certain tentativeness.[20] For this reason the approach suggested will inevitably appear to many to be tepid and hesitant.

Unfortunately, at this moment in man's development most men seem capable of being ethically involved only by isolating one or a few factors in a situation, and giving them an aura of certainty which demands absolute and unyielding commitment. Mankind is better served by reflective men who attend to as many relationships and factors in a situation as they possibly can, who evaluate their relative weight and importance as best they can, who have the courage to decide and act while remaining open to the discovery of new factors, and who at all times are willing to review their judgments and commitments in the light of ongoing experience.

[20] The irreducibility of the free individual decision is, of course, a central tenet of various existentialisms. The ethic I am proposing would be, in this regard at least, existential. It differs from "existentialism," however, in its metaphysics, in the fundamental way in which it views the world. "The world that is disclosed in experience," according to my perspective, "is neither the eternally ordered world of Greek thought nor the absurd and fundamentally chaotic world which undergirds certain forms of existentialism. The world in which we live is responsive to our need for order. It does not meet this need, however, by presenting us with order final and complete but by confronting us with the possibility of achieving order through our activities, intellectual and other." "Religious Truth," *op. cit.*, p. 289.

Introduction to Charles DeKoninck

In the following article, the late Professor Charles DeKoninck answers the charge that according to Thomistic natural law ethics, practical moral judgment consists simply in the application of general moral standards to particular situations. The alleged fault is a devastating one, he holds, but one of which authentic Thomism is not guilty. Such an interpretation is a misinterpretation for it neglects two crucial aspects of the Thomistic position, the role of prudence and the role of right appetite.

How does one bridge the gap between rules or precepts and the particular situation in which action is called for? For the Thomist the answer is: Prudence. This is a kind of practical wisdom which directs the choice of means to ends, and is necessary in order to bring moral precepts to bear on the particular case; for no rule can be found or formulated which adequately determines the right thing to do in the irreducibly particular situation in which moral decision is called for. One cannot invent a non-tautological moral rule, no matter how nuanced, which has no exceptions; but since rules, general and particular, are certainly relevant to moral decision and action, the appropriate rule or rules to be applied must be chosen, a function performed ideally with the aid of the intellectual virtue of prudence or practical wisdom.

Now it might appear that morality is wholly a matter of reason. After all, prudence which directs us in the choice of the best means to the right ends, is an intellectual virtue; one can be taught both general and particular rules, and taught how to evaluate the particular situation in which action is called for. So perhaps the moral man is simply the knowledgable man, the man possessed of a certain sort of "smartness". But this is not the Thomistic position. In point of fact, prudence and its subordinates—principles, precepts, and detailed knowledge of the situation—are impossible or of no avail unless one has a "rectified appetite," unless, that is, one is virtuous and is thereby inclined to the right ends. Prudence is sufficient for right action, but a necessary condition of prudence is a right or virtuous appetite. Not only will the man whose appetites are bad or distorted generally be unable to choose the right means, he will be unable to see what the right means is, for he will want the wrong end. In sum, unless one is inclined by virtue to the right end, it is impossible that one choose prudently, choose, that is to say, the best means *to the right end.*

General Standards and Particular Situations in Relation to the Natural Law*
by Charles DeKoninck

Speaking of Orthodox Catholicism's concept of the natural law, Reinhold Niebuhr, in his Gifford Lectures, makes the following reservation: "The difficulty with this impressive structure of Catholic ethics, finally elaborated into a detailed casuistic application of general moral standards to every conceivable particular situation, is that it constantly insinuates religious absolutes into highly contingent and historical moral judgments."[1] And so he speaks of "the mistake of Catholic moral casuistry to derive relative moral judgments too simply from the presuppositions of its natural law . . ." Perhaps we should add that the same author considers "Thomistic ethics" as an instance of this rationalism.[2]

Yet I believe every disciple of St. Thomas would, no less than Reinhold Niebuhr, condemn any moral doctrine which would have that note. No practical judgment could be true if it were simply the result of an "application of general moral standards" to a particular situation. Moral standards are not universal in representation, and in the field of action there is no such thing as "every conceivable particular situation." No amount of casuistic "if's" could meet and be adequate to the contingent circumstances of conduct. There can be no universal file of proximate norms for behaviour. The proper precepts of individual actions are to be found in the particular precepts of prudence—not in the law, which, natural or human, retains a certain degree of

---

* First published in *The Proceedings of the American Catholic Philosophical Association, XXIV* (1950).
[1] *The Nature and Destiny of Man* (New York: 1949), p. 220–21.
[2] *Ibid.*, 221.

generality. No law can be the particular premise of an operative syllogism in which one infers what is to be done *here* and *now*. The outcome of reasoning from law alone could be no more than a general conclusion pertaining to practical science. If, on the other hand, the particular premise of a syllogism were no more than the statement of a fact that is speculatively true, the syllogism would not be what we call operative; and if it alone were taken as a sufficient basis for action, this action would be practically false.

An instance of such a type of reasoning was pointed out recently by Gabriel Marcel in his *Preface* to Gheorghiu's novel entitled *La vingt-cinquième heure*. Although the general premise is taken from positive law, the result would be the same if the law were a natural one:

The writer Traian Koruga and his wife Nora, though they were always sympathetic to the cause of the Allies, the more so as she was a Jewess and barely managed to escape from persecution, have travelled, at the time of the German collapse of '45, hundreds of kilometers on foot in order to reach the American zone, of which they fondly dream as a haven of refuge. At last, they find themselves in Weimar. But it is certainly not the spirit of Goethe which inspires the American governor of that city. He cares little about what Traian and his wife are or think. What matters is only this: they are bearers of a Roumanian passport; Roumania is officially considered by the United States as an enemy Power; *ergo* Traian and his wife must be treated as enemy subjects, and put in prison. It is most remarkable, let it be noted in passing, how easily the method of syllogistic reasoning—in which, until a comparatively recent date, so many short-sighted thinkers imagined to hold *the* very instrument of Reason—comes to subserve whatever aberrations of Reason. It is really a machine, with which (as with all other machines, for that matter) one may do what one likes. True thought is something entirely different.

Why is the conclusion, in this particular instance, a practical error? Not because it is reached by "syllogistic reasoning", but because the official in question " cares little what Traian and his wife are or think." Insofar as such a disposition is the reason why he infers that " Traian and his wife must be treated as enemy subjects, and put into prison," the conclusion is practically false—and his reasoning is a good example of a bad operative syllogism. For practical truth does not consist in the mind's conformity to what is, but in its conformity with the rectified appetite.[3] Let us note, then, that even if the official were well-informed and knew who those two people are and what they think, he could still draw a false conclusion as to what is to be done, so long as he " cares little".

Practical reasoning is not a matter of reason alone, not even of the kind of practical knowledge which is confined to reason. "Prudence is not in reason alone, but has something of the *appetite* about it. . . . For insofar as ethics, economics, and politics are in reason alone, they are called practical sciences".[4] And so we may well agree with Gabriel Marcel in condemning the kind of syllogistic reasoning he illustrates by the example we have seen. No amount of such reasoning could ever reach a practical truth. And this is the same as to say that practical reasoning, in matters of conduct, cannot consist in the simple application of a general rule to a particular so-called objective case. With Reinhold Niebuhr we must admit that a doctrine which propounds such a method as a guarantee of practical truth in action is wholly inacceptable. We share Niebuhr's views for reasons we may quote from St. Thomas, with whom the Church has found no fault on this score.

We, too, have "too strong a sense of the individual occasion, and the uniqueness of the individual who faces the occasion, to trust in general rules." [5] We must do and pursue the good, and avoid evil. This is the most general of natural laws. Yet, with this generality alone we can meet no particular situation whatsoever. To know what to do in a given instance, we must not only have some knowledge of the particular situation, but also of more particular rules. From this we may feel tempted to infer that, at the limit, the particular rules would embrace, in advance, every conceivable particular situation. Yet, St. Thomas holds just the reverse, and in doing so, he condemns that very casuistry which Reinhold Niebuhr believes to be ours. "Thus," St. Thomas says, "it is right and true for all to act according to reason, and from this principle it follows, as ('quasi') a proper conclusion, that goods entrusted to another should be restored to their owner. Now this is true for the majority of cases. But it may happen in a particular case

---

[3] " . . . Bonum practici intellectus non est veritas absoluta, sed veritas 'confesse se habens,' idest concorditer ad appetitum rectum." St. Thomas, *In VI Ethicorum*, lect. 2 (ed. Pirotta), nn. 1130–1301; *Summa theologiae* IaIIae, q. 57, a.5, ad 3.

[4] St. Thomas, In VI Ethicorum, lect. 7 (ed. Pirotta), n. 1200. *Cajetan, Comm. in Summa Theologiae* Iam IIae, qq. 57–58.

[5] R. Niebuhr, *op. cit.*, 60.

that it would be injurious, and therefore unreasonable, to restore goods held in trust; for instance, if they are claimed for the purpose of fighting against one's country. And this principle will be found to fail the more, according as we descend further toward the particular, e.g., if one were to say that goods held in trust should be restored with such and such a guarantee, or in such and such a way; because the greater the number of conditions added, the greater the number of ways in which the principle may fail, so that it be not right to restore or not to restore." [6]

In other words, the application of increasingly proper rules, far from becoming automatic, requires greater circumspection. This is true of natural law, but it is no less true of human law. The multiplication and refinement of particular rules provides no excuse for neglecting the irreducible peculiarity of the individual case; on the contrary, they should help to appreciate that peculiarity which no just law was ever meant to overlook. The application of any law must always be an act of prudence, which is "circa singularia contingentia", and whose judgment depends upon the condition of the appetite. No law could possibly render irrelevant either the knowledge of this contingency or the disposition of the appetite. To overlook these two factors would spell intolerable tyranny. Reality, in this order, is never simply rational.

Reinhold Niebuhr said that the "difficulty with this impressive structure of Catholic ethics, finally elaborated into a detailed casuistic application of general moral standards to every conceivable particular situation, is that it constantly insinuates religious absolutes into highly contingent and historical moral judgments. Thus the whole imposing structure of Thomistic ethics is, in one of its aspects, no more than a religious sanctification of the relativities of the feudal social system as it flowered in the thirteenth century." We presume that the author of these lines does not take the term "ethics" in the usual sense, since the precepts which correspond to the relativities of the feudal social system are not held to be natural law: they are viewed as judicial precepts established by men. But such laws are variable, as St. Thomas points out in the following passage: "The judicial precepts established by men retain their binding force forever, so long as the state of government remains the same. But if the state or nation pass to another form of

---

[6] *Summa theologia*, Ia IIae, q. 94, a. 4, c. (Transl. from *Basic Works*, A. Pegis, Random House, New York: 1945).

government, the laws must needs be changed. For democracy, which is government by the people, demands different laws from those of obligarchy, which is the government by the rich, as the Philosopher shows. Consequently, when the state of that people changed, the judicial precepts had to be changed also."[7]

In the sentence immediately following the one we have just quoted, Reinhold Niebuhr says: "The confusion between ultimate religious perspectives and relative historical ones in Catholic thought accounts for the fury and self-righteousness into which Catholicism is betrayed when it defends feudal types of civilization in contemporary history as in Spain for instance."[8] We are not concerned here with the truth or error of this statement. It is relevant to our discussion only insofar as it reflects a judgment on doctrine. Supposing that the attitude of the Church toward a particular form of government, at a given place and time, is really such as the author describes, could it not be precisely by virtue of its solicitude to take into account, even in the fact of widespread criticism, the contingent circumstances which our sometimes oversimplified generalities about "contemporary history" tend to overlook and which we are apt to convert into general standards for every situation regardless of its peculiarity?*

[7] *Ibid.*, q. 104, a. e., ad 2.
[8] *Op. cit.*, p. 221.
* Cf. "The Moral Responsibilities of the Scientist", *Laval Theologique et Philosophique*, VI (1950), pp. 352–56; and for a contrast between Thomistic and existentialist ethics, see DeKoninck's "The Nature of Man and his Historical Being", *loc. cit.*, V, pp. 271–77.

Introduction to Charles Fried

In the article from which the following selection is taken, Professor Charles Fried argues that natural law theory (i.e. it is possible rationally to discover and determine the proper ends for men) entails the concept of justice (i.e. all human persons have an equal right to equal liberty in the pursuit of their interests.) In the course of prosecuting this argument, he sketches a version of natural law morality which proves to be of interest here.

The problem for a natural law ethics is to show convincingly how human nature can be taken as normative, for everything human beings do can in some sense be referred to as "natural." How then, on what grounds, can we pick out a subset of these natural human actions and legitimately refer to these as in accord with natural law, as moral, as acts that ought to be done?

According to Fried it is possible to come to know a thing's nature by coming to know its way of acting; and if one compares a certain thing's way of acting with other things' ways of acting, one can come to know that thing's characteristic way of acting. Man himself can first be characterized as a being that knows natures, his own and others', those that can be sensed and those that cannot. Secondly, man can act freely, is capable of grounding his action in a knowledge (a) of the situation, (b) of his own nature, and (c) of conclusions about appropriate responses of nature to situation. Characteristically human acts are free acts; and free acts are rational acts, acts for which it is possible to find good reasons; and good reasons are reasons sufficient and appropriate to move that agent and any other agent to the same action.

Not only means but even ends can be chosen by human beings for themselves. Evaluation of ends depends on evaluation of natures, which in its turn depends on understanding of characteristic acts, acts

221

which best express that nature. "Morality" systematizes right deliberation about human acts, and identifies the subset of acts that ought to be done as those which most fully express human nature; as most fully expressive, these are most natural.

This understanding of natural law differs radically from those versions which rest on divine authority for specification of the content of morality. And it differs radically, too, from modern relativistic views which rest on the will of the individual; for it is a view which says that if one looks, one will find not a variety of standards or ideals among which one must perforce freely choose, but a single rationally ascertainable standard for action.

Natural Law*
By Charles Fried

The term "natural law"[1] is misleading in its implication that the average, the usual, that which normally happens constitute the standard for moral evaluation. The term depends rather on the theory—we might now call it a metaphysical theory—that every entity exhibits a rationally ascertainable nature, by virtue of which it is, and therefore can be known as, the very entity which it is and not something else or nothing at all. And, for reasons which shall be indicated, it is this nature which is normative for that entity. To grasp this it is necessary to accept the premise that to exist at all is to act. Every existing entity has a definite potential for self-assertion, for interaction with the rest of the universe of entities. It is this self-assertion and this interaction

* From "Natural Law and the Concept of Justice", *Ethics*, LXXIV, Number 4 July, 1964, by permission of The University of Chicago Press.

[1] The account which follows is a composite of several philosophical systems. It seems to me that it is compatible with the system of Aristotle, Aquinas, and perhaps even that of Hegel. . . . The many, often fundamental points on which these systems differ seem to me to allow, nonetheless, so much common ground as I have provided here. In my account the crucial notion of a hierarchy of being is developed in terms of the degree of inclusivity of involvement with the rest of the universe. This may be close to the Aristotelian doctrine and also parallels the Hegelian account of the progressive stages of self-awareness of Spirit (see generally, J. Plamenatz, *Man and Society*, II (1963), 129–268; and F. Grégoire, *Études Hégéliennes* (Louvain, 1958)). The Thomistic system is not incompatible with my account either. It differs from the Aristotelian system by its affirmation of a God who created all other entities *ex nihilo*. In metaphysics this is a crucial difference, but for my purposes it leads— within the confines of natural theology—to the same view of human nature and morality as seems to have been put forth by Aristotle. In each case it is the capacity of human persons to comprehend the principle of the system of the universe which defines their nature and gives them this special status. For Aquinas that principle is God; for Hegel it is Absolute Spirit as manifested and realized in the very act of comprehension.

which is the act of the entity, and it is the sort of this self-assertion, the form the self-assertion takes and can take, which is the nature of that entity. Act is everything, for in the fullest sense an entity's act is its existence; and an entity which performed no act at all would not exist at all. There is here, of course, an extension, almost by way of a metaphor, of our ordinary concept of an act. But the metaphor is intended, for what is meant is that even a stone acts to the extent that it exerts the pressure of its characteristic weight, displaces air of its particular mass, reflects light of certain frequencies, etc.[2] (Perhaps in terms of atomic theory the notion that even an object like a stone "acts" insofar as and in the way that it "is" anything at all is not so difficult to accept after all.)

Entities exist by virtue of their acts and these acts and their entities are intelligible because they take a form, which is the entity's nature. When we recognize an entity we recognize its activity. We comprehend its identity, we comprehend that it is what it is by virtue of the form—the pattern, as it were—that activity takes. This (metaphysical) account of the universe of entities and our comprehension of it may not after all be impossible to appreciate. What is much more difficult is the further notion—crucial to the natural law philosophy—of a hierarchy of natures, of degrees of being or of intensity of action. This hierarchy has usually begun at inanimate entities, going on to plant life, animals, and to humans. Is this a plausible conception?

The first step depends on some such argument as this: A vegetable entity in its act, in its intelligible assertion of itself, goes beyond inanimate matter in that it maintains itself in existence by drawing new entities to itself (vegetation) and that its act, its self-assertion, also includes reproducing itself. Thus it is the nature of this lowest of living entities to assert itself by maintaining itself in existence and to assert itself by bringing forth new entities like itself. Its act is an act of self-maintenance and of active self-preservation through time and in new entities.

It is the yet more active response of animal life to its environment which sets it off as a more intense and inclusive form of being. The animal performs both acts which have been ascribed to plant life but

[2] Those readers who are not persuaded that the metaphor is apt and in any case are uncomfortable about this Thomistic use of the term "act" might prefer to read for the verb "to act," "engage in activity" throughout. I find the latter term awkward and prefer the shorter one.

adds to them a new capacity, the perception of other entities and the response, in aid of its acts of self-preservation and self-extension through reproduction, to this perception which reveals a limited but true appreciation of those entities. Certain plants may grow toward the sunlight but their perception of the sun is less comprehending of the nature of the sun than is the perception of one animal, for example, of another animal which it stalks and kills as prey. The judgment that we have a more intense mode of action here does not depend on greater efficiency in self-preservation or reproduction, but rather on the more inclusive nature of the activity vis-à-vis the totality of existence. The nature of a stone in relation to other entities is fully asserted by merely excluding other things from being where it is. A plant's mode of activity is more expansive in that it thrusts itself onto other entities and thrusts its reproduced forms forward. While an animal does all these things, it does so by taking into account in its perceptions a part of the nature of other entities, and thus its own life or activity includes after a fashion the activity of other entities. An animal may see the moon and thus its sphere of reference and of activity—for seeing is an activity—can embrace even so remote an entity as that. An animal is a higher existent because in its activity-existence it more fully includes the rest of existence. And it is this sentient response which partly defines animal nature.

Natural law is a philosophy of human morality in this sense of nature, and human nature depends on the kinds of acts which humans can perform and which sets them aside as the kind of entities they are. Most important of such acts is knowing. In knowing, the human person is able to apprehend the nature of the object and not only manifestations of that nature, as does the animal in its merely sensuous apprehension. Further, a human person can, in knowledge, abstract from his sensuous perception to the understanding that all entities in the universe must exemplify some form of intelligibly structured act, and thus the human person can apprehend to a degree even entities of which he has no sensuous perception.[3] For this reason the human act of knowing involves a higher degree of activity: It is both a more thorough taking

[3] In accordance with the generality I attempt to maintain in this account, see n. 1., this proposition can apply to the apprehension both of sensible entities not yet apprehended—e.g., at some past time the planet Pluto or now the craters on the far side of the moon—and of entities of which we can in principle have no direct, sensible apprehension—e.g., Aquinas' doctrine of angels.

to itself of outside entities—the act of knowing exposing the principle by which an entity is what it is—and also a more inclusive act than animal perception, allowing as it does some apprehension of the whole universe of entities whether sensuously perceived or not and of the principle by which these enties are differentiated.

Finally, the act of knowing permits the knowing entity a kind of perception of itself, which an animal, deprived of human powers, presumably cannot share: The knowing subject can comprehend itself as an object of knowledge not in principle different from other objects of knowledge.

There is another aspect of human acts which defines human nature: Only of human acts can it be said that they are free. This freedom is closely related to the capacity for knowledge. (Let us call this capacity for knowledge "rationality.") Freedom is the capacity of human persons to ground their action in their understanding of the situation in which they are, their appreciation of their own nature as a nature among other natures, and their conclusions about the appropriate response of such nature to its situation. Hume has said that reason is the slave of the passions, whereas by contrast the freedom referred to here may be thought of as depending on the capacity of reason not only to propose appropriate means to ends, which are posited and unexaminable, but to propose ends for human action.

I have deliberately used the term "ground their action" to denote the relation between free human acts and their basis in rationality, since it would be misleading to assert that the full rational comprehension and the act appropriate to that comprehension, to which it leads, are linked by a relation of causation. It is not at all misleading to say for instance that sunlight is a cause of a plant's growing in a certain direction or that hunger is the cause of an animal's behavior in some circumstances. The relation between the understanding of what reason requires and the consequent action in a free human act appears to be different, and yet it explains that act as fully as do the relevant causes of animal behavior. The relationship is more like that between the separate steps of understanding in a logical demonstration than the physiological necessity we would ascribe to animal behavior. Perhap this relationship can best be expressed by saying that only free agents have reasons for their acts, while the acts of unfree agents have not reasons but only causes. And perhaps the point of the distinction can be sensed in this: A free agent's action is felt to be fully accounted for when that agent gives—or could give—reasons for that action which another human agent would—or could—acknowledge as being sufficient and appropriate [4] to move him to the same action.

The freedom of a human agent consists, then, in this: that he can propose to himself not only the means to his ends but his ends themselves by coming to understand his nature as an entity among entities and coming to understand what acts are most expressive of that nature. It is this freedom and rationality of human agents which alone make morality possible. Only free and rational agents can deliberate about their acts to any effect, and morality is that branch of knowledge which systematizes right deliberation about human acts. It is the possibility of choice that makes morality possible. Unfree natures must be what they are, must act according to their natures. Free agents *ought* so to act, in the sense that if they do not they are less than what they could be, and only by doing what they ought are they all they can be; it might be said that only by doing what they ought can they be what they are. This is why voluntarist theories of natural law, which treat the natural law as simply a positive divine command, are out of harmony with the main tradition of natural law, since natural law is in no sense external to the agent but in fact is the very definition of what he is. Similarly the natural law view differs from prevalent modern views of morality which, while ascribing to reason an important role in morality, found themselves again in voluntarism, not this time the voluntarism of the arbitrary and positive divine will but of the positive will of each individual. Thus R. M. Hare in his recent excellent book *Freedom and Reason* argues (1) that moral judgments are like objective judgments about reality in that they must be fully generalizable, that is, applicable to all relevantly similar cases, but (2) that no conclusive arguments are available to choose between or even rule out any "ideal" (to use Hare's term), which a person may have and which he is prepared to apply in all cases, even where he himself will suffer. (An example Hare uses is the person whose ideal it is that all Jews be exterminated and who sincerely is prepared to hold to the ideal even should it turn out that he himself is a Jew.)

---

[4] Appropriate, because a sympathetic man may well concede that the temptation which another suffered and which led that other to err is a temptation to which he too might have yielded. But still he could wish that he would not, if tempted, yield. It is quite a different matter to wish that one would not, if shot through the heart, die.

Human nature, on this view, is a rationally ascertainable standard for action. It is also a concept which depends upon a philosophy which holds that there are degrees of being, corresponding to the levels of comprehensiveness with which an entity may interact with the rest of the universe.

C. Old or New Morality? Kolnai vs. Fletcher

Aurel Kolnai

> Professor Aurel Kolnai teaches philosophy at Bedford College of the University of London and has written extensively in the fields of ethical theory and social philosophy.

Joseph Fletcher

> Dr. Joseph Fletcher is a professor at the Episcopal Theological School in Cambridge, Mass. He is the author of *Morals and Medicine* (1954), *Situation Ethics* (1966) and *Moral Responsiblity* (1967).

Introduction to Aurel Kolnai

One may find in Professor Kolnai's article three sorts of things: careful, brief analyses of a number of important moral issues and movements; a critique of situationism; and a defense of intrinsicalism.

Among the important analyses found here, three might be mentioned. The first is that of the concept of *legalism*, developed by a discussion of its various meanings, of the relations between moral law and civil positive law and of the sense in which the "legalist" can properly be said to be emphasizing law at the expense of situation. Another useful analysis is that of Aristotelian-Thomist *Prudentialism*, its relative strengths and weaknesses vis-à-vis utilitarianism and situationism. A third discussion analyzes ends and means in the light of the question: does the end justify the means, and if so how, and if not why not?

Kolnai's critique of situationism and defense of intrinsicalism are closely tied together, as the full title of his article indicates. He indicts situationism as a form of extrinsicalism, and extrinsicalism, Kolnai argues, ought to be rejected in favor of intrinsicalism; there are other grounds for rejecting situationism, its being infected by the errors of existentialism, for example, but the intrinsicalism vs. extrinsicalism issue is central. In part the issue seems to be over the proper way to look at kinds of action. Does it, or does it not, make sense to think of some kinds of action as intrinsically good and others as intrinsically bad? Is it useful to think this way? Is it necessary to think this way if one is to capture the *moral* quality of actions? For Kolnai some descriptive qualities of an action are intrinsically good; but none is sufficient of itself to override all else, circumstance and consequence, and fully determine the rightness or wrongness of an individual act. Thus for example, though promising is neither good nor bad intrinsically, promise-keeping is intrinsically right, and it is always right to keep one's promise unless it clashes with another promise, or the circumstances have changed, etc. For the intrinsicalist the morality of an individual act depends on many things, but one of these is the kind of action it is. For the extrinsicalist, all the moral qualities of an act come from the outside, as it were, and there is nothing within the act to which he is sensitive; he is concerned with the action only as a vehicle for the expression of agapé or concern for human welfare or the like.

It might be useful, in reading the article which follows, to focus one's attention by keeping in mind these questions: (1) who offers the better account of moral experience, the intrinsicalist or the situationist? (2) do the theoretical differences between the two entail or imply any practical moral differences about what is right or wrong to do?

A Defense of Intrinsicalism against "Situation Ethics"
Aurel Kolnai

1. THE THESIS TO BE ARGUED IN THIS PAPER

Situationism or Situation Ethics, a current of ethical thought that has mainly emerged in a Christian—both Catholic and Protestant—context, is opposed, on the face of it, primarily to "Legalism" and may so far be represented as a move towards, or a position approaching, or again a moderate form of, "Antinomianism". It may be defined as equating morally right action to "doing what is best in the particular situation in which the action is taking place" or "giving the proper answer to the moral problem inherent in a situation with its peculiar circumstances" in contrast with "duty-fulfilment" or "action in conformity to a moral law". This antithetic schema in itself raises, of course, a host of conceptual problems with some of which we shall have to deal. In spite, however, of the situationist aversion to "Law" and distaste for "Duty", the antithesis is *not* identical with the classic controversy between the (broadly speaking) Aristotelian moral philosophers of "Virtue" and the (broadly speaking) Kantian formalists—the former defining the "good man" in terms of "having the right wishing in the various morally relevant respects" and the latter, in terms of "acting from duty-consciousness regardless of his wishes". In a sense, Situationism is actually not greatly interested in the build-up of a "virtuous personality" (a theme, anyhow, more closely concerning Moral Education than Ethics proper), and again, what it opposes is not so much the claim of Duty as the objective meaning and validity of "*duties*". Although, for essential reasons, Situationism often *looks* like a *laxist* as opposed to a rigorist moral attitude, its emphasis is not on a negation of moral Right and Wrong

232

or a (relative) depreciation of what is morally right in favor, say, of what the agent likes or wants; rather, its central point lies in its rejection or at any rate devaluation of any detailed moral *code* or codes, not only in the sense of a "table of laws" (or "commandments") but also in the sense of a table of particularized moral *standards* or values or points of view. While inveighing against "Legalism" and inevitably hostile to rigoristic insistence on certain moral taboos, the Situationists see an unbridgeable gulf set between their principle and that of *Intrinsicalism*, i.e. the attribution to such specified moral values as, say, truthfulness or promise-keeping, or again monogamy, of an intrinsic and unbarterable meaning and validity of their own. Situationists, then, operate with the concept of a *unique*—a supreme, all-embracing and uniformly decisive—moral *criterion* which also embodies an unconditional *demand*, and to which all other, specified or particularized, moral aspects or motifs or "duties" are not merely subordinate but simply instrumental, of which they are mere applications proper to some situations but unsuited to others (being, in this second case, expendable without further ado). Whereas a non-rigoristic Intrinsicalist would recognize that moral laws, to say nothing of moral desirabilities, may in some situations come to be mutually incompatible *in concreto* (e.g. I cannot fulfil two contradictory promises I have carelessly or indeed frivolously made; by truthfully answering or even trying to evade a question I may deliver an innocent person into the hands of his malignant enemies) and that in such cases it must be "decided" which is the "lesser evil" and *that* must be chosen, a Situationist would deny that in such a case value stands against value or evil against evil and would speak, not of doing right by breaking a less urgent obligation or of choosing the lesser evil, but simply of doing the right thing or in other words, of intelligently conforming to the *one* omnipresent moral imperative, say that of producing the "maximum good" (classic Utilitarianism) or that of "Love" (*Agapé* or "agapéic love": Christian Situationism).[1]

---

[1] See the recent work principally treated here: Joseph Fletcher, *Situation Ethics: The New Morality* (Philadelphia, Westminster, 1966). Of the titles of its ten chapters, I quote here those of III–VIII: "Love only is always good. Love is the only Norm. Love and Justice are the same. Love is not Liking. Love justifies its means. Love decides there and then."—Instead of "Love," a possible monistic supreme principle of a situationalist concept of Morals may be e.g., "Evolution," "History" or "Progress", as in Marxism and various other forms of Historicism.

Supposing that I have presented here the Situationist doctrine, very incompletely of course but by no means unfairly or misleadingly, I propose to argue against it on the following grounds.

The terms "Situation Ethics" and "Situationism" are infelicitously chosen; they blur the real issue and set the mind on a false track. This may not constitute a very serious objection; it applies perhaps to most technical terms in Philosophy and to most "-ism" words. Nevertheless, the objection is worth making, for its significance reaches beyond a question of mere verbal usage; it leads us on to a critique of the antinomian emphasis suggested by the word. The target-fetish of the Situationists, "Legalism", similarly connotes a false scent. As I hope to show, the perversity attaching to the "legalistic" and the "puritanical" attitudes, and, likewise, the traditional misconception of Morality as a "Law of Nature" can perfectly well be exposed without falling a prey to the antinomian emphasis of Situationism and, above all, without lapsing into the *extrinsicalism* which constitutes its ultimate core. By its extrinsicalist negation of Moral Standards as really experienced by men, Situationism falsifies and subverts the concept of Morality; by the arbitrary monistic simplification inherent in its doctrine it aims at separating the conceptual appearance and emotive zest of moral consciousness from moral common-sense and its wealth of contents. In other words, Situationism *substitutes* for Morality or Ethics *something else*, though that "something else" is not unconnected with *one aspect* of Morality; the connexion is clearer in the case of Situationism than in the case of Existentialism: if, therefore, it may be excessive to label Existentialism as a form of Immoralism, it would be even more unjust so to label Situationism.[2] It is nevertheless a fact that Situationism is more concerned with a *reform* of our moral experience than with its *interpretation*; this feature in itself, interpretation ordained *ad hoc* to a reformatory bias, tends to disqualify it from a philosophic point of view;[3] but the nature of its reformatory intent is such as to render it particularly open to immoralistic *misuse*. It has not unreasonably been branded as "dangerous" by a number of critics. Like all

---

[2] Some writers, however, consider on the contrary Situationism as a form of "extreme" Existentialism. Thus Karl Rahner and Herbert Vorgrimler, "Situationsethik," *Kleines theologisches Wörterbuch* (Freiburg: Herder, 1961), p. 336; cf. our Note (10).

[3] Characteristically enough, Fletcher's above-quoted book carries the sub-title *The New Morality*. Such a caption alone justifies the profoundest mistrust. I would

naturalistic types of ethics, i.e. types of ethics that tend to conflate moral with non-moral values or desirabilities and identify Morality with the well-advised and effective conduct of Practice as a whole, it invites *laxism*, a proclivity to underestimate the majesty of Duty and neglect moral demands in favour of extra-moral advantages; but it may invite also *rigorism*,[4] the ideal of moral "perfection" as the sole guide of Practice and interpretation of all unsatisfactory and unlucky dealing with practical problems in terms of moral guilt or weakness. The focal point of the aberration, once more, lies in the theorist's negation of, or insensibility towards, the inherent moral properties—values and disvalues—of certain definite and basically important *kinds of action* (conduct, intention) and accordingly, on the level of methodic approach, in a style of ethical thinking divorced from Moral Experience.

It should be added at this point that in spite of the Christian background and presuppositions of most varieties of Situation Ethics it constitutes a structurally definable possibility of ethical speculation apart from any accepted religious position—it may bear a Catholic or a Protestant tinge but may also be conceived in a non-Christian, a non-religious or an atheist spirit[5]—; that it may reveal a characteristic kinship with *some* specifically Christian points of view but may at the same time be hard to reconcile with *other* specifically Christian modes of valuation; and that it is in no way (and does not generally claim to be) representative of traditional Christian orthodoxy, and much less of Christian Moral Theology, as such. The present paper is about

---

not commit myself to a condemnation of Ethical Relativism in *all* its — very different — forms; in particular, there exists such a thing as an historical change in some of the contents of Moral Consensus, notably as regards the variable apportionment of moral *emphasis*, and the change can be for the better as well as for the worse. But "the new morality" sounds like "the new look," or "fashions for the coming season." Nothing is more inherent in Moral Experience as such than the overall concept of Morality as a *Constant Standard* by which the varying forms of personal collective behaviour are *judged*. Our epoch may not produce a Caligula or Nero; in their epoch, Hitler and Stalin would have been impossible. But those two eminent rulers did evoke considerable moral resentment in their time, and the same applies to ours. As men, our paramount business is to *comply* with the demands of Morality; as philosophers, to *analyse* and *interpret* it — to "change" it is an altogether minor and secondary concern, though it may be meaningful as applied to some limited and well-defined points.

[4] In D. von Hildebrand's words, a "blindfolded radical legalism": cf. our note (16) on Hildebrand.

[5] Fletcher would recognize this, in the sense of a secular humanistic Utilitarianism scarcely different in contents from his own "Christian Love Ethic." Cf. our Note (1).

Situation Ethics as a philosophic construction; it refers to the problem of an authentically "Christian Ethics" only in an accidental and illustrative, not in a systematic, manner.

2. THE MEANING OF THE "SITUATION" EMPHASIS

On the face of it, the principle "Rather than mechanically conforming to a Law, suit your action to the particular situation" (or "meet the demand of the situation", etc.) has something about it that sounds attractive. Surely the important thing for the physician is to cure the patient—this patient, here and now—not to faithfully observe a traditional or current medical—: e.g. *Ubi pus, ibi evacua* (Where "matter" is collecting, evacuate). Even supposing this rule to be predominantly valid, we feel it to be more satisfactory if the sick person recovers (owing, perhaps, to a course of antibiotics) *without* the pus having been drained surgically than if the draining *is* carried out carefully and in due course the patient dies. Medical rules exist for the sake of curing patients, not patients for the sake of reverently applying medical rules.[6] However, the simile may well be misleading; it presupposes a conception of Morality or "moral action" on the model of a *Craft* like Medicine or Engineering in which, primarily and ordinarily, one definite purpose is paramount and "laws" or rules are nothing but pieces of fact-knowledge pointing to a probable or average means appropriate to securing that purpose. (The practice of any craft, and very largely of that of medicine, *may* of course *involve* thorny moral problems [7]; e.g. a doctor may sometimes have to ask "his conscience" whether or not to apply a *risky* method of treatment, or whether he ought to save the patient at the cost of endangering another person's life or welfare,

[6] Nevertheless, the popular adage "The physician ought to endeavour to cure the patient rather than the disease," its cheap humor resting on the syntactic ambiguity (in English and also in other languages) of the verb "cure", does not amount to more than that a careful and open-minded medical mind is a better medical mind than a hoodwinked and schematic one. Obviously every physician knows that he would most surely and promptly eliminate the typhoid fever by cutting off the typhoid patient's head but that his task is of a quite different nature, yet that "curing the patient" *means* curing him *of his typhoid*, not for example providing for his happiness or physical invulnerability. Berdyaev's pompous phrase (see Fletcher, p. 143) "Every moral action should have in mind a concrete living person and not the abstract good" is a similar mixture of portentous platitude and logical muddle. "The abstract good" is the only meaning and standard of morality, and it can be only secured, attained, performed, displayed, encouraged etc. by "concrete living persons."

[7] Cf. my paper "Deliberation is of Ends" in *Proceedings of the Aristotelian Society*, LXIV (1963), pp. 27–50.

or whether he should tell a serious lie which may help the patient psychologically for the moment but hurt him in the long run by destroying his hope—and above all, his *trust*—on his subsequent discovery of the truth). Suppose I may avert some grave evil by uttering a crucial falsehood. Very well: perhaps I ought to do that; perhaps I will do that. But I shall do it with a most significantly different state of consciousness than the one I should feel if repairing a broken object successfully with some unconventional tool, flying in the face of some established technical maxim; perhaps, having resolved myself to tell the lie in question, I shall not despise myself but I should indeed feel myself very despicable in reflecting (subsequently) on the fact that I have told the lie quite simply as a matter of course, without having had to override the protest of my sense of self-respect. And, for the matter of that, why exactly was it "situational" behaviour to tell that lie, whereas it would have been "non-situational" behaviour to stick to the truth? *Either* took place or would have taken place—like every concrete choice, every action—in the context of the given situation. "My situation" was that of giving a statement about a certain matter, though it was also a great deal else. To decide *against* telling the lie, perhaps because the alternative evil consequence appeared to me not very grave or rather uncertain, or because the lie in question might commit me to a *sustained policy of deceit* in the sequel would have been as "situational" as the opposite choice; what might be *comparatively* "non-situational" would be the doing of some irrelevant action quite out of context: e.g. if I had suddenly started roaring the Chilean national anthem.

What, after all, does a "legalistic" type of conduct mean? Applying, so one would suppose, a moral Norm precisely to a situation *to which it* "*applies*", a situation that as such falls under its terms of reference. Confronted with a problem such as whether I should save my friend X's or a distinguished man's, Y's, life in an acute situation of crisis (to do *both* being impossible), or whether I should try to save a drowning man's life (considering that I am a very poor swimmer myself), it would *not* be "legalistic" but just insane to decide "on no account to commit adultery" or "to pay punctually my debt to my creditor". For these praiseworthy resolutions do *not* apply to the problem on hand and provide no answer, not even a remote or tentative answer, to it; therefore they do not suggest answers that might even seem objectionable or "false"; whenever we do feel inclined to object to a "legalistic" attitude it is not irrelevance to the "situation" we have in mind. "Legalism" in another sense—and it is here that the word appears to be most appropriate—is more to the point. Some (very primitive and unthinking) people may tend to assume, though perhaps only occasionally and inconsistently, that whatever is not prohibited by a code of "positive", *jural* law, in especial that of their own country, is *eo ipso* also *morally* permissible—for example, prostitution (though not procuring), or any kind of heartless and callous behavior, or any unscrupulous grabbing or "sharp practice" short of actual fraud— and that whatever is prescribed by the law of the land is necessarily also a moral duty: thus, obedience to the orders of tyrannous and inhumane authorities; nay, that anything ordained by the law is therefore also *intrinsically* right. Again, what is wrong here is not reverence for "the law" in contrast with response to "the situation", but confusion of the moral with the jural "law": in other words: mistaking for a moral norm of what is enjoined by state-power. The stipulations of legal codes are indeed, as a rule, closely tied to moral norms of certain important kinds, e.g. respect for the life and property of others, or loyalty to one's country; but they never as such *mean* moral norms, and normally and justifiably leave vast areas of morality uncovered. Marked unfriendliness to "little" people and obsequious cringing to people whose good-will or resentment may easily be conducive or harmful to our interests is a morally base and contemptible kind of behaviour, but it does not and cannot fall under any paragraph of the criminal law; wilful indulgence in "impure thoughts" is, as many of us firmly believe, morally bad, but the idea of its being penalized by the legal code is utterly ridiculous and revolting.

Yet it remains true that a "legalistic" spirit, in one sense, may be present in moral judgement itself which still fully deserves the criticism levelled against it by Situationists, by sensitive Christians, and indeed by sensible ethical thinkers. The mistaken and unlovely—and perhaps crudely perverse—"legalistic" spirit I have in mind reveals a certain *similarity* to the "juridicalism" as described above. Without going so far as to confuse moral norms with codified positive laws, it conceives of moral norms unilaterally and misleadingly *on the model* of such laws. Unaware of the complexity of many moral problems or anxious to evade awareness thereof and to arrive as quickly as possible at a rigorous, unequivocal and massively unproblematic moral appraisal, it is only interested in finding some moral norm that *obviously* and conspicuously applies to the situation in question, and turns a blind eye to *other* moral norms which may apply to it less conspicuously and which are less calculated to yield an unequivocal "directive" but which may not a whit less essentially be relevant to the problem. It is *easier* [8] to cling to the strict norm "Thou shalt not lie" than to weigh the greatness of the evil I am likely or quite foreseeably almost certain to work by telling the truth in some cases: "I must not lie" simply stands then, the rest is lost sight of. Some promise I have made, perhaps one whose content is *per se* morally dubious, is of no great consequence to the promisee; whereas by keeping it I have to renounce providing some great and genuine, objectively valuable, benefit for others: no matter at all; such considerations are *a priori* illegitimate; "*a promise is a promise*" and I have to keep it without stopping for a moment to reflect. Or again, "divorce is divorce" regardless of whether divorce in the given case implies perhaps the saving of two lives from interminable agony or is perhaps only the means and expression of an evil, lustful, promiscuous mode of life. In "legalism" of this type, we do indeed find a reluctance to look carefully into the proper nature, the problem-content and the value-and-disvalue implications of the situation in question. True, but just as much do we find a reckless less lack of regard for "abstract" and universally valid moral standards or categories, possibly even of actual norms, which happen to have a bearing on that situation. The appraiser has arbitrarily and superficially selected *one* relevant norm, one category-label invoking that one relevant norm, and discarded others likewise relevant, perhaps equally so, perhaps even more so. What he has done is *not* thinking of the norm only while neglecting the situation: such an interpretation makes no sense, for situation (the configuration of facts that demands practical attention) and "relevant" moral norm or standard or point of view are mutually correlated and *complementary*. From the situation as such, from it *alone*, absolutely nothing—no moral imperative or direction, nor even a practical incentive or counsel—follows. The approach, say, of a large carnivorous beast does not "necessitate" me to flee; it "occasions" me to flee *given* my urge of self-preservation which in itself is *not* "situational" at all but is "actualized", set in motion, brought into action by, or "responds to", the threatening situation. If a person is collapsing near me and I, instead of quietly

---

[8] In this respect, we cannot but fully agree with Fletcher.

walking away without any move to help him (taking as it were the "I can't be bothered" position of callous selfishness), rush to his help and do what I can to save his life, alleviate his pain or call in the succour of others, I choose to be actuated by my compassionate feelings or my formal sense of duty, in a word by moral sentiments (to some extent at least crystallized into "principles" I have accepted): again a non-situational constant "responding" to the situation. But, of course, I do not run away at the sight of a kitten, nor offer a robust, athletic-looking man merrily walking towards the station to carry him on my back. Situations do not mysteriously "produce" moral motives to act (or to refrain from doing something); and moral norms have no meaning except by reference to (ultimately) actual but (proximately and more essentially, in the sense of permanent awareness) conceivable or possible situations. If, as I too admittedly think, there is such a thing as a misdirected "legalism", it is a kind of attitude that *fails to do justice to abstract and universal moral principles* as well as to "the situation".

It should be further admitted, to be sure, that Legalism is also open to the more specific objection, often advanced by Situationists, that it tends to exaggerate what I call "the thematic primacy of moral evil", in other words to overemphasize abstention from evildoing and under-emphasize active (so-called "creative") good-doing. (The State maintains an extensive system of criminal jurisdiction but no similar system of "recompensing virtue"; Society and in some ways the State do also manifoldly honour and reward virtuous conduct but chiefly in the form of recognizing and recompensing useful or admirable and distinguished *accomplishments* which involve and include a great deal of moral virtue but are not straightforward "right actions" or manifestations of "moral goodness" as such.) But Legalism is guilty, on this score, of *bluntness of vision* rather than of any fundamental perversion. For evildoing *in fact* stands out in sharper contours against the background of the general practice of life than does the exercise of virtue. Thus, veracity is a positive moral virtue just as mendacity is a positive moral vice but any single act of "truth-telling" is very much less ethically remarkable than any single act of lying. Again, cruelty and malice are very much more noticeable, but also incomparably more evil, than mere passive indifference to the fate of another or others. Again, to refuse help to others in need, to callously avert one's glance from the sufferings of others instead of trying to alleviate them whenever possible, is of greater ethical moment in a bad sense than the endeavour to procure a superabundance of good for others and procure gratuitous pleasures for them is in a good sense. Lastly, good-doing as the contrary opposite of evildoing is essentially less susceptible of being cast into precise rules on the same footing with the prohibitions which bear on evildoing—the moral restrictions, taboos or "Don'ts". Active moral good-doing is, for reasons inherent in the very structure of life, largely a matter of the agent's free choice, his self-chosen ideals, his moral genius as one might say; to refrain from wrongdoing is more urgent and more stringent, more duty-like, and is more easily testable. To find fault with these basic facts is not to criticize Legalism but to challenge the constitution of the world or the human condition; it amounts to an attempt at substituting for *Morality* a utopian subversion of the universe. Legalism deserves blame, not for recognizing the irremovable thematic primacy of moral evil [9] but for its tendency to confine the moral outlook to what is *easier* to notice and what is easier to codify and to apply: an attitude conducive to an all too mediocre, trivial and inadequate but not to an essentially mistaken or perverse conception of Morality.

3. THE AMBIT OF SITUATION ETHICS: ANTINOMIANISM AND EXISTENTIALISM; PRUDENTIALISM AND UTILITARIANISM

"Antinomianism" means the contrary opposite of "Legalism", i.e. the negation of the validity or relevancy of the Moral Law or moral laws, rules or imperatives. Situationism is more closely antinomian as regards moral laws in the plural than as regards "the Moral Law" inasmuch as it impugns the idea of a moral *code* rather than of moral *obligation* as such. While "pluralistic" in the sense of asserting that moral obligation has a different content and attaches to different kinds of action according to each different (perhaps "unique") situation, it is *anti*-pluralistic (monistic) in the sense of denying the meaning and validity of *several* autonomous moral norms, standards or points of view. The situationist mood may tend to emphasize, at the same time, the concept of a unitary "moral principle" or even more of an identical "moral goodness" rather than of an all-embracing "moral *law*", but, this is a comparatively inessential aspect of it. Thus, so far as

---

[9] On this point, see my paper "The Thematic Primacy of Moral Evil," *Philosophical Quarterly*, VI (1956), pp. 27–42; but above all, Bernard Mayo *Ethics and the Moral Life* (London: Macmillan, 1958), esp. chapter XI on "Negative and Positive Morality."

antinomianism means the position that Morality is not basically "imperative" ("Ought"-like, obligational, deontic, imperative etc.) but say, "evaluative" in nature, i.e. reposes on the distinction between Good and Bad or Better and Worse rather than between Right and Wrong, Situationism may be regarded as akin to but by no means necessarily identical with antinomianism; again, so far as autonomianism means the more extreme doctrine which simply denies, or equates to mere superstition, moral distinctions as such and proclaims our right do do as we please (though obviously it may often be "wiser" not to pursue our pleasure directly and uninhibitedly), Situationism appears to be even more definitely *not* antinomian, since it purports to be the right *conception* of moral goodness and not a *negation* thereof. Yet even on this interpretation of antinomianism (understanding it as equivalent to immoralism, that is), a point of kinship between the antinomian and the situationist attitudes or "atmospheres" is undeniably present: what is common to them is the formal gesture "Never mind if what you do infringes this or that widely accepted moral rule or standard; the one thing that matters is . . ." (to wit, the "good" you intend to achieve).

Existentialism, which has significantly different varieties and cannot properly be treated here at all, is much like both Antinomianism and Situationism in its rejection of moral codes and its monistic conception of Value; but it is founded on a specific type of value-emphasis which cannot be defined in terms of antinomianism and is certainly not characteristic of Situation Ethics. It is no more pleasure-centered than "right"-centered or "good"-centered; what constitutes its conceptual core may be variously described as "freedom", "selfhood", "authenticity", "personhood"—coincident or not with a closely-knit "Community"—or the agent as a true embodiment of "Being". Whether conceived in an explicitly atheist or in a vaguely religious or in a professedly Christian spirit, whether denying or affirming the possibility of a "salvation" of man, Existentialism is *interested* in what stands for something like a divine *stature* of man [10] rather than either his *goodness* or even his *good*. It has a predilection for the extraordinary, the heroic or the deviant, the irreverent and even the irrelevant ("gratuitously" elevated to supreme relevance by arbitrary

---

[10] Perhaps it is this point—that Existentialism at any rate represents a conception of the *qualitative worth of man*—which Rahner (see out Note (2)) has in mind when censuring Situationism as a more extreme deviation.

choice) but also possibly for excessive and mystical—chiefly, un-conventional—religiosity; for the state of "crisis" and for "marginal situations". Existentialist and Situationist attitudes will easily interfuse and we are often reminded by situationist utterances of existentialist motifs and inversely; existentialism has surely exercised a strong impact on Situation Ethics. There are, none the less, reasons for keeping the two concepts apart. What is common to the two doctrines is, once more, their identical aversion to moral codes and, what I think to be more essential, to moral *categorization*. Situationism is undoubtedly the *wider* concept; existentialism ineluctably entails an emphasis on "situational decision" by the agent as contrasted with his conformance to "abstract" but contentual standards, whereas a situationist doctrine *need not* have anything to do with the conceptual idols specific to existentialism.

Prudentialism, a salient feature of Aristotelian-Thomist ethics, as well as Utilitarianism reappear in a somewhat refurbished—perhaps, clarified—shape in Situation Ethics, and here too the point of kinship lies in the displacement of emphasis from fixed particular types of Value and Disvalue towards the "unique", "here-and-now" situation—or agential behaviour evoked by it. The question, in other words, is not whether the agent's conduct answers such and such moral standards (*quâ* relevant to the situation, of course) but whether the agent deals with the situation in a well-designed or well-adapted or conducive or expedient manner. The criterion is in each case a *unified* (i.e. monistic) and an ultimately *non-moral* one. Morality is interpreted as *identical* with right, correct, wise, reasonable, capably directed, etc. *Practice* as such.[11] Within this framework, however, the divergencies appear to be considerable. Prudentialism tends to be an *agent*-ethic rather than an act- or a norm-ethic. It sees the criterion of right acting in the virtuous character of the agent itself: a character and a conjunction of habits governed and permeated by "Reason", more exactly "practical reason" (in its turn not only underlying, but dependent on, specific habits of virtuous conduct); reason as the *art*, so to speak, of applying the agent's permanent and all-embracing purpose, *scil.* the pursuit of

---

[11] As for the delimitation of Morality from Practice, see for example the particularly enlightening papers of Professor A. M. MacIver, *Practical Philosophy and Morals*, Inaugural Lecture at the University of Southampton, 1962, and Timothy L. S. Sprigge, "Definition of a Moral Judgment," *Philosophy*, XXXIX (1964), pp. 301–22.

his own "true" good, correctly and with full awareness and certitude to the given here-and-now situation. Right is what a good or virtuous— a well trained, well educated, shrewd and percipient, as also experienced —person would do, his reason not being swamped and obfuscated or momentarily perverted or swept away by the impetus of extraordinary or quasi-irresistible passion. Thus Prudence, the guiding light of Morality, is also its substantive unitary content, and at the same time the mark of man's natural "perfection" *quâ* man (Reason being man's distinctive feature). This is a highly complex and largely circular notional construction; the use of expressions like *"true* good", *"right* reason", "conformity of reason to the *rectified* will" and the role attributed to "virtuous habits" betray a surreptitious or shamefaced leaning on ordinary, traditional moral valuations and a shy evasion of radical utilitarianism or situationism. Aristotle already distinguishes Practical Wisdom or Prudence from mere "cleverness", i.e. an able strategy in the pursuit of any kind of pleasure or inferior advantages; and his Catholic followers and interpreters or, in part, revisers, will— misleadingly enough—warn occasionally against mistaking "false prudence" and "prudence of the world" for what Prudence "truly" means. If on the one hand such a mistake is obviously *invited* by the basic drift and conceptual atmosphere of prudentialism and if countless immoral schemes *have* in fact been salved with the chrism of sophistical "justification" in prudential terms, on the other hand Prudentialists with a rigoristic bent have chided their opponents, the Conscientialists— i.e. the typical "legalistic" casuists of Moral Theology—for providing too many loopholes for moral laxity by limiting moral obligation to what is clearly and beyond reasonable doubt prescribed by moral "laws" and thus extending the realm of the "permissible" to the point of securing a space of freedom for such milder kinds of unvirtuous, mundane and morally indifferent sorts of conduct as may escape from "legal" definition. Many things we do are not prescribed or expressly sanctioned by our conscience but do not provoke its protest either or can extort a "free pass" from it; whereas prudence "governs" every step of him who "possesses" it and impregnates his conduct with a positive and omnipresent morality: prudentialism is linked to the Thomist doctrine of *all* single, concrete human acts being either morally good or morally bad and none morally indifferent. Morality *means* right practice, and *all* right practice is *eo ipso* moral: prudence in itself implies morality; but again everything we do ought to be morally good, or else we are *not* governed by *true* prudence. A nomistic and categorical ethic cannot but reject this doctrine together with its implicit alternative of a laxist or rigorist conception of life. The agent is urged by the prudential moralist to be as virtuous as possible, "perfect" as it were; but, objective yardsticks being underemphasized if not altogether denied, analytical checking of transgressions and judgement of conduct by an "impartial spectator" tend to be evaded. As opposed to Conscience, the "inner judge" or "man in the breast" surveying and appraising but not actually decreeing or commanding the agent's conduct, "Prudence" is as it were its own guarantee: it is the agential power itself and, so far as it is operative, the epitome of its goodness at the same time. Yet, obviously, *moral discourse* is tuned to the conceptual key not of Prudence but of Conscience, i.e. the idea not of relying on the hypothetical virtue-wisdom of the supposedly virtuous but of calling the agent to account for his actions (which can be read and appraised only in terms of right and wrong *kinds* of actions as involved in any single "situation"); and Moral Theology and confessional practice have on the whole been definitely tied to conscientialism, with prudentialism inorganically affixed in the background as an ostensible metaphysical "basis", in fact rather an ornamental appendage.[12]

Situationism, so far it expects the agent to deal with every "unique" situation "rationally on its merits"—not from caprice, blind sentimental impulse, flash-like "intuition" etc.—comes very close to prudentialism. But, on the one hand, it will simplify that many-faced doctrine and render it more consistent, doing away with the built-in residuum of traditional valuations and virtue-categories; on the other hand, as a compensating means of orientation it has to postulate some handier *overall* principle of morality than the agent's own "true good" and

---

[12] For the Prudentialist side, esp. for the tension between a Prudence-orientated and a Conscience-orientated ethic, see Th. Deman O. P.'s edition and annotations of Aquinas's *Summa Theologiae* (2ª-2ᵃᵉ, Questions 47–56), *La prudence* (Paris-Tournai Rome: Desclee, 1949), particularly pp. 378–84 and 460–78. The gist of these tortuously involved discussions seems to be that Prudence is superior to Conscience, for Conscience does no more than (imperfectly and discontinuously) show the agent (as a "theoretical" fact) what he ought to do, whereas Prudence quasi-inerrantly "governs" his behavior and makes him do what he ought. The author is interested in the effectiveness of virtue once its presence is granted rather than in a cognitive penetration of Right and Wrong. He does not conceal his awareness of the delicately ambiguous status of the word "prudence" but, as the zealots of a school are sometimes fond of doing, tries to construe precisely this obscurity into an "admirable" richness of meaning.

"natural perfection". This might be a humanitarian concept of "the greatest good of all" as the supreme and exclusive "end" to which every action *ought* to be and every *moral* action *is* ordained; or, under a Christian varnish, universal "Love" or "Agapé" or "Charity" as the source from which every action ought to spring, shaped in its here-and-now content by a rational commensuration and calculus of the facts that make up or are relevant to the situation. Thus we might say that while Prudentialism already displays a definitely situational slant, this emerges more clearly in Situationism which abandons the ego-directed and perfectional emphasis with the *qualitative* biases clinging to it, replacing them with *altruism* as a straightforward moral principle. Altruism does indeed make more sense a as *moral* principle than does prudence or reason, or again "virtuous *habits*"; yet in another important respect situationism, recognising Universal Benevolence (with or without a Christian overtone) as the supreme moral principle but also as the *sole* substantive and irrefrangible moral principle, veers farther than does prudentialism from congenial acceptance of moral values and from an authentic interpretation of moral experience. For altruism thus exclusively inthroned (under whatever name) means the reduction without a remainder of all *moral goodness* to the "good *of* man": that is, to a concept that in itself is purely *non*-moral. The prudential pursuit of the agent's own good was less obviously moral, but more genuinely moral in so far as in the agent's "own good" it included (in however obscure and tortured a fashion) the agent's own goodness: that is, virtue, dignity, distinction, "tempered" and in some sense "purified" quality. Altruism as such, however, is directed to the welfare of men alone, its only ultimate theme and teleology. We thus come to locate Situation Ethics in the closet vicinity of Utilitarianism, with which Prudentialism displays an equally indubitable but a more remote and qualified parentage.

Utilitarianism itself, to be sure, has no single and unambiguous meaning. In its prototypic primary form, it is hedonistic, egoistic and consequentialist. In its modified forms, it may adopt a concept of "welfare" not wholly reducible to "the balance of pleasure and pain" but embracing, say, health, vigorous and well-ordered activity, harmoniously developed dispositions etc. as autonomous components; or again it may transpose selfish into "universal" hedonism (as derived, pretty fictitiously, from self-interest, or frankly accepted—on Sidgwick's model—as a valid moral "intuition"); and, lastly, it may throw consequentialism overboard in favor of a merely wholesale justification of a traditional (consensual, intuitional, experiential) body of autonomous moral standards *in terms* of general utility. As regards the first distinction, that between hedonism and welfare-emphasis, the position of Situationism seems to be an open and indeterminate one; but then, anyhow, a comprehensive policy devoted to the aim of promoting pleasure and suppressing "pain" (i.e. unpleasure, sorrow, suffering) will even on purely immanent grounds be hardly able to refrain from encouraging some kinds of pleasure rather than others or endurance of some kinds of suffering rather than of others. As regards the second distinction, Situationism as a humanistic and especially as a Christian doctrine plainly sides with altruism or universalism against egoism— though strictly speaking this may not be *essential* to its peculiar distinctive principle or inherent in its definition: the agent's adequate response to the here-and-now situation, regardless of "intermediate" permanent standards of value and disvalue. It is on the third point, that of consequentialism versus "normative" utilitarianism, or in other words *act*-utilitarianism versus *rule*-utilitarianism,[13] that Situationism ranges entirely, indeed coincides, with the unmodified prototypic form of the Utilitarian conception.

The Utilitarian imperative runs: "Always act with a view to maximizing good and minimizing evil" (we now disregard the distinction between the good/evil of self and of others, and the question whether good/evil strictly reduces to pleasure/suffering). The agent, then, when taking a decision should weigh the respective consequences of his possible alternative actions in terms of a balance of desirability and undesirability, and make his choice accordingly. That is what morality "means"; of course, the presupposition is implied that he also should be properly equipped with intellectual power (*cf.* "prudence"), relevant information, and experience concerning various similar models of practice, enabling him to perform such a calculus of foreseeable consequences pertinently, with a high degree of objective probability. The preparation of the act itself should consist in considerations of utility: hence the term "act-utilitarianism". But it might not unreasonably be assumed that such an extensive thinking out of the foreseeable

---

[13] The denomination originates, I think, from Professor Hare; it is established in recent English-speaking philosophy, and the subject has been much discussed by a great number of writers.

consequences in regard to every single here-and-now problem of practice would constitute an extremely wasteful method and that to apply it competently is anyhow beyond the reach of the ordinary man. This reflection suggests the passage to rule-utilitarianism, which could perhaps also be labelled "conservative utilitarianism" and which prevails in Aristotelian and prudentialist ethics and in a different form also, e.g., in Hume, and is discernible in the outlook of both Bentham and Mill. To act morally, the agent should conform to a received system of rules which is ordained to, or expresses, the principle of utility; the code or codes of moral norms in "civilized society" *are* in fact so interpretable to a large extent, and so far as they are not—so far as in some respects they are irrelevant or indeed run counter to the principle of utility—they ought to be intelligently revised and reconstituted. I would myself agree with this mitigated version of utilitarianism up to a certain point: that is to say, I would in no sense agree with the tenet that morality *means* utility but do admit that moral conduct is on the whole consonant with a wise management of the business of life conducive to the interests of society, and that this is not so merely as at matter of contingent fact but that the nexus is a somehow essential one; for standards of human goodness not on the whole subservient of the good of men would never have come to be registered as valid in the consciousness of mankind or solidified into a moral *consensus* of society. Thus truthfulness, honesty and contractual morality in general are not morally right simply because they are calculated to promote communication, the dissemination of knowledge and the effective ordering of social cooperation (and thereby, the aims of human striving in their all-round conspectus), but the high importance attached to them in civilized society as a whole is very largely due to their being thus beneficial.

But rule-utilitarianism certainly does not suit the situationist temper. For what appeals to this is, in the first place, not the principle of utility as such but precisely the agent's *direct* recourse to a "situational" decision over and above any intermediate moral normativities: and that means, so far as consequential utility is called in as the discriminating test of good and bad action, act-utilitarianism. The agent should not bring "ready-made" universal and contentual preferences to the shaping of his right behaviour in the given situation but make his decision "in freedom", in the spirit of "the situation" and animated by the *one* principle alone that is supposed not so much to claim his obedience (analogously to conscience) as to inform his volition as a whole (analogously to prudence). According to Prof. J. Fletcher, that prominent, extreme and articulate champion of Situation Ethics,[14] the agent's will is not good unless it is fully steeped in "Agapé" (agapéic love, or shortly "Love" in this sense), but again if it *is* good it is not bound by any specified rule or standard about kinds of action obligatory or forbidden, commendable or condemnable, but "free" to do anything rationally fitted to the aims emergent, under "Love", from the situation. The much-quoted sentence from St. Augustine, "Love and then do what thou wilt", is to be taken seriously and literally. Fletcher calls his moral doctrine, proudly—and rightly—"monolithic", "pragmatistic", "totalitarian" and "utilitarian". It certainly is all that; for the last word we might more precisely substitute "act-utilitarian".

4. SITUATIONAL EXTRINSICALISM

Above all, to use another of Fletcher's self-descriptive terms, it is *extrinsicalist*—in full consonance, of course, with the rest. This means that moral goodness and badness are not intrinsic but extrinsic to any of the materially descriptive categories into which actions may be classed. Lying is not as such bad; promise-keeping is not as such good. What can be said is only that this act of truth-telling (or lying), given its circumstances and its relation to Universal Benevolence, is (or was, or would be) good, while *that* act of promise-breaking (or promise-keeping), similarly viewed, is (or was, or would be) bad. As Fletcher also formulates it, moral characteristics are not properties but *predicates*. I would paraphrase it thus: chess-playing is neither good nor bad, but it was good of you to provide entertainment for this poor sick man by playing a couple of games with him, or bad of you to waste your time on chess-playing instead of devoting yourself to that urgent and useful task incumbent upon you. It is much like the logical structure of the judgement that Vitamin B pills are good for many people but bad for me since they upset my digestion, whereas sugar and bread or noodles are good for me who am too thin but are bad for

---

[14] See our note (1). Fletcher's later book *Moral Responsibility: Situation Ethics at Work*, (Philadelphia, Pa.: Westminster, 1967), is not being considered here, since, apart from a briefer restatement of the principles exposed in *Situation Ethics*, it deals with detailed concrete problems of business ethics, sexual ethics etc. which fall outside the scope of the present article. With some of his reformatory casuistry I would be disposed to agree, at any rate more than with his ethical approach as such.

diabetics and for the fair number of people who are too fat.[15] Fletcher's "Predicates, Not Properties" watchword may be criticized by logicians, but it is enlightening inasmuch as it reveals that, beyond the legalistic strictness which is the proximate target of his attack, his guns are trained at a more fundamental one: the objective validity of moral standards (except "Agapé" alone) as distinct from purely practical appropriateness "to the situation". But he makes his point even more explicit by stating that traditional marks of moral goodness and badness, e.g. those derived from the Ten Commandments or any other widely accepted moral codes or tables of virtues and vices are *per se* morally meaningless: actions orientated by such injunctions and commendations are good if inspired by "Love" and fit to secure single concrete ends thus inspired, bad if contrary to "Love" or ill fitted to the ends it suggests. Fletcher's radicalism—and consequently, sometimes, clarity—compels our admiration: he caps the climax by declaring that whether "The End Sanctifies the Means" ever was or wasn't, in historical fact, a principle professed by the Society of Jesus, it certainly is not only a defensible but a well-nigh self-evidently true and right principle. He invokes Lenin's answer given to an interlocutor who complained of the cruelty and tyrannical harshness of the "means" applied by the Bolsheviks in furthering their allegedly good "end", as if the end sanctified the means. "Well," said Lenin with disarming candour, "what *else* but the end could sanctify the means?"; and he was utterly correct.

Fletcher also credits the moral agent, as envisioned by him, with "freedom" and "responsibility". Freedom is notoriously a word

---

[15] Fletcher, (*Situation Ethics*, p. 13) delights in the story of a man who, like his father and grandfather before him, had invariably voted Republican but on one occasion after some pondering decided to vote against the Republican candidate and justified his decision in the words: "There are times when a man has to push his principles aside and do the right thing." It sounds odd that it is only at some rare times that a man ought to do "the right thing," and that — apparently — he should do so in defiance of his principles and on the other hand hold "principles" that do *not* direct him to do "the right thing." It seems that Fletcher, along with the "hero of his book" — for so he calls him — cannot distinguish "principles" which are in fact personal *maxims* of practice, having much or little or nothing to do with moral norms as the case may be, from moral principles proper. One's political position may have moral grounds and implications among others, but it is something *essentially* different from a moral principle; and nothing can be "the right thing" unless it represents a moral principle (or several such) decisively relevant to the practical problem on hand.

with several meanings. What he has in mind here is obviously not the classic philosophical concept of free-will, which is at least equally compatible with traditional "legalistic" ethics—I freely obey or disobey the moral norms relevant to my practical situation; I freely choose between two "goods", one of which represents or involves duty-fulfilment, whereas the alternative good, whose attraction may be very potent, objectively involves disregard for an obligation and perhaps even tempts me subjectively all the more by dint of the spicy lure, the perverse zest, of doing the illicit thing (the experience of pleasure enhanced by overlapping its intrinsic obstacle). Again, he cannot have in mind physical freedom, which is presupposed by every "action" proper and is irrelevant to the debate; nor, finally, the concept of "freedom under the Law", i.e. freedom from arbitrary authority, from the despotic whim and compulsive fascination of another—against which the impersonal majesty of a normative and objectified Table of Values and Wrongs provides the securest bastion. He can only mean a kind of "freedom of spontaneity": the freedom of snapping one's finger at rules and taboos and of "doing what one likes", though, in contrast with rank immoralism or pure antinomianism, on the pre-supposition only of being imbued with the principle of "Agapé" or "Love" or Universal Benevolence. Indeed, by committing himself to the hyperbolic—and strictly speaking, wholly nonsensical—Johannine phrase "God is Love", and putting on it the preposterous construction that it defines not God in terms of Love but Love in terms of God, Fletcher comes perilously near to the degrading and irrational doctrine of the so-called "Ethics of Divine Imperatives" ("Right is what God commands", instead of "God commands us to do right"), i.e. the kind of extreme "Legalism" which is the negation of all moral experience and of all rational cognition in the realm of morality.[16] This religious fantasy is not, as he himself rightly observes, essential to the concept

---

[16] Our Note (4) on Hildebrand. Chapter X of D. Hildebrand, *True Morality and its Counterfeits* (New York: McKay, 1955), "Basic Errors of Circumstance Ethics," pp. 130–154, is probably the most profound and most devastating criticism of "Situation Ethics" ever written, though its highly strung professedly Catholic emphasis may evoke in non-Christian readers a totally deceptive impression of philosophical irrelevance. "Circumstance ethics in denying the existence of general morally relevant and moral values, as well as the existence of moral commandments and moral laws rooted in these values, in effacing the difference between a moral commandment and a mere positive commandment, . . . leaves no other beacon for our moral life than a private relevation of God's will . . ."

of Situationism; but apart from showing us his fanciful and inauthentic reading of Christianity, it throws additional light on the *extrinsicalist* turn of mind. Better blind submission and infatuated, obsessive discipleship than bowing to the intrinsic evidence of Moral Cognition. But a kind of experience of "freedom", which however misguided may be intense, remains. And what of "responsibility"? This seems, if possible, more paradoxical. What we ordinarily mean by responsibility is precisely the testability, "checkability", appraisability, judgeability, or shall we say the ethical intelligibility of an agent's conduct in term of recognised (though not, in general, strictly definable or exhaustively enumerable) moral norms and standard of value, and "before" an informal and indefinite "tribunal" of others "onlookers", "appraisers", "judges"—who constitute a *consensual medium* of moral response, sensibility and evaluation.[17] And it is just *against* this concept of moral discourse and arguable appraisal that Situationism is directed, placing as it does—reservation made for "Love"—all emphasis on the agent's "freedom", not in the sense of free-will or of "freedom under the Law" but in the sense of a sort of moral "sovereignty", i.e. freedom to "decide" *in actu* what *for him* is *here and now* right or wrong to do. Short of certain very simple and blatant cases of good-doing and evil-doing (succouring others in danger with heroic self-abnegation, perhaps, or on the contrary assault and robbery or sadistic child-murder practised on a large scale), nobody could on such presuppositions form any reasoned judgement on the behaviour of a fellow-member of society, since he is precluded from analysing it into categorically tangible aspects of right and wrong. Almost everything can be "justified" in virtue of a "Love" (an "agapéic") motivation: a man may shoot his eight children so as to spare them the horrors of an atomic war he fears to be impending; and almost every such justification may be plausibly or arbitrarily called in doubt: Mr. X's sustained display of irreproachable conduct and manifold beneficence might be underlain entirely by his "base" concern, quite alien to "Love", for his security and "respectability" or "smooth-running" life. I cannot even see how an agent imbued with the situationist doctrine can be

[17] Cf. the situational, ambiguously antinomian emphasis of the two short articles in favour of Prudentialism as against Deontic Ethics published by the late Prof. C. De Koninck in *Laval Théologique et philosophique*, "The Nature of Man and his Historical Being," V (1949), pp. 271–77; and "General Standards and Particular Situations in Relation to Natural Law," VI (1950), pp. 335–38.

"responsible before *himself*", i.e. before his *conscience*;[18] for Conscience is an argumentative and analytical function (*cf.* "examination of conscience"): what I can really and concretely, in terms of professed norms and standards, justify "before my own conscience" I can also intelligibly justify *to others*, even though (what may very possibly occur) on a specified point my conscientious emphasis appreciably diverges from the emphatic opinion current in my social environment. (A person who is a vegetarian on *moral* grounds can wholly intelligibly and lucidly convey his point—his moral repugnance to having other sentient beings slaughtered in order to feed on their flesh—to others: he will fail to convince most of them and elicit some counter-arguments, Christian or other; but his attitude will strike few of them as a mere opaque whim, and though it may not earn him much sympathy, it will compel respect rather than inspire contempt.)

Nevertheless, however ill the epithet "responsibility" is applied by existentialists and situationists, I feel inclined to suppose that they must mean *something* by it. In a *distinctive* sense, we attribute responsibility—differently from our calling a person responsible for what he does—to a man arranging his policy, in a certain domain of affairs, according to his own judgement as opposed to simply carrying out the instructions of his superiors on every problematic point and at every important turn or juncture. In every hierarchy of office, a higher position is (normally) a more "responsible" position. For successes and achievements of State policy, as also for the moral integrity and nobility displayed therein, high-ranking Government leaders are praised, and for failures and immoralities blamed, rather than their scribes, subordinates and technical executives. But their "responsibility" lies in the policies' being imputed to them and in their liability to being "called to account", not in their range of power and latitude of decision. The alleged "responsibility" of the "sovereign" agent of Situation Ethics, an agent over and above any hard-and-fast appraisability of his actions, is one of the ornamental slogans, the euphoric hurrah-words well familiar to students of "emancipatory" ideologies; the concept of that "responsibility" is empty of content. And the main point is not that situationism fails to threaten the agent with sufficient "distinct

---

[18] See, against illusions of hubris attaching to the concept of Redemption and the notion of commandments, principles and laws being "no longer needed," Hildebrand, *op. cit.*, pp. 149–52, esp. the Footnote on p. 150.

damnations" or specified reasons for social ostracism but that it deprives him of seriously applicable moral orientation and makes havoc of the conceptual scaffolding of his conscience. With sonorous magnificence, Fletcher disposes of the commonsensical objection that the human agent is not in general able to determine Right and Wrong, in regard to a given practical problem, merely from the all-comprehensive principle of "Agapé" and his overall calculus of "foreseeable consequences" (including, of course, their respective probability and their comparative weights!) but, in order to "choose Right as against Wrong," nay even to work out a more or less meaningful and valid "moral decision" where plain, unequivocal "Ought" or "Don't" really fails to yield and indubitable and adequate direction, absolutely needs a differentiated body of contentual rules and standards. This might be true so long as men were children unthinkingly going astray unless treated to the drill of minutious catechisms of behaviour (with their often inevitably silly and disproportionately emphatic details); but after all it is time now that at long last they should mature to the status of adult persons.[19] Why exactly now? The ineptitude of this random historicism defies description; by contrast, it appears to lend the Marxist brand of historicism an air of scientific respectability in virtue of its dubious but comparatively real historical basis in the sociology of classes and of technological equipment. The only similar basis that Christian Situationism might conceivably claim for itself is the increasing prevalence in modern industrial society of Atheism and Irreligion. Were I an historicist anxious to espouse the fashion of his epoch I would boldly celebrate the so-called "death of God" but certainly not amuse myself with a "Theology without God," and perhaps adopt the ethic of a humanistic utilitarianism but with a hearty contempt refuse to deck it out with a Christian paint and tags of a pious biblical or mystical phraseology. Utterly remote from the authentic religious ideal of *imitatio Christi* (this, to be sure, is itself no substitute either for an elaborate code of morals, which on the contrary it presupposes and postulates, or for an analytical ethic based on the phenomenology of moral consciousness, which is a demand of Philosophy), what the new slogans of man's "maturity" or "adulthood" and "responsibility", meaning his promotion beyond judgeability in

---

[19] About Conscience presupposing *universal* value categories (and its primarily "negative", i.e. warning and accusing function), see Hildebrand, *op. cit.*, p. 139.

terms of moral laws and categories, really express is the Utopian *hubris* of the *Divinity of Man:* the conceit of an omniscience of man, the infantile fancy of his all-goodness ensured by pressing the *one* magic button of Love, and the trance-like experience of his apparent technological omnipotence. That this radiant optimism should emerge in the epoch of Bolshevism and of Fascism, of a universal wallowing in "crisis"-consciousness and an all-prevading helpless dread of a possible universal suicide of the species, of carnages on an unexampled scale, and of an irresistible invasion by meretricious and pornocratic features of the surviving islands of Liberal Civilization—that remarkable coincidence is neither a paradoxy nor a *mere* coincidence, but, so far as history is not a realm of random contingency alone but also possesses features of a dimly intelligible "process", may well be regarded as an only too natural connexion. The horrors listed above are intertwined with elements of a real and indubitable progress (mainly but I think not exclusively technological); and the more monstrous the horrors the louder the self-reassuring noises of Progress-consciousness is likely to grow.

5. THE POVERTY OF EXTRINSICALISM

Returning, however, from the nebulous spheres of historico-cultural criticism to the sober level of philosophic argument, we must admit that Situationism is not refuted by an unsympathetic reference to its modernistic backgrounds and associations. There are indeed, in spite of the presence of much solid substance hardly compatible with them, situationist overtones in the New Testament: the Moral Law is expressly confirmed, presupposed as a matter of course, supplemented in one respect or another, beautifully reaffirmed by St. Paul but at the same time somehow given a suppler note and certainly incorporated as a whole in the lofty and unitary religious experience or "command-ment" of "loving God with one's whole heart" and for His sake "one's fellow-men as oneself". Again, the Augustinian "Love and then do what thou wilt" really originates from the ardent and versatile mind of St. Augustine—who, it may be worth to remember, also lived in a time of "crisis" and decadence—and is only jubilantly quoted by Fletcher, as it has been by many others before. We should, though, I feel confident, vainly look in any text by Augustine for any such concretizations of the principle as that, e.g. marital fidelity or honesty in business matters are "good" *when* conducive to the ends of "Love" and "bad" *when* they disserve the cause of "Love". What he meant was presumably that a person "truly" pervaded and guided by the spirit of "Love" need not slavishly tremble before the "letter" of the Law and meticulously strain himself to "observe" it in all its ramifications: rather, surrendering and entrusting himself to Grace, he will again and again with nimble feet tread *the objectively right path* and avoid what is objectively wrong, repelling temptations with spontaneous ease and in a mode of radiant security. Dedicated to God and, in organic unity therewith, to the good (*including* the virtue) of your neighbour, you will seldom even feel a temptation to immorality, and if you do you will elude it in a smilingly self-possessed way as it were, with little effort and pondering. (To my knowledge, he did so in fact once a Christian, and though the institution was already established he never went to confession.) Perhaps the "ideal" Christian can afford to live "above" the Law—in the "freedom of the children of God"[20]—yet not in the sense of living *unaware* and much less *in defiance* of the Law. Even so, the hyperbolic temperamental style in which this maxim of Augustine's (like some others) is couched is misleading, dangerous and open to serious criticism; the maxim lends itself all too easily to a situationist interpretation closely approaching antinomianism and moral nihilism. Prefaced by *whatever* condition, "do as thou wilt" is unsound and inadmissible counsel, and argues a magical rather than a rational state of mind. Presupposing the highest and most fundamental "motivation" conceivable does not dispense the ethical thinker (nor of course the moralist) from the task of going accurately into the question what the various specified dimensions of morality mean or of sundering the praiseworthy from the morally second-rate and mediocre, and more urgently the permissible from the wrong. Certainly, "Agapé" being granted, some more concrete moral implications seem to follow: thus, the exclusion of acts of wilful offence or cruelty, or even ruthless pursuit of one's advantage at the grave detriment of others; and even—though more vaguely—attitudes of sincere and equitable cooperation. Even so, to "deduce" moral truths immediately evident to a high degree and more generally recognized, such as the wrongness of deceit and the rightness of promise-keeping, from an injunction to "love God with our whole heart"—something

---

[20] About the antinomian misinterpretation of the "freedom of the children of God," see the quoted Chapter by Hildebrand, esp. p. 134.

that we do not even properly understand and that is not even in our power to do except in an indirect dispositional sense; and a God "ye have not seen", as Jesus rightly said—is pretty reminiscent of putting the cart before the horse, or, in Scholastic idiom, of explaining *obscurum per obscurius*. Again, it is hard to see how "Love", for God or even for men or mankind, could imply the values and standards of uprightness, fortitude, sobriety or chastity. St. Paul candidly enjoins the duties of chastity reminding his hearers that their bodies, awaiting their resurrection in the end, should be kept *undefiled*, destined as they were to be worthy "vessels of sanctity"; but why and in what sense promiscuity, modes of sexual gratification contrary to "norm", and non-matrimonial connection "defile the body", i.e. the real contentual meaning of sexual morals, is left by Paul in total obscurity—presupposed, obviously, as a matter of self-evidence quite independent of any reference to God or to altruism as opposed to egoism. From a Christian point of view, it is not Fletcher's interpretation (and that of some previous enthusiasts of the Faith, including *partly* St. Augustine) but the Church's traditional interpretation of the supreme and summative Commandment that is valid: the "Love God, etc." principle does not actually contain and condense "the Law and the Prophets", it is not a self-sufficient compendium of their teachings,[21] but envelops, sanctions and enhances it; places it in an all-important perspective and a context of ultimate decisiveness. Some of the more simplifying Christian text-books actually *equate* "loving God" to just "loyally obeying His Commandments", it being of course understood, with St. Thomas Aquinas, that those "commandments" prescribe what is "naturally", i.e. intrinsically good, "defining" it not in the sense of making it a mere function of the arbitrary fancies of a Supreme Ruler but in the sense of pointing it out and casting it into higher relief as willed by a *good* and *holy* Creator who has designed "Nature" and enlightened men about how to order their actions as free beings in "conformity" with the "laws" written into the constitution of that "Nature". This construction, not free of some metaphysical confusion, undoubtedly also reveals an aspect of untenabl: "legalism": whatever "Love" for God (or for any person whatever) means it cannot mean

---

[21] Above all, the two comprehensive commandments given by Christ are in no way meant to *invalidate* either "the law and the prophets" or the so-called "natural" Moral Law outside the Judaeo-Christian revelation of which St. Paul says that "even" the "Gentiles" had it inscribed in their hearts. Cf. Hildebrand, *op. cit.*, p. 152.

"obedience", i.e. practical subordination, alone; to speak of love while prescinding from its appreciative core and its emotive and "sentimental" aura, as if love could be a position of the Will alone, is a misuse of the word. In that respect and up to that point, one may agree with Fletcher.

But he gets caught himself in a very similar pitfall when, obstinately clinging to an indefensible unitary ethic of "Love" yet—most praise-worthily—unable to deny response to the majestic dignity of Justice, he proclaims the bizarre thesis, utterly symptomatic of inept philoso-phizing, that "*Love is Justice*". He grounds this on the universal, impartial and rational character of true Agapé as opposed to the aberrant and contemptible sanctification of love as a merely psychological, arbitrarily selective, and blindly emotive impulse. And this attitude, with which I am to a large extent in vivid sympathy—his strictures upon Tolstoy, in especial, filled me with deep pleasure—bears out his contention that "Situationism" as he understands it must not be identified with Immoralism and Antinomianism. Now if Fletcher said that Love was not enough but must be supplemented with Justice, or the other way round, and that indeed the two essentially conspire, that Universal Benevolence is the natural background of Justice and that all love other than idolatrous infatuation for some arbitrarily singled-out object inevitably tends to foster attitudes of justice, all would be well. (Except, of course, that the whole of Morality would still not have been "accounted for", since the demands of sobriety, chastity or a "high" or "spiritual" tone of life are not convincingly derivable from either love or justice which are both bearing on the theme of the relations between persons with divided and harmonizable interests rather than on that of the quality of their lives as such.) But Fletcher's craving for unity, perhaps the worst source of danger to philosophic thought, drives him on to distort the somewhat pedestrian thesis about the reconcilability or indeed convergency of love and justice into a glittering paradox: the forced establishment of an identity between them, or more exactly, the arbitrary assertion that justice was a necessary corollary or implication of love. Such a sleight-of-hand requires on the one hand a mutilated concept of Justice and on the other an impoverished, prefabricated concept of Love. The truth is that I can have an extremely keen sense of justice and at the same time no more than a minimal, anaemic and atrophied sense of sympathy for my fellow men (both universally and singly), for justice connotes *something* that has nothing at all to do with love, *scil.* a cold but intense passion for "correctness", "fittingness", exactitude and "fidelity to the *object*" (to "*what is the case*"), wherefore I may be remarkably truthful and reliable but at the same time pretty callous, heartless, unsocial and unamiable; whereas on the contrary I may be definitely warm-hearted, eager to help (whenever I come across people who suffer, but also on a more extended scale and in a more sustained and planned fashion) and capable of frequently sacrificing my own interest for the good of others yet at the same time possessing no more than a very loose sense of justice, prone to lavish money on "the deserving poor" but sluggish in paying my debts to well-to-do or institutional creditors, disposed to treat offenders all too mildly or to waive my claims all too light-heartedly as well as to accord privileges with little justification, and so forth. Fletcher would in all probability call this "ungenuine" love or not the "right kind" of love; he certainly makes it clear that what he means by "agapéic love" is *not* erotic attraction nor being-in-love (*amor*), nor impulsive sentimentality, nor again the *selective* love typified by friendship, but that active and intelligent universal benevolence "for God's sake" (*sub specie aeternitatis*, we might paraphrase it) which in traditional Latin is properly called *dilexio* (albeit the language of the Church freely uses expressions like *amor Dei, amor proximi, amor benevolentiae*—as distinct from *amor concupiscentiae*; and *ordo amoris*—the right preferential scale of love—, not to speak of the supreme theological virtue of *charitas*, a term that carries a suggestion of tender sympathy). Whether Fletcher's interpretation of Christian "Agapé" is historically correct I am by no means sure, but I would not labour the point. What I am sure of, however, is that his picture of Love is psychologically misdrawn and that this gravely interferes with the validity of his Ethics, for love *is* a primarily psychological concept, and an ethic centered in a psychological concept that is misrepresented as such cannot help being false. Fletcher's concept of Love is arbitrarily pruned and doctored so as to "include", to produce from a conjurer's hat as it were, the concept of Justice and thus be made to serve as a naturalistic (and supernaturalistic; above all, monistic) "Moral Principle". At the same time, *in practice* a situationist ethic will of course reveal itself as favouring a "love-morality" rather than a "justice-morality", not only in virtue of the magic of the word but also because a "free decision" born in the heat of the "situation", improvised without regard to any specified and permanent rules or codified points of view, is, so far as it may in any sense be "moral" at all, likely to spring from kind and generous sentiments as elicited by the circumstances rather than from the rational and in some sense impersonal suasion of justice.

Fletcher is inclined—so am I—to see the inmost essence of love, aside from sexual passion (however personalized), expressed in the term *dilexio*. But *dilexio*, as the word itself shows, has an essential and ineliminable *selective* connotation. Selective love is an emotive attitude that pervades mental life at all levels; its extension immensely outranges the narrow domain of the particular Greek concept of "friendship"—it may, e.g., be unrequited in fact, but also one-sided in a necessary sense, for we may selectively love, that is to say passionately appreciate, admire and long for, non-personal objects which cannot reciprocate our love: thus, works of art or again places, but also persons "beyond our reach" or no longer alive; it would be silly, insane or nonsensical of me to expect or even to desire certain paintings by El Greco, Rembrandt or Cezanne, or places like Madrid, Berne, Brussels, etc., or dead philosophers like Meinong or Moore, but even some living persons, to love me as I love them. Now selective love is for a large party wholly or almost wholly irrelevant to morality; it is obviously relevant to morality in so far only as it expresses particular appreciation of objective excellence of quality [22] and in especial, of course, a discriminating respect and admiration for a note of high morality attaching to a character, an action, or an institution; but however complex the relations are between selective love and the

---

[22] According to Moral Theology, the human act derives its "essential" or "specific" morality from the value of the *object* to which it adheres—an eminently selective type of *dilexio*. Thus, in the O. T., Hosea (9. 10): Facti sunt abominabiles, sicut ea quae dilexerunt. (They became abominable, according to the things they loved.) And St. Augustine (Tr. 2, on 1. *Epist. S. Joann.*, n. 14): Talis quisque est, qualis est ejus dilexio. Terram diligis? terra es; Deum diligis? quid dicam? quasi Deus es. (What a person is worth is measured by what he loves. Is it "earth" you love? Earth you are. Is it God you love? What shall I say? You are almost God-like.) The point, then, even of "loving God" is *not* "Love" as such, but the selective adherence of man to God's supreme *holiness*, goodness and purity: what Hildebrand in his basic works calls *response to value*. The Christian "love for sinners" refers, of course not to some mystical superiority or to an ultimate "indifference" of "being a sinner" but to the intrinsic and supreme *evilness* of sin, of which the "sinner" is the *author* but by which he is also *beset*, and the paramount urgency of helping the "sinner" to *repudiate* and *break away from* his sin. About the disgusting perversion of a romantic glorification of sin, see chapters VIII–IX of Hildebrand's quoted book.

morality of the man who feels it, selective love most organically and integrally pertains to *love*. Even in one who recognizes and tries to obey the "commandment" of "love for all men" (universal benevolence), a poor capacity for selective loves argues not only an insipid but stifled, if not crippled, personality. (Some would doubtless so regard even a person incapable of a strong and fully experienced love-attitude in the field of man-woman relationships, not necessarily negating thereby the specific values of "virginity" as an aspect of supernatural dedication to God or to a highly meaningful spiritual task.) Love for the "next" person (*le prochain;* one's "neighbour"; the man one "happens to come across") is also in a sense a species of "selective", i.e. non-universal and privilege-creating love; Fletcher arbitrarily underrates the utterly essential Christian emphasis on this modality of love and reduces the concept of "Love" to that of a universal, not to say neutral "universal benevolence (whose moral relevancy I am, however, the last to deny) and the frigid utilitarian calculus it practically involves (the importance of which I am again far from denying, though I regard it as much more fallible and its effectual range as much more circumscribed than Fletcher does). He, then, in my view, not only fails to do justice to Justice by interpreting it as a mere function of Love but also denatures Love by forcing it into the procrustean bed of a simplifying moral preconception; and I even see an unresolved tension between his situationism as such and his depreciation for acting on direct and unreflective sentimental impulse. Moreover, I consider it an open question how far his "Christian situationism" is Christian—seeing, first, that the situationist overtones of the authentic Christian attitude suggest a very much less utilitarian brand of situationism, and secondly, that in spite of the teleological bent of Thomist ethics and the pastoral and diplomatic pragmatism manifoldly revealed in Church policies, traditional Christian ethics—Aquinas's doctrine of the "Law and Nature", and Moral Theology—have never committed themselves to extrinsicalism but on the contrary strictly insisted on the validity of specified moral norms and on the concept of intrinsic Right and Wrong. I have never yet observed any encouragement by the Church of a contentually uniform kind of confession in which the petitent declares that he "has sometimes acted from motives other than Love and has sometimes poorly calculated the foreseeable consequences of his action" (without mentioning the so and so many acts of theft or embezzlement or adultery or assult, etc., he has committed); and in a theologian as "modern" as Rahner [23] I find confirmation of my view that it is essential for the penitent not just to "confess" that he "is a sinner" (which we all do as casually as we mention having had a poached egg for breakfast) but to confess himself guilty of the definite sins the stating of which really inflicts upon him the "medicinal pain" of shame and humiliation.

On the extrinsicalist view, it would indeed appear that "the end sanctifies the means" ; and in proclaiming this openly and adorning it with Lenin's quip "What else but the end should sanctify it?" Fletcher certainly achieves, particularly as seen against his Christian background, an effect of crude piquancy. The point is here not so much that "ends" of course do *not* sanctify or justify means, but that ends are not themselves means which could be "derived from" or "put in the service of" some comprehensive principle of Practice such as Love—just as keeping one's promises is not a means but a manifestation and specification of Justice, or as a succulent dish is not a means but a fit part of a good dinner and its eating not a means but a specification of good nourishment and of an adequate response to gustatory values. In the name and even in the spirit of Love, very different and discrepant good—but also, less naturally, bad—ends can be conceived; and the monstrous system of Leninist government (formally interpretable in terms of "Love", i.e. a zealous vision of promoting men's material welfare and even their freedom), notwithstanding its uninhibited and systematic use of criminal means, embodies an evil end much rather than a mere evil means or class of means. What extrinsicalism involves is not just the freedom of using any kind of efficacious and technically apposite means in the service of putatively good ends but the freedom of choosing any kinds of end which the agent, given the scale of his predilections and aversions, may be inclined to set up as colourably "good" ends. This position is as it were retroactively supported by the blatantly false doctrine of "ends sanctifying means". The cynical witticism Fletcher quotes from Lenin typifies the kind of well-turned *apparent* triviality that is really essential falsehood enwrapped in clever sophistry. In one sense indeed every means is "sanctified" by its respective end, otherwise it would not be a "means"; a means is precisely *defined* by its instrumental relation to

[23] See the articles on Penitence and Contrition (Repentance) in the *Theological Dictionary* quoted above.

a foregiven end. My end of doing some transaction or some sight-seeing in the town of X, where I do not live, "sanctifies" (informs, determines and brings about) the "means" of my buying a railway ticket to X. This unassailable truth is well known to everybody and never has been in doubt at all; only, needless to say, it is totally irrelevant to any ethical consideration and notably to the queston whether or no "the end sanctifies the means" as ordinarily understood. That question is not what sanctifies a means but *whether* a morally permissible or even highly laudable end makes an *intrinsically wrongful* end *licit* (or perhaps even laudable: "sanctifies . . ."). And to that question the answer is, generally speaking at least, No. In our epoch of Marxist-Leninist Communism, I can conceive of no morally better end than the annihilation of Communism; to bring Lenin's name into disrepute might (to a modest extent at any rate) contribute towards that end; yet in my firm view I should *not* be justified in disseminating the lie—for a lie it would be—that Lenin led a dissolute life, or that personal power was his central aim, or that his paramount aim was to enjoy a life of opulence and that *this* made him the paid agent of the national enemy in 1917. Similarly, I am *not* allowed to kill a rich man and steal his money in order to improve my own standard of living (though this is a permissible end) or even to establish a new and finer clinic for sick children or a vast home for stray cats (though these would be morally high-ranking aims). Naturally, a morally good end accredits and even in a sense "sanctifies" a means that in itself is indifferent as to its intrinsic moral quality—for an end is not really "willed" unless the agent earnestly seeks to find some efficacious mean to achieve it—but the intrinsically bad moral quality of a means, which is independent of the quality of the end, precludes it from justification by that end. And Fletcher ought to be aware of this in so far at least that he does hold that "agapéic" action implies the pondering by the agent of the foreseeable consequences of what he is doing and that, accordingly, a "means" well adapted to some definite end conceived in the spirit of "Love" may yet have to be rejected because its foreseeable consequences, unlike its end, are gravely incompatible with the intent of "Love". He at least ought to say that what "sanctifies the means" is not the "end" but the compatibility of its foreseeable consequences with *other ends* the agent *must* keep in mind if he is "really" guided by "Love". I say more simply that what justifies a means is its intrinsic moral permissibility. Admittedly, though, its end *may* justify it *when* the alternative can be described in such terms as that both applying the means and renouncing the end (or pursuing it by some other available means) entail the risk of dangerous consequences but the risk attending the use of the means in question appears to be less grave and less certain. However, it will be the natural *drift*—though not a rigorous implication—of Situationism with its emphasis on an ultimate monistic concept of goodness and on the merely extrinsic rightness or wrongness of action to exalt the instrumental value of the "means" even at the cost of a conscientious examination of its possible harmful "side-effects".

6. THE CONCEPT OF INTRINSIC RIGHT AND WRONG

The rightness or wrongness of an action (of a volitive attitude, a "tract" of conduct, a policy, an habitual direction of the will, etc.) is neither a descriptive quality on the same footing with the size, the shape, the colour or the weight of a material object or with psychological characteristics such as being excited or depressed, pleased or pained, vivacious or slow-minded, interested in this or that subject and so on, nor a mystical and unitary "non-natural quality", and least of all a mere expression of the *appraiser's* state of mind. For I cannot "approve of" or "disapprove of" something except in virtue of some objective quality of it, nor mean anything by "commending" or "condemning" some conduct *morally*—as distinct from simply being "for" it or "against" it, glad about or irked by it, for any practical reason of my own—except by reference to this or that commend*able* or condemn*able* descriptive *feature* or *features* of it. Rightness and wrongness can only be approbatively/disapprobatively attributed to action (a note of "obligation" or "duty" and "prohibition" or "transgression" always somehow attaching to this class of judgements) but the unitary "pro" or "con" attitude herein expressed is of logical necessity closely tied to known and describable qualities inherent in the act (conduct, etc.) and differentially colored according to the distinctive "moral quality" referred to. Thus, terms like honesty, loving kindness, cruelty, lewdness, etc., all denote, respectively, tangible describable qualities, and may mostly be used also just descriptively, with favourable or adverse evaluation "bracketed" as it were; though in some such terms, such as "correctness" or "impurity", the evaluative meaning appears primarily expressed. And again, our approval of honesty seems tinged rather with the note of respect, that of magnanimity rather with the note of admiration; cruelty evokes a condemnation tinged with horror, lewdness one tinged with disgust. Moral experience thus forms a kind of conceptual "universe" furnished with richly manifold contents; and extrinsicalism means in the first place a negation of that "universe".[24] There is, furthermore, one purely and strictly descriptive, factual *moral* quality, though it could not logically exist without a reference to other moral qualities nor be (as Kantian formalism would have it) the only and all-comprehensive moral quality: namely, the conscious and conscientious concern *to behave morally* (its contradictory opposite being amorality or moral indifference; its contrary opposite, the "satanic" defiance of morality). This "second-order" intrinsic moral quality, to which may be added the less weighty but equally evident moral goodness of approving everything morally good and even of appreciating everything in any way distinctively valuable *per se*, makes it easier to understand the basic ethical fact that some descriptive qualities of an action, behavior or emotive attitude are intrinsically good and constitutive for the moral value of the behavior in question (and more remotely of the character from which it issues) as well as directive for our right evaluation of it, *although* no intrinsic moral quality as such, including that of being concerned about morality, determines by itself (regardless of *other* good and bad qualities) the rightness of that action or the degree of goodness attributable to the agent's intention (let alone, to his character).

Value- and disvalue-features, translatable to some extent into the language of discordant or mutually competitive value-features, will balance each other, and so may "colliding obligations" in a problem-laden moral situation. In Aristotle's doctrine of the "right mean" this is expressed somewhat hazily and misleadingly but characteristically enough; in the analysis of the goodness and badness of an action by Moral Theologians the theme has received ample treatment; among more recent discussions of it, Sir David Ross's theory of "*prima facie* obligations" or competitive moral "claims" is rightly regarded as classic. Perhaps the best example available is promise-keeping or

---

[24] Cf. Hildebrand, *op. cit.*, p. 148: "If matters were as circumstance ethics claims, no moral *pattern* would exist, no moral education" (my italics). About concrete commandments—the "Divine Mandates," interpreted in a chiefly institutional sense akin to Prof. E. Brunner's "*Ordnungen*" (*The Divine Imperative* (Philadelphia: The Westminster Press, 1947))—see the late Dietrich Bonhoeffer's posthumous (Lutheran) *Ethics* (London, SCM, 1955), pp. 252 ff. We may also mention here that on p. 173 Bonhoeffer rightly refers to Luther's magnificent phrases: "Love without Truth is *accursed love*" (my italics).

"contractural fidelity", a more evident form of right-doing and a most stringent obligation, the observance of which may yet be morally bad rather than good (or again intrinsically impossible, or in some cases definitely bad) by reason of the circumstances. Fletcher utterly distorts the datum in affirming that traditionally "commanded" kinds of action—of which promise-keeping is one—are neither right nor wrong *per se* but may be either according as they conform or disconform with the intent of "Love". Contrast the absurdity of this position with the truly maintainable intrinsic moral indifference of some other kinds of action, e.g. precisely *promising* itself, which is indeed neither right nor wrong *per se* but may be right when the arrangement of some reciprocal services calls for contractural regulation or any good purpose is essentially promoted by, or even necessitates, contractual commitment, but may be bad when it runs counter to another obligation already contracted or when the undertaking cannot be given without levity and mental reservation. Complying with one's promise is always necessarily and unequivocally right and obligatory, without any recourse to a good purpose or a praiseworthy content being necessary or even relevant at all, *unless* it clashes with another promise given and thus implies promise-*breaking*, or the action promised is intrinsically bad (and definitely and seriously so), or the circumstances have in an unforeseen fashion so changed as to make the fulfilment of the promise completely meaningless or factually impossible or definitely evil in view of its certain or almost certain consequences.

Circumstances may certainly modify the rightness or wrongness of an action, but that has nothing to do with the allegedly fictitious character of the intrinsic rightness or wrongness of some nameable and describable *kinds of action*, which alone provide the necessary standards for the moral appraisal of any concrete single action here and now. The *description of actions* is, as it has been much emphasized recently by analytical philosophers, essentially variable and a difficult matter: some typically relevant "circumstances" may change the nomenclature under which the action can fall, others may not; but even in the latter case circumstances are relevant *because*, or *in so far as*, they subsume the action performed or contemplated *also* under *another* morally significant *category* of actions. It is morally even worse to murder one's own father or brother than to murder a stranger, and we may designate the first two kinds of murder by the special names "parricide" and "fratricide"; it is also, though special nouns are missing here, worse to murder one's own uncle or again one's benefactor than a stranger to whom one owes no special duty of family loyalty or gratitude; but in all these cases the "aggravating circumstance" involves transgression of a further moral norm on top of "Thou shalt not kill", i.e. the prohibition of simple "homicide". Similar considerations apply to the (physically identical) act of sexual intercourse which may be conjugal intercourse (not illicit at all), "simple fornication" or (worse) adultery or incest, the specification depending not on the direct qualitative description of the action but on the "attendant circumstances" or "background of states of affairs". However, relevant circumstances do make a difference as to the *intrinsic content* of the action simply inasmuch as the agent is supposed to be *aware of these circumstances*, and that he does the action being aware of them means that he is actually *doing* something (perhaps significantly) *different* from what he would be doing if he was unaware of them. Leaving the point of "simple" homicide out of consideration, Oedipus was *not* guilty either of parricide when slaying his father or of incest when marrying his mother, for, being ignorant of the "circumstances", he did not yield *assent* to committing either a parricidal or an incestuous action. Again, a "pleasure-murder" (*Lustmord*, whether or no the pleasure of killing connotes a tinge of sexual "lust") is *per se* an act of even graver malice than a murder committed for gain or for revenge; and (as Moral Theology establishes it theoretically, though it inclines to regard the distinction as practically negligible) adultery committed knowingly but simply out of desire for "this attractive woman" though a grave sin, is an act less depraved than it would be if the transgressor were taking a special delight in committing adultery as such.

While it is evident that most of the intrinsically good actions we might meaningfully think of doing or wish to do are not obligatory or indeed practically not within our reach at all, our moral sense is hard put to it to stomach the idea that sometimes we cannot help having to choose between several courses of action each of which is tainted with a feature of intrinsic malice: to break a promise in order to keep another, to tell a lie lest we should knowingly (and perhaps decisively) contribute to the success of some criminal project, to kill aggressors rather than submit to their intent or to allow one life (which it would be in our power to save) to perish in order to save another, and the like. *Some* such situations, but by no means all, could have been avoided by the agent (e.g. by exercising due caution, discretion, modesty, or fortitude), in other words their coming about itself implies guilt on his part, and all of them necessarily involve an element of the "morally deplorable"—though in different degrees and fashions which cannot here be discussed. Linguistic strategems such as reserving the intrinsic malice of taking human life for cases that can properly be qualified as "murder" or at least "manslaughter", or the Moral Theologians' efforts to veil the intrinsic malice of lying (or deliberately deceiving) by the phraseology of "mental reservation", cannot dispose of the unpalatable fact that we sometimes *have* to do intrinsically bad kinds of things, though of course in *all* such cases, including those conditioned by antecedent guilt, it is possible and obligatory to seek *bona fide* to determine the morally best course available and to follow it. The moral-theological axiom that to do something intrinsically bad is never permissible (*nunquam licet*) cannot be upheld, since it analyses into *either* demanding the impossible (yet *ultra vires nemo obligatur* is an absolutely unchallengeable principle) *or* making nonsense of the concept of intrinsic moral qualities and admitting, thus approaching situationism, the reduction of the concept of right and wrong to that of what is "concretely", "on balance", morally preferable "in the circumstances". Nevertheless, the above-quoted moral-theological axiom has a sound core inasmuch as it expresses the greater stringency of prohibitive as contrasted with prescriptive norms and the greater dependence on circumstances of right-doing than of wrong-doing (*cf.* the axioms that "laws of commission" *obligant semper sed non pro semper* while "laws of omission" *obligant semper et pro semper*, and that what the agent does is *bonum ex integra causa, malum ex quocumque defectu*); more briefly, the valid principle that abstention from specifiable forms of evildoing, *not barterable* against any aspects of motivational goodness or consequential advantages, provide the *primordial basis of moral orientation*. The moral-theological predilection for pointing to acts of "lust" or "impurity" as the most obvious example for "intrinsic moral badness", whether or not psychologically linked to a possibly misguided and obsessive habit of looking askance at sex as such, also reveals a sound *logical* substance. Sexual activity, tending to culminate in the ecstatic condition called "orgasm", is inherently permeated with a well characterized species of pleasure to which, while it lasts, the agent tends to fully "abandon" himself; this by itself marks a certain contrast with the characteristically "moral"—self-distanced, self-judging, self-tempering state of consciousness, and *if* the action by any further specific standard is a morally inordinate one, the agent inevitably comes close to more totally and unreservedly assenting to a mode of immorality than does, e.g., a transgressor who disregards the welfare or even infringes the rights of others for the sake of his own advantage. That does not make "lust" the gravest of sins, generically graver for example than injustice, deceit and dishonesty (which call for "retribution" in a logically more evident and practically more urgent sense); but it does make "lust" a more paradigmatic and illustrative form of *intrinsic* moral disvalue, that disvalue being as it were fused more intimately and indissolubly with the activity to which it adheres. However, the incomparably graver "satanic" sins of cruelty and "malice" (in the narrower sense), i.e. delight taken in the suffering of others and in harming them, as well as delight taken in morally corrupting others, also exhibit "intrinsic" immorality in a paradigmatic fashion; this has sometimes been overlooked by moralists obsessed with the more ubiquitous nature and conspicuous power of venereal temptations. But Aquinas is supremely right when he says that a man who never indulges in adultery himself but who disseminates the teaching that there is nothing wrong with adultery is so far a much worse man than an inveterate adulterer who "teaches" no such thing but just stifles the voice of his conscience or turns a deaf ear to its protests.

Fletcher condenses his extrinsicalism in the formula that moral values and disvalues are "not properties but predicates of actions". This grammatical distinction is undoubtedly not only of stylistic interest but may also stimulate a discussion of certain logical subtleties. Mostly if I say that this cardboard box is round I can just as well describe it as a round cardboard box, or if I can say that Jimmie is ten years old I can equally refer to him as ten-year-old Jimmie; but "These apples are sour" need not mean that they are "sour apples" (i.e. the variety of apples, perhaps the same as crab-apple?, produced by the kind of tree of which Jeff Davis is proposed to be hanged in *John Brown's Body*), and if "this worm is round" it is not necessarily a roundworm. But the difference, largely verbal, does not amount to much; so far as predicates are purely relational ("Jimmie is John's son"="John is Jimmie's father", "This is pleasant to me"="I am pleased by or with it", "Guinness is good for you"="Guinness benefits your organism", etc.) they would not be confused with qualities; but so far as they are qualitative, they are *qualities predicated of* an object. Apples as sweet as honey cannot be "sour apples", worms as flat as a strip of thin paper cannot be roundworms; and to distinguish "sour apples" from unripe standard apples and roundworms from some other breed of round worms I would need the criteria of further descriptive qualities, though I don't happen to know which. Fletcher obviously means that although we may call one action good and another bad, actions are not classifiable into "good actions" and "bad actions" as they perhaps are into carefully prepared and impulsive actions or plants into phanerogamous and cryptogamous. True; but that does not a whit alter the fact that neither can we "predicate" goodness or badness of them except by pointing to their establishable "properties". Yet no such property (quality, category, criterion) can unequivocally justify us in predicating of them definitely that they are good or bad: it depends on the "situation" with its various elements, ingredients or circumstances. True again, on the whole; but these, precisely, enter into the description of their "properties". That no two situations are absolutely identical has nothing to do with their imaginary "uniqueness"; otherwise it would be simply empty of meaning to call any action in any sense morally appraisable. The differences between any two situations (in which actions somehow comparable as to their categorical character have been performed) are analysable in terms of universals capable of description and comparison. In a world of "unique" situations as dreamed of by Existentialists and Situationists and in which actions, as extrinsicalism would have it, would not possess universally knowable and designable good and bad qualities—relevant and applicable to the assessment of moral problems and conduct in an infinitude of "situations", so far as happening and behavior can be articulated into distinct "situations"—no moral judgements would be possible at all but only a chaotic welter of arbitrary pro and con "reactions". It is undeniable that moral problems, rooted partly in the complexity of situations, are frequently difficult to "decide", and that there is a "legalistic" temptation of complacently slurring over the difficulty by dint of a schematic and conventional application of categories ready at hand. But to propose to remedy our imperfection by grotesquely magnifying it on the one hand and transvaluating it into an imaginary perfection on the other, by debasing man as an appraiser into an idiot and inflating man as an agent into an embodiment of creative godhead, is a counsel of despair which is indefensible on all counts and has nothing to commend itself.

In rejecting—however reluctantly—pure Antinomianism, Fletcher admits the necessity of some "order". Man's instinct for survival, and survival at the level of a modicum of civilization, is so sensitive to that necessity that it impels him to turn to Tyranny once the autonomous, impersonal code of objective norms has been devaluated and destroyed. He who pits his freedom against the Golden Rule, Chesterton said, lays himself open to subjugation by an Iron Rule. When Fletcher bids fair to supersede "Legalism" with (in his own words) a "Totalitarian" and "Monolithic" Imperative of Utility, of "Love" as he also calls it, he is more right than he probably thinks to be; that is, he inaugurates a more literal, far-reaching and sinister truth than he may be aware of. And Kipling's battle-cry launched against the same general tendency in 1912

> Whatsoever, for any cause,
>   Seeketh to take *or to give*
> Power above and beyond *the Laws*,
>   Suffer it not to live!
>
> Holy State or Holy King—
>   Or Holy People's Will—
> Have no truck with the *senseless* thing.
>   Order the guns and kill

might well be re-written to-day so as to include "Holy Agent".

Introduction to Joseph Fletcher

What follows is Fletcher's response to Kolani's article. Among the merits of his rejoinder is that of directing our attention to issues crucial in determining the nature and function of moral philosophy. (a) Is there, one might ask, any rational way to decide whether goodness should be taken to be a property of kinds of acts, or rather to be an accidental predicate that belongs to some particular acts because they promote human welfare? (b) Does it make any difference theoretically or practically whether one relativizes the obligation to obey a law (i.e. to say that a law always holds, but that one may have no obligation to obey the law if the consequences of obedience are very bad) as Kolnai allegedly does, or whether one relativizes the moral "law" itself (i.e. to say that no law is anything more than a rule of thumb), as Fletcher confessedly does? (c) Can one distinguish between the intrinsicalist and the situationist on the basis of preferences for different courses of action in various hypothetical cases, asking each, for example, what Oedipus ought to have done if the only way he could have saved Thebes was to marry the woman he knew to be his mother?

A Situationist's Feedback
by Joseph Fletcher

The widening debate about situation ethics—it covers more areas than philosophy, such as education and psychology—draws in Marxists and humanists and Jews as well as Catholics and Protestants. It is bound to deepen and sensitize our moral reasoning.[1] Ethics is *thinking* about morality, essentially, and therefore competitive or contending thought can be highly profitable. Books like this one have been for the most part competent and dignified. Occasional drops of acid in the pot only help the brew to reach its payoff point.

In Aurel Kolnai's paper (the only one in this volume I am asked to consider) there are fairly long sections of an acute and correct restatement of my views, often with a warmth and color I could not myself bring to their service. Occasionally, even, he permits a little admiration of my views to creep in, in spite of his basic and sustained rejection of them, and for this I am grateful and eager to reciprocate.

[1] Other works debating situation ethics are, e.g.: Harvey Cox, ed., *The Situation Ethics Debate* (Philadelphia: The Westminster Press, 1968); The Editor, *Storm Over Ethics* (Philadelphia: United Church Press, 1967); P. Ramsey and G. Outka, *Norm and Context* (New York: Charles Scribner's Sons, 1968); Wesley C. Baker, *The Open End of Christian Morals* (Philadelphia: The Westminster Press, 1967), W. G. Muelder, *Moral Law and Christian Social Ethics* (Richmond, Va.: The John Knox Press, 1967); H. H. Barnette, *The New Theology and Morality* (Philadelphia: the Westminster Press, 1967); James A. Pike, *You and the New Morality* (New York: Harper and Row, 1967; Joseph Fletcher, *Moral Responsibility* (Philadelphia: The Westminster Press, 1967); Paul Ramsey, *Deeds and Rules in Christian Ethics* (New York: Charles Scribner's Sons, 1967); Paul Hessert, *Christian Life*, Vol. V, New Directions in Theology Today (Philadelphia: The Westminster Press, 1967); Dietrich and Alice von Hildebrand, *Morality and Situation Ethics* (Chicago: Franciscan Herald Press, 1966); J. G. Milhaven, S.J., and D. J. Casey, S.J., "Introduction to the Theological Background of the New Morality," *Theological Studies*, XXVIII (1967), pp. 213–34.

But also there are several important points of debate and disclaimer to be made where I will have to raise questions as to Kolnai's accuracy or reasoning or learning. In a paper as rich as his, on a subject so moot, one cannot possibly deal with everything—at least not without being unconscionably long and wearisome. Therefore I have chosen only a few things for reference: I trust the more significant ones.

First off I want to agree with Kolnai that while it may bear a Protestant or Catholic "tinge", situation ethics could just as likely be adopted by non-Christians and atheists. Indeed, in fact it is. The point, of course, is that situation ethics is a methodological thesis; it, like pragmatism, follows a certain method of approach to ethical cognition and decision making without, of itself, determining what substantive values are to be in control. The highest good or first-order value could be love (and so it is, in my case) or power or self-aggrandizement or obedience to authority or national interest, et cetera. Too much of the time *my* demonstration of the situational way to do ethics (by using it in the explication of agapism) is taken to mean that *all* situationists are agapists. This is no more the case than that they have to be theists or atheists, Catholics or Portestants.

Again, I want to assert with great alacrity that, even though Kolnai appears a bit hesitant about it, situation ethics is as he says a *craft*. And I suppose, as he suggests, that the exercise of a craft entails something in the nature of craftiness, such as a doctor's or a nurse's telling a lie in order to help a patient. (This, I am willing to confess, is a departure somewhat from what I once argued, rather moralistically, back in 1954, in my *Morals and Medicine*.[2] I have had to change my stance, due to the crystalization of situation ethics.) I get the impression that Kolnai, bless his heart, is very unhappy about such a "hang loose" posture vis-a-vis truthtelling—that moral laws such as "we should tell the truth" are a real part of *him*, even though rationality calls for a little craft sometimes!

There are issues posed but not resolved by Kolnai: e.g., why does he say that cruelty and malice are "incomparably more evil" than passive indifference? He knows that I have held to the contrary, that indifference is more opposed to *agapé* (loving concern) than ill will; that callous "I don't care" is worse than caring-enough-to-will-ill. *Why* does he

---

[2] (Princeton, N.J.: Princeton University Press, 1954) and (Boston: Beacon Press, 1960), Ch. 2.

say so? He doesn't explain—and for the agapist such a declaration needs explaining. In the same way he says that there is a "kinship" between antinomian and situational morality, but without really saying why. For the most part he polarizes, speaking (like Karl Rahner) as if the choice logically is between spontaneous moral decisions and a rules-bound approach.[3] Of *course* situation ethics has an aspect in common with legalism (using principles as helpful guidelines, but not being bound by them) just as it has as aspect in common with antinomian or extemporist ethics (viz., a refusal to be bound by any rule, but willing to illuminate the situation with all relevant moral generalities). Yet situation ethics is neither of these strategies and Kolnai's *als ob* discussion, as it were really antinomianism, is both misguided and undefended.

There are also a few rhetorical declarations made without answers. For example, he declares that my thesis that love and justice are one and the same is "bizarre" and "utterly symptomatic of inept philosophizing." Why so? Assertedly it counters the classical tradition and conventional wisdom, but *why* is it bizarre and inept? He does not say. Nor does he explain (you would think he would, eh?) why my view that goodness is a predicate of human acts, not a property, "may be criticized by logicians". We all wait for *that* assertion to be exegeted!

Early in his paper Kolnai reveals that in his opinion situation ethics is (1) a prey to an "antinomian emphasis" (there is his persistent polarization again) and (2) an extrinsicalist theory of the locus of value—i.e., that acts are right or wrong according to the situation *ex casu, per accidens*, and not *per se*. On the second score he is quite correct, and it is this one that bothers him more—hence the title of his essay. He and the reader may therefore be interested in the following anecdote.

In September of 1967 I spent a week with thirty-some members of the faculty of the University of Alberta (Canada). Among them was Charles Davis, ex-Jesuit and English *peritus* at the Second Vatican Council, now turned Anglican. In a summation dialogue after six days of debate (I tell this to pinpoint the issue) Davis was asked if he could "buy" situation ethics. He replied, "Yes and No." He was, he said, a situationist "practically" but he could not accept the

---

[3] See my "Reflection and Reply" in Harvey Cox, *The Situation Ethics Debate*.

"philosophical underpinnings". The "underpinnings" he identified as the *extrinsicalist* theory that value is contingent on the situation; he thought that goodness, or at least badness, must be inherent in some acts, if not all.

"There must be," he said, "some things that are always wrong; there must be at least a few universal negatives." [4] When I asked "Why?" he replied very intelligently, "I think so because I am, I realize, an intrinsicalist." Then when I asked "Why are you an intrinsicalist?" his answer was, "I prefer Aquinas' realism to Ockham's nominalism." Then I put the basic, metaethical question: "Do you think there is any rational way to resolve the issue at stake between them, whether goodness and badness are *in* acts or *of* them, a property or a predicate?" To this his considered response was, as mine is too, "No." I repeat what I said in *Situation Ethics*: in the last analysis one's ethics comes down to a decision, not a conclusion; it is a matter of faith posited, not of fact verifiable empirically.[5] Call it emotivist, attitudinal, *gessingsethik*, positivist, what you will—there it is.

Kolnai and I are agreed at least about how unlovely legalism is, in the sense of an oversimple adherence to code rules. We would agree, I take it, that classical casuistry made a responsible and compassionate effort to deal with conflicts between loving concern and obedience to law, under such headings as "perplexity" (when two or more conflicting moral laws seem to oblige) and "doubt" (whether a particular law really obliges or not). Our divergence comes because situation ethics goes farther, to say that classical casuistry was wrong to hold that there is any intrinsic validity at all in any moral law, whether obeyed, suspended or sidetracked. Kolnai, because of his intrinsicalism, cannot go with me this far towards situational or relative morality. He insists on "objective" or "real" morality. His position is still one of "right is right, wrong is wrong"—so that he must say "a lie is a lie" or "a promise is a promise," even though he *is* willing to extenuate or excuse

---

[4] In dialogue with me Fr. Charles Curran of the Catholic University of America has contended that there are only a very few unexceptionable obligations—such as honor to God, truthfulness, respect for the sanctity of life, the finality of sex functions. It is interesting to speculate on how far this reductionism might go eventually. Maybe to the zero point, thus satisfying situationists! The only Catholic moral philosopher I know who has gone as far as to say that there are *no* universal negatives is Thomas A. Wassmer, S.J., in "Is Intrinsic Evil a Viable Term?" in *Chicago Studies*, V (1966), pp. 307–14.

[5] *Situation Ethics*, pp. 46–50.

or exculpate the liar and the promisor in some situations, for the sake of loving concern. (All reasoning based on absolute moral "laws" is necessarily tautological.)

He relativizes only the *obligation* of a moral law, whereas I and any other situationist would relativize the moral "law" itself! As Kolnai puts it, he is opposed to "misdirected" legalism; I am opposed to legalism as such, however compassionately employed. The point here is central to our whole debate and merits careful consideration. Situationists seriously mean it when they say, "Morality was made for man, not man for morality." On their view so-called "confessional" or retrospective ethics would have no reason whatever for forgiveness or absolution of any act which was lovingly intended or benevolent (good-willed), no matter what some "abstract law" prescribed. (This is, actually, just another way of expressing the logic of *conscientia semper sequenda est*.)

When, in another vein, Kolnai complains that situation ethics identifies right and good with "correct" and "wise" and "reasonable" he is again only expressing his intrinsicalist premise that some things are wrong no matter how expedient or constructive in love's interest. As an intrinsicalist he is not much moved by how pragmatic or prudent or utility-minded or Success-seeking an action may be. But the situationist obviously has much more sympathy with what Kolnai denigrates as "prudentialism"—an emphasis of other Catholic philosophers, such as Joseph Pieper.[6]

Even Kant's old term for ethics, "practical reason," comes closer to the bone here, for whatever else he assigned by way of meaning to "practical" he meant it to be realistic and situationally knowledgeable—*effective*. Indeed, I urge Professor Kolnai to return to Aristotle. He will find that he (the Stagirite) analysed *praxis* in such a way that all wisdom is prudential and down-to-earth—an elemental feature of his teaching which set him apart from Plato. Kolnai's legalistic orientation exposes itself in his setting of prudential agents over against "conscientialist" agents: prudential *versus* consciential—prudence distinguished from conscience! Aristotle would find that antinomy an interesting one, to say the least.

Let me directly challenge the idea that "altruism" or *agapé* or "universal benevolence" means, as Kolnai puts it, "the reduction of

[6] See his *Prudence* (London: Faber and Faber, Ltd., 1959), pp. 45 and 48.

all moral goodness to the 'good of man',," and let me also challenge his statement that to reduce goodness to human welfare is a "concept that in itself is purely non-moral." Here we have the unmistakable accents of legalism or ethical absolutism. Agapistic situationists are pretty plainspoken about this; to the contrary, we say, there is no good except the good of people, of human beings. To paraphrase Sartre's famous statement about atheism, "Situationism is a humanism." Some of us may make the further theological assertion that God too is a "people" or person, or that the only way to please God is to seek the good of human beings (Luther: "only through the neighbor can we love God"). But this is additional; the ethical baseline is the proposition that only what helps people (is loving) is good—not adherence to any rule. This sharply joined issue, What is the good? is as much at the heart of this whole debate as the issue over situation *versus* moral rules.

It is helpful, I grant, to relate this controversy over situation ethics to utilitarianism and the difference between the *act* and *rule* versions, as well as to the question about the careful (I would say "loving") calculation of consequences. But now we must pay close attention to the problems at stake. The situationist with an ultimate criterion of the agapistic kind is willing, even happy and candid, to accept "general utility" as a synonym for "love." [7] Yes. I go along with Kolnai on that score; it is nothing to be denied or evaded! Situation ethics find the utility or goodness in the actual deed and its foreseeable or projected consequences, not in any norms or general rules or maxims of conduct. Yet *nota bene*, this is not a simplistic consequentialism of the sort defended by G. E. Moore, who said an act is right if it has good effects, even if it was intended maliciously; in short, consequences determine an act's moral value, not intentions. Sir David Ross and H. A. Prichard held that some acts are right independently of their consequences. Among the ancients, Socrates would back Moore and Abelard would back Ross. An agapist, however, whether a situationist or not, is both consequential and intentional; he rejects the either-or way of using them as antinomies. There is no reason logically or empirically for setting them in opposition. I, for one, say that an act is "good" if it has good consequences, "bad" if they are evil (i.e. hurtful to human

---

[7] I have done so in detail in my Fenton Lecture, "American Pragmatism and the Problem of Theological Ethics," in William Baumer, ed., *Religion in Modern Society*.

beings); and it is "right" if its intention was loving, "wrong" if it was done with either malice or callous indifference. Consequences don't make an act right, intentions don't make it good.

It is certainly true, as Kolnai sees, that the temper of situational agapism (that is my whole position in a phrase) is not suited to rule-utilitarianism, but he errs in thinking that it is a form of act-utilitarianism. Indeed, it is neither of these. It is, instead, a "modified" or "summary" rule-utilitarianism, in the sense that it finds general rules or maxims helpful in deciding what the utility (most loving thing) is in any situation, yet is prepared to bypass the rule. It is also, therefore, a "modified" act-utilitarianism, in the sense that it is willing to advert to rules but keeps free to act without them if love seems better served thereby.[8] It is due to Kolnai's fundamental intrinsicalism or absolutism that he calls this *act*-utilitarianism, and this is because (I repeat) he really polarizes the issue: he cannot help reducing the issue simplistically to either legalism or antinomianism, absolutism or chaotic spontaneism —he cannot perceive or concede a middle way or third alternative mediating between the two extremes. It may well be that he is right about this, but at least he has not established it. If he *can*, then situation ethics might lose all claim to being a discrete method. (The point is well worth noting by those who want further analysis and discussion.)

Theologically the nut of the whole matter may lie in Kolnai's startling remark that "God is love" (St. John's basic theological tenet—a kind of ultimate religious ontology) is only "hyperbolic" and "wholly nonsensical." It would be interesting to hear how he justifies this repudiation of a central concept in Christian ethics and moral theology. (He offers nothing but the *dicta*.) But connected with this stance he makes three points which I want to speak to very briefly:

(1) He rejects "the ethics of divine imperatives." This takes us back to old debates in theological ethics of the realist-nominalist, Aquinas-Ockham kind. Admittedly, professedly, a situationist is much closer to the nominalist's model ("Right is what God commands") than to the realists' model ("God commands what is right"). Leaving a side the theological dilemma of accounting for a value or imperative which pre-exists the *mens creatrix*, I judge that the most succinct way to

---

[8] W. K. Frankena did so in "Love and Principle in Christian Ethics," *Faith and Philosophy*, ed. Alvin Plantinga (Grand Rapids, Mich.: Eerdmans Publishing Company, 1964), pp. 203–205.

put the position is like this: the Thomist would say, "God wills whatever is right," the Ockhamist would say "What is right is whatever God wills," while the situationist would say, "If and when anything is right God wills it." All this means, really, is that for the situationist God commands one thing only, to have loving concern, and therefore whatever happens to be loving in any particular situation is "the will of God." God, too, is a situationist.

(2) He says it is "hard to see" how love for God or man could imply virtues or standards such as fortitude, chastity, sobriety, and the like. On the basis of common sense and experience most people would say that love (i.e. *agapé* or concern for one's neighbors) frequently or even usually entails the moral dispositions Kolnai mentions, and in addition the other familiar norms of the *sophia*.[9] St. Augustine subsumed all moral principles under *caritas* and inferred them from *caritas*. Kolnai mentions St. Paul in this connection, and yet it was Paul even more radically than Jesus who reduced all moral "law" to love, as in Galatians 5:6 and 14. Love is obviously, yet not always, expressed through and by means of the classical virtues and norms of conduct; these are virtuous and normative only when and because they find expression for love in the situation. They do not stand alone, self-validated.

(3) At bottom Kolnai is betrayed by his erroneous idea that "love is primarily a psychological concept." Evidently he means that it is a psychic phenomenon (which, as far as it goes, is true enough). Therefore, since he defines love emotionally rather than attitudinally, he cannot accept an agapistic ethic, whether situational or not. Defining love as *philia* or *erōs* makes it affective and interpersonal. "Charity" might have helped him, as a synonym, but it is interesting that he does not bring that glorious term of the Christian heritage into play at all. His main point of contention is that as he understands love it is *selective*; in short, non-agapéic. But his connotation (the romantic one) simply isn't to be found anywhere in what the New Testament says about *agapé*. He has burked the issue, rather cavalierly, by saying, "Whether Fletcher's interpretation of Christian 'agapé' is historically correct I am by no means sure, but I would not labour the point." In the future, one hopes, he will see fit to "labor" the question; it is conceptually vital to the whole debate.

---

[9] See my "Tillich and Ethics: The Negation of Law," in *Pastoral Psychology* (1968).

Now I make two objections as to accuracy. The first is that my thesis about the relations of love to justice is that they are one and the same, coterminous in meaning and interchangeable as terms. I do not say, and never have, that justice is a "mere function of love." There is a world of difference between the two positions. This too is something I'd have appreciated Kolnai's critique of—but I mustn't be greedy. In the second place, what he says about the means-ends problem is, I am afraid, beside the point. A rejection of the bromide "The end does not justify the means" seems to demoralize Kolnai. I have never said, of course, that any end will justify any and all means. And I must protest his description of Lenin's remark "If the end does not justify the means, what does?" as a "cynical witticism." Lenin was being entirely serious in his *Philosophical Notebook*. I might add another critical query: "Does the means justify the end?" If anything needs fresh examination, this means-ends problem does.

To make an end. Kolnai tries in a generous and judicious spirit to meet me half way. He agrees that *even an intrinsicalist* ought to "be aware" of what he calls "relevant circumstances" (the situation), and that in so being aware he might be "actually doing something (perhaps significantly) different from what he would be doing if he were unaware of them." On this ground, but by a *non sequitur*, he states that Oedipus did not commit either parricide or incest because he acted ignorantly of the circumstances. But in moral theology, and I would add common sense, Oedipus *did* commit both parricide and incest, yet his acts were not *imputable* because of his ignorance; he was materially guilty, but not formally.

However, let us suppose or hypothecate—for the sake of sharpening up the core "quarrel" between us—that Oedipus *had* actually known that the queen Jocasta was his mother, that as soon as he had reached the city he had learned the awful truth that his roadside victim had been his own father, and further, that the only way he could forestall a bloody uprising and dynastic revolution in Thebes, entailing the destruction of the city and its people, was by accepting the crown he'd won by guessing the riddle of the Sphinx, marrying his mother and siring her issue. Would it be a right thing to do, a good deed? Some situationists would say Yes. I would. Here, then, is a question that ought to smoke Professor Kolnai and his fellow intrinsicalists out of their Platonic cave of shadows, their absolute abstractions called "objective moral principles."